In Defence of Animals

Edited by

PETER SINGER

Basil Blackwell

© Peter Singer 1985

First published 1985
Basil Blackwell Publisher Ltd
108 Cowley Road, Oxford OX4 1JF, UK

Basil Blackwell Inc.
432 Park Avenue South, Suite 1505,
New York, NY 10016, USA

British Library Cataloguing in Publication Data

In Defence of Animals.
1. Animals, Treatment of
I. Singer, Peter, *1946–*
179'.3   HV4708

ISBN 0–631–13897–8
ISBN 0–631–13896–X Pbk

Typeset by Freeman Graphic, Tonbridge, Kent
Printed in Great Britain by
Whitstable Litho Ltd., Whitstable, Kent

Contents

Acknowledgements

It is, of course, the contributors who have written this book, and its merits are due to their work. I take this opportunity to thank them for the enthusiasm with which they set about their task, the diligence with which they met their deadlines, and the good-natured way in which they responded to my editorial suggestions. I am also grateful to Lori Gruen, who read the typescript and made several valuable suggestions, and to Jean Archer (again!) for excellent secretarial assistance. Finally, the book owes its existence to René Olivieri of Basil Blackwell: his advice at all stages of production has improved almost every aspect of it.

Melbourne   P.S.

The Contributors

DONALD J. BARNES is director of the Washington DC office of the National Antivivisection Society. Having studied psychology at the University of Colorado and Ohio State University, he worked first as a clinical psychologist and then as a research psychologist at the United States Air Force School of Aerospace Medicine at Brooks Air Force Base, Texas, before rejecting vivisection to work with the animal rights movement.

DEXTER L. CATE is a high school teacher and environmental activist from Hilo, Hawaii. He has worked with Greenpeace and the Fund for Animals on several projects involving protection of whales and dolphins. He is currently writing children's stories to promote the cause of Cetaceans.

STEPHEN R. L. CLARK is Professor of Philosophy at Liverpool University and author of *Aristotle's Man*, *The Moral Status of Animals*, *The Nature of the Beast* and *From Athens to Jerusalem*.

MARIAN STAMP DAWKINS is Tutor in Biological Sciences and Fellow of Somerville College, Oxford. She teaches animal behaviour in the Animal Behaviour Research Group of the Department of Zoology and researches into the behaviour of hens, with an emphasis on behavioural measures of welfare.

CLIVE HOLLANDS is Director of the Scottish Society for the Prevention of Vivisection and Secretary to the St Andrew Animal Fund. He also holds a number of other appointments, including Secretary to the Committee for the Reform of Animal Experimentation, and is an Advisory Director of the World Society for the Protection of Animals. He is author of *Compassion is the Bugler: The Struggle for*

Animals Rights and a contributor to *Animal Rights: A Symposium* and *Humane Education: A Symposium*.

DALE JAMIESON is Assistant Professor of Philosophy and Associate of the Center for the Study of Values and Social Policy at the University of Colorado. He has published articles on ethical aspects of the treatment of animals, on aesthetics, and on the philosophy of language.

JIM MASON is an attorney and freelance journalist. He is also co-author, with Peter Singer, of *Animal Factories*; a founder of Animal Rights Network, Inc, a non-profit organization that publishes educational material for animal rights groups; and both founder and editor-in-chief of *Agenda*, a bi-monthly news magazine for animal rights activists.

MARY MIDGLEY, formerly Senior Lecturer in Philosophy at the University of Newcastle-upon-Tyne, is the author of *Beast and Man*, *Heart and Mind*, *Wickedness*, *Animals and Why They Matter* and, with Judith Hughes, *Women's Choices: Philosophical Problems Facing Feminism*.

ALEX PACHECO co-founded People for the Ethical Treatment of Animals (PETA) along with Ingrid Newkirk in the USA in 1980. They and PETA often serve as spokespeople for the Animal Liberation Front and are active in sponsoring civil disobedience training sessions for animal rights. Anna Francione, who worked with Alex Pacheco on his contribution to the present volume, is a former editor of *PETA News*.

TOM REGAN is Professor of Philosophy at North Carolina State University, where he has twice been named Outstanding Teacher and, in 1977, was selected Alumni Distinguished Professor. He has written or helped to edit ten books, including *The Case for Animal Rights* and *All that Dwell Therein*.

LEWIS REGENSTEIN is vice-president of the Fund for Animals in Atlanta, Georgia, and author of *The Politics of Extinction: The Story of the World's Endangered Wildlife* and *America the Poisoned: How Deadly Chemicals are Destroying Our Environment, Our Wildlife – and Ourselves*, both about subjects on which he lectures at colleges throughout the USA. He has served as president of the Monitor Consortium, a coalition of conservation and animal-protection organizations in Washington DC and has contributed articles to several leading newspapers.

RICHARD D. RYDER is chairman of the Animal Experimentation Advisory Committee of the Royal Society for the Prevention of Cruelty to Animals and chairman of the Liberal Animal Welfare Group. He is the author of *Speciesism* and *Victims of Science* and co-editor of *Animal Rights: A Symposium*.

HARRIET SCHLEIFER is a social and political activist, who works part-time as a freelance photographer and translator. She is the co-founder of Quebec's Animal Liberation Collective, and an editor of *Agenda*.

PETER SINGER is Professor of Philosophy and Director of the Centre for Human Bioethics at Monash University, Melbourne, Australia. He is the author of *Animal Liberation*, which has been described as 'the bible of the new animal rights movements'. His other books include *Practical Ethics*, *The Expanding Circle*, *Animal Factories* (with Jim Mason) and most recently, with Deane Wells, *The Reproduction Revolution*. He continues to work actively with the animal liberation movement in Australia.

HENRY SPIRA co-ordinates coalitions to abolish the Draize rabbit eye and LD50 tests. He has been a merchant seaman, an auto assembly line worker, a journalist and a teacher. He was active in campaigns for civil rights and trade union democracy.

PHILIP WINDEATT is a journalist and film researcher. He was co-film-maker and researcher for *The Animals Film*, directed by Victor Schonfeld, which was transmitted by Channel Four Television in November 1982, and he is the author of *The Hunt and the Anti-Hunt*.

Prologue

Ethics and the
New Animal Liberation Movement

PETER SINGER

This book provides a platform for the new animal liberation movement. A diverse group of people share this platform: university philosophers, a zoologist, a lawyer, militant activists who are ready to break the law to further their cause, and respected political lobbyists who are entirely at home in parliamentary offices. Their common ground is that they are all, in their very different ways, taking part in the struggle for animal liberation. This struggle is a new phenomenon. It marks an expansion of our moral horizons beyond our own species and is thus a significant stage in the development of human ethics. The aim of this introduction is to show why the movement is so significant, first by contrasting it with earlier movements against cruelty for animals, and then by setting out the distinctive ethical stance which lies behind the new movement.

Although there were one or two nineteenth-century thinkers who asserted that animals have rights, the serious political movement for animal liberation is very young, a product of the 1970s. Its aims are quite distinct from the efforts of the more traditional organizations, like the Royal Society for the Prevention of Cruelty to Animals, to stop people from treating animals cruelly. Even these traditional concerns, however, are relatively recent when seen in the context of 3,000 years of Western civilization, as a brief glance at the historical background to the contemporary animal liberation movement will show.

1

Concern for animal suffering can be found in Hindu thought, and the Buddhist idea of compassion is a universal one, extending to animals as well as humans, but our Western traditions are very different. Our intellectual roots lie in Ancient Greece and in the Judeo-Christian tradition. Neither is kind to those not of our species.

In the conflict between rival schools of thought in Ancient Greece, it was the school of Aristotle that eventually became dominant. Aristotle held the view that nature is a hierarchy in which those with less reasoning ability exist for the sake of those with more reasoning ability. Thus plants, he said, exist for the sake of animals, and animals for the sake of man, to provide him with food and clothing. Indeed, Aristotle took his logic a step further – the barbarian tribes, which he considered obviously less rational than the Greeks, existed in order to serve as slaves to the more rational Greeks. He did not quite have the nerve to add that philosophers, being supremely rational, should be served by everyone else!

Nowadays we have rejected Aristotle's idea that less rational human beings exist in order to serve more rational ones, but to some extent we still retain that attitude towards non-human animals. The social reformer Henry Salt tells a story in his autobiography, *Seventy Years Among Savages* (an account of a life lived entirely in England), of how, when he was a master at Eton, he first broached the topic of vegetarianism with a colleague, a distinguished science teacher. With some trepidation he awaited the verdict of the scientific mind on his new beliefs. It was: 'But don't you think that animals were sent to us for food?' That response is not far from what Aristotle might have said. It is even closer to the other great intellectual tradition of the West – a tradition in which the following words from Genesis stand as a foundation for everything else:

> And God said, Let us make man in our image, after our likeness: and let them have domination over the fish of the sea, and over the fowl of the air, and over the cattle, and over all the earth, and over every creeping thing that creepeth upon the earth.
>
> So God created man in his own image . . ..
>
> And God blessed them, and God said unto them, Be fruitful, and multiply, and replenish the earth, and subdue it; and have dominion over the fish of the sea, and over the fowl of the air, and over every living thing that moveth upon the earth.

Here is a myth to make human beings feel their supremacy and their power. Man alone is made in the image of God. Man alone is given dominion over all the animals and told to subdue the earth. One may debate, as environmentally concerned Jews and Christians have done, whether this grant of dominion entitles human beings to rule as petty despots, doing as they please with the unfortunate subjects placed under their jurisdiction, or whether it was not rather a kind of stewardship, in which humans are responsible to their Lord for the proper care and use of what has been placed in their custody. One can point to one or two Christian figures, like John Chrysostom and Francis of Assisi, who have shown compassion and concern for non-human Creation. (Though even the stories about Francis are conflicting. There is one episode in which a disciple is said to have cut a trotter off a living pig in order to give it to a sick companion. According to the narrator, Francis rebuked the disciple – but for damaging the property of the pig owner, not for cruelty to the pig!) So far as the history of Western attitudes to animals is concerned, however, the 'dominion' versus 'stewardship' debate and that over the true nature of the teachings of Francis are both beside the point. It is beyond dispute that mainstream Christianity, for its first 1,800 years, put non-human animals outside its sphere of concern. On this issue the key figures in early Christianity were unequivocal. Paul scornfully rejected the thought that God might care about the welfare of oxen, and the incident of the Gadarene swine, in which Jesus is described as sending devils into a herd of pigs and making them drown themselves in the sea, is explained by Augustine as having been intended to teach us that we have no duties towards animals. This interpretation was accepted by Thomas Aquinas, who stated that the only possible objection to cruelty to animals was that it might lead to cruelty to humans – according to Aquinas, there was nothing wrong *in itself* with making animals suffer. This became the official view of the Roman Catholic Church to such good – or bad – effect that as late as the middle of the nineteenth century Pope Pius IX refused permission for the founding of a Society for the Prevention of Cruelty to Animals in Rome, on the grounds that to grant permission would imply that human beings have duties to the lower creatures.

Even in England, which has a reputation for being dotty about animals, the first efforts to obtain legal protection for members of other species were made only 180 years ago. They were greeted with derision. *The Times* was so dismissive of the idea that the suffering of animals ought to be prevented that it attacked proposed legislation that would stop the 'sport' of bull-baiting. Said that august newspaper: 'Whatever meddles with the private personal disposition of man's time or property is tyranny.' Animals, clearly, were just property.

That was in 1800, and that Bill was defeated. It took another twenty years to get the first anti-cruelty law on to the British statute books. That any consideration at all should be given to the interests of animals was a significant step beyond the idea that the boundary of our species is also the boundary of morality. Yet the step was a restricted one because it did not challenge our right to make whatever *use* we chose of other species. Only cruelty – causing pain when there was no reason for doing so but sheer sadism or callous indifference – was prohibited. The farmer who deprives his pigs of room to move does not offend against this concept of cruelty, for he is considered to be doing only what he thinks necessary to produce bacon. Similarly, the scientist who poisons a hundred rats in order to determine the lethal dose of some new flavouring agent for tooth-paste is not regarded as cruel, merely as concerned to follow the accepted procedures for testing the safety of new products.

The nineteenth-century anti-cruelty movement was built on the assumption that the interests of non-human animals deserve protection only when serious human interests are not at stake. Animals remained very clearly 'lower creatures' whose interests must be sacrificed to our own in the event of conflict.

The significance of the new animal liberation movement is its challenge to this assumption. Taken in itself, say the animal liberationists, membership of the human species is not morally relevant. Other creatures on our planet also have interests. We have always assumed that we are justified in overriding their interests, but this bald assumption is simply species-selfishness. If we assert that to have rights one must be a member of the human race, and that is all there is to it, then what are we to say to the racist who contends that to have rights you have to be a member of the Caucasian race, and that is all there is to it? Conversely, once we agree that race is not, in itself, morally significant, how can species be? As Jeremy Bentham put it some 200 years ago:

> The day *may* come when the rest of the animal creation may acquire those rights which never could have been withholden from them but by the hand of tyranny. The French have already discovered that the blackness of the skin is no reason why a human being should be abandoned without redress to the caprice of a tormentor. It may one day come to be recognized that the number of the legs, the villosity of

the skin, or the termination of the *os sacrum* are reasons equally insufficient for abandoning a sensitive being to the same fate.

Someone might say: 'It is not because we are members of the human species that we are justified in overriding the interests of other animals; it is because we are rational and they are not.' Someone else might argue that it is because we are autonomous beings, or because we can use language, or because we are self-conscious, or because we have a sense of justice. All these contentions and more have been invoked to justify us in sacrificing the interests of other animals to our own.

One way of replying would be to consider whether non-human animals really do lack these allegedly important characteristics. The more we learn of some non-human animals, particularly chimpanzees but also many other species, the less able we are to defend the claim that we humans are unique because we are the only ones capable of reasoning, or of autonomous action or of the use of language, or because we possess a sense of justice. I shall not go into this reply here because it would take a long time and it would do nothing for the many species of animals who could not be said to meet whatever test was being proposed.

There is a much shorter rejoinder. Let us return to the passage I have quoted from Bentham, for he anticipated the objection. After dismissing the idea that number of legs, roughness of skin or fine details of bone formation should 'trace the insuperable line' between those who have moral standing and those who do not, Bentham goes on to ask what else might mark this boundary:

> Is it the faculty of reason, or perhaps the faculty of discourse? But a full-grown horse or dog is beyond comparison a more rational, as well as a more conversable animal, than an infant of a day or a week or even a month, old. But suppose they were otherwise, what would it avail? The question is not, Can they *reason?* nor Can they *talk?* but, *Can they suffer?*

Bentham is clearly right. Whatever the test we propose as a means of separating human from non-human animals, it is plain that if all non-human animals are going to fail it, some humans will fail as well. Infants are neither rational nor autonomous. They do not use language and they do not possess a sense of justice. Are they therefore to be treated like non-human animals, to be fattened for the table, if we should fancy the taste of their flesh, or to be used to find out if some new shampoo will blister human eyeballs?

Ah, but infants, though not rational, autonomous or able to talk, have the potential to become adult humans – so the defender of human supremacy will reply to Bentham. The relevance of potential is another complicated argument that I shall avoid by the stratagem of focusing your attention on another class of humans who would fail the proposed test: those unfortunate enough to have been born with brain damage so severe that they will never be able to reason, or talk or do any of the other things that are often said to distinguish us from non-human animals. The fact that we do not use them as means to our ends indicates that we do not really see decisive moral significance in rationality, or autonomy, or language, or a sense of justice, or any of the other criteria said to distinguish us from other animals. Why do we lock up chimpanzees in appalling primate research centres and use them in experiments that range from the uncomfortable to the agonising and lethal, yet would never think of doing the same to a retarded human being at a much *lower* mental level? The only possible answer is that the chimpanzee, no matter how bright, is not human, while the retarded human, no matter how dull, is.

This is speciesism, pure and simple, and it is as indefensible as the most blatant racism. There is no ethical basis for elevating member-ship of one particular species into a morally crucial characteristic. From an ethical point of view, we all stand on an equal footing – whether we stand on two feet, or four, or none at all.

That is the crux of the philosophy of the animal liberation movement, but to forestall misunderstanding I had better say something immediately about this notion of equality.

It does *not* mean that animals have all the same rights as you and I have. Animal liberationists do not minimize the obvious differences between most members of our species and members of other species. The rights to vote, freedom of speech, freedom of worship – none of these can apply to other animals. Similarly, what harms humans may cause much less harm, or even no harm at all, to some animals. If I were to confine a herd of cows within the boundaries of the county of, say, Devon, I do not think I would be doing them any harm at all; if, on the other hand, I were to take a group of people and restrict them to the same county, I am sure many would protest that I had harmed them considerably, even if they were allowed to bring their families and friends, and notwithstanding the many undoubted attractions of that particular county. Humans have interests in mountain-climbing and skiing, in seeing the world and in sampling foreign cultures. Cows like lush pastures and shelter from harsh weather. Hence to deny humans the right to travel outside Devon would be to restrict their rights significantly; it would not be a significant restriction of the rights of cows.

Here is another example, more relevant to real problems about our treatment of animals. Suppose we decided to perform lethal scientific experiments on normal adult humans, kidnapped at random from public parks for this purpose. Soon every adult who entered a park would become fearful of being kidnapped. The resultant terror would be a form of suffering additional to whatever pain was involved in the experiments themselves. The same experiments carried out on non-human animals would cause less suffering overall, for the non-human animals would not have the same anticipatory dread. This does not mean, I hasten to add, that it is all right to experiment on animals as we please, but only that if the experiment is to be done at all, there is *some* reason, compatible with the equal consideration of interests, for preferring to use non-human animals rather than normal adult humans.

There is one point that needs to be added to this example. Nothing in it depends on the fact that normal adult humans are members of our species. It is their capacity for knowledge of what may happen to them that is crucial. If they were not normal adults but severely brain-damaged humans – orphans perhaps, or children abandoned by their parents – then they would be in the same position as non-human animals at a similar mental level. If we use the argument I have put forward to justify experiments on non-human animals, we have to ask ourselves whether we are also prepared to allow similar experiments on human beings with a similar degree of awareness of what is happening to them. If we say that we will perform an experiment on monkeys but not on brain-damaged human orphans, we are giving preference to the humans just because they are members of our own species, which is a violation of the principle of equal consideration of interests.

In the example I have just given the superior mental powers of normal adult humans would make them suffer more. It is important to recognize that in other circumstances the non-human animal may suffer more because it cannot understand what is happening. If we capture a wild animal, intending to release it later, it may not be able to distinguish our relatively benign intentions from a threat to its life: general terror may be all it experiences.

The moral significances of taking life is more complex still. There is furious controversy about the circumstances in which it is legitimate to kill human beings, so it is no wonder that it should be difficult to decide whether non-human animals have any right to life. Here I would say, once again, that species in itself cannot make a difference. If it is wrong to take the life of a severely brain-damaged abandoned human infant, it must be equally wrong to take the life of a dog or a pig at a comparable mental level. On the other hand, perhaps it is *not* wrong to take the life of a brain-damaged human infant – after all, many people think such infants should be allowed to die, and an infant who is 'allowed to die' ends up just as dead as one that is killed. Indeed, one could argue that our readiness to put a hopelessly ill non-human animal out of its misery is the one and only respect in which we treat animals better than we treat people.

The influence of the Judeo-Christian insistence on the God-like nature of human beings is nowhere more apparent than in the standard Western doctrine of the sanctity of human life: a doctrine that puts the life of the most hopelessly and irreparably brain-damaged human being – of the kind whose level of awareness is not underestimated by the term 'human vegetable' – above the life of a chimpanzee. The sole reason for this strange priority is, of course, the fact that the chimpanzee is not a member of our species, and the human vegetable is biologically human. This doctrine is now starting to be eroded by the acceptance of abortion, which is the killing of a being that is indisputably a member of the human species, and by the questioning of the value of applying all the power of modern medical technology to saving human life in all cases.

I think we will emerge from the present decade with a significantly different attitude towards the sanctity of human life, an attitude which considers the quality of the life at stake rather than the simple matter of whether the life is or is not that of a member of the species *Homo sapiens*. Once this happens, we shall be ready to take a much broader view of the wrongness of killing, one in which the capacities of the being in question will play a central role. Such a view will not discriminate on the basis of species alone but will still draw a distinction between the seriousness of killing beings with the mental capacities of normal human adults and killing beings who do not possess, and never have possessed, these mental capacities. It is not a bias in favour of our own species that leads us to think that there is greater moral significance in taking the life of a normal human than there is in taking the life of, for example, a fish. To give just one reason for this distinction, a normal human has hopes and plans for the future: to take the life of a normal human is therefore to cut off these plans and to prevent them from ever being fulfilled. Fish, I expect, do not have as clear a conception of themselves as beings with a past and a future. Consequently, to kill a fish is not to prevent the fulfilment of any plans, or at least not of any long-range future plans. This does not, I stress, mean that it is all right, or morally trivial, to kill fish. If fish are capable of enjoying their lives, as I believe they are, we do better when we let them continue to live than when we needlessly end their lives, though when we cut short the life of a fish, we are not doing something as bad as when we needlessly end the life of a normal human adult.

The animal liberation movement, therefore, is *not* saying that all lives are of equal worth or that all interests of humans and other animals are to be given equal weight, no matter what those interests may be. It *is* saying that where animals and humans have similar interests – we might take the interest in avoiding physical pain as an example, for it is an interest that humans clearly share with other animals – those interests are to be counted equally, with no automatic discount just because one of the beings is not human. A simple point, no doubt, but nevertheless part of a far-reaching ethical revolution.

This revolution is the culmination of a long line of ethical development. I cannot do better than quote the words of that splendid nineteenth century historian of ideas, W. E. H. Lecky. In his *History of European Morals* Lecky wrote: 'At one time the benevolent affections embrace merely the family, soon the circle expanding includes first a class, then a nation, then a coalition of nations, then all humanity, and finally, its influence is felt in the dealings of man with the animal world.' Lecky anticipated what the animal liberationists are now saying. In an earlier stage of our development most human groups held to a tribal ethic. Members of the tribe were protected, but people of other tribes could be robbed or killed as one pleased. Gradually the circle of protection expanded, but as recently as 150 years ago we did not include blacks. So African human beings could be captured, shipped to America and sold. In Australia white settlers regarded Aborigines as a pest and hunted them down, much as kangaroos are hunted down today. Just as we have progressed beyond the blatantly racist ethic of the era of slavery and colonialism, so we must now progress beyond the speciesist ethic of the era of factory farming, of the use of animals as mere research tools, of whaling, seal hunting, kangaroo slaughter and the destruction of wilderness. We must take the final step in expanding the circle of ethics. The essays which follow show how this can be done, both in theory and in practice.

Part I

The Ideas

The Case for Animal Rights

TOM REGAN

I regard myself as an advocate of animal rights – as a part of the animal rights movement. That movement, as I conceive it, is committed to a number of goals, including:

- the total abolition of the use of animals in science;
- the total dissolution of commercial animal agriculture;
- the total elimination of commercial and sport hunting and trapping.

There are, I know, people who profess to believe in animal rights but do not avow these goals. Factory farming, they say, is wrong – it violates animals' rights – but traditional animal agriculture is all right. Toxicity tests of cosmetics on animals violates their rights, but important medical research – cancer research, for example – does not. The clubbing of baby seals is abhorrent, but not the harvesting of adult seals. I used to think I understood this reasoning. Not any more. You don't change unjust institutions by tidying them up.

What's wrong – fundamentally wrong – with the way animals are treated isn't the details that vary from case to case. It's the whole system. The forlornness of the veal calf is pathetic, heart wrenching; the pulsing pain of the chimp with electrodes planted deep in her brain is repulsive; the slow, tortuous death of the racoon caught in the leg-hold trap is agonizing. But what is wrong isn't the pain, isn't the suffering, isn't the deprivation. These compound what's wrong. Sometimes – often – they make it much, much worse. But they are not the fundamental wrong.

13

The fundamental wrong is the system that allows us to view animals as *our resources*, here for *us* – to be eaten, or surgically manipulated, or exploited for sport or money. Once we accept this view of animals – as our resources – the rest is as predictable as it is regrettable. Why worry about their loneliness, their pain, their death? Since animals exist for us, to benefit us in one way or another, what harms them really doesn't matter – or matters only if it starts to bother us, makes us feel a trifle uneasy when we eat our veal escalope, for example. So, yes, let us get veal calves out of solitary confinement, give them more space, a little straw, a few companions. But let us keep our veal escalope.

But a little straw, more space and a few companions won't eliminate – won't even touch – the basic wrong that attaches to our viewing and treating these animals as our resources. A veal calf killed to be eaten after living in close confinement is viewed and treated in this way: but so, too, is another who is raised (as they say) 'more humanely'. To right the wrong of our treatment of farm animals requires more than making rearing methods 'more humane'; it requires the total dissolution of commercial animal agriculture.

How we do this, whether we do it or, as in the case of animals in science, whether and how we abolish their use – these are to a large extent political questions. People must change their beliefs before they change their habits. Enough people, especially those elected to public office, must believe in change – must want it – before we will have laws that protect the rights of animals. This process of change is very complicated, very demanding, very exhausting, calling for the efforts of many hands in education, publicity, political organization and activity, down to the licking of envelopes and stamps. As a trained and practising philosopher, the sort of contribution I can make is limited but, I like to think, important. The currency of philosophy is ideas – their meaning and rational foundation – not the nuts and bolts of the legislative process, say, or the mechanics of community organization. That's what I have been exploring over the past ten years or so in my essays and talks and, most recently, in my book, *The Case for Animal Rights*. I believe the major conclusions I reach in the book are true because they are supported by the weight of the best arguments. I believe the idea of animal rights has reason, not just emotion, on its side.

In the space I have at my disposal here I can only sketch, in the barest outline, some of the main features of the book. It's main themes – and we should not be surprised by this – involve asking and answering deep, foundational moral questions about what morality is, how it should be understood and what is the best moral theory, all considered. I hope I can convey something of the shape I think this theory takes. The attempt to do this will be (to use a word a friendly critic once used to describe my work) cerebral, perhaps too cerebral. But this is misleading. My feelings about how animals are sometimes treated run just as deep and just as strong as those of my more volatile compatriots. Philosophers do – to use the jargon of the day – have a right side to their brains. If it's the left side we contribute (or mainly should), that's because what talents we have reside there.

How to proceed? We begin by asking how the moral status of animals has been understood by thinkers who deny that animals have rights. Then we test the mettle of their ideas by seeing how well they stand up under the heat of fair criticism. If we start our thinking in this way, we soon find that some people believe that we have no duties directly to animals, that we owe nothing to them, that we can do nothing that wrongs them. Rather, we can do wrong acts that involve animals, and so we have duties regarding them, though none to them. Such views may be called indirect duty views. By way of illustration: suppose your neighbour kicks your dog. Then your neighbour has done something wrong. But not to the dog. The wrong that has been done is a wrong to you. After all, it is wrong to upset people, and your neighbour's kicking your dog upsets you. So you are the one who is wronged, not your dog. Or again: by kicking your dog your neighbour damages your property. And since it is wrong to damage another person's property, your neighbour has done something wrong – to you, of course, not to your dog. Your neighbour no more wrongs your dog than your car would be wronged if the windshield were smashed. Your neighbour's duties involving your dog are indirect duties to you. More generally, all of our duties regarding animals are indirect duties to one another – to humanity.

How could someone try to justify such a view? Someone might say that your dog doesn't feel anything and so isn't hurt by your neighbour's kick, doesn't care about the pain since none is felt, is as unaware of anything as is your windshield. Someone might say this, but no rational person will, since, among other considerations, such a view will commit anyone who holds it to the position that no human being feels pain either – that human beings also don't care about what happens to them. A second possibility is that though both humans and your dog are hurt when kicked, it is only human pain that matters. But, again, no rational person can believe this. Pain is pain wherever it occurs. If your neighbour's causing you pain is wrong because of the pain that is caused, we cannot rationally ignore or dismiss the moral relevance of the pain that your dog feels.

Philosophers who hold indirect duty views – and many still do – have come to understand that they must avoid the two defects just noted: that is, both the view that animals don't feel anything as well as the idea that only human pain can be morally relevant. Among such thinkers the sort of view now favoured is one or other form of what is called *contractarianism*.

Here, very crudely, is the root idea: morality consists of a set of rules that individuals voluntarily agree to abide by, as we do when we sign a contract (hence the name contractarianism). Those who understand and accept the terms of the contract are covered directly; they have rights created and recognized by, and protected in, the contract. And these contractors can also have protection spelled out for others who, though they lack the ability to understand morality and so cannot sign the contract themselves, are loved or cherished by those who can. Thus young children, for example, are unable to sign contracts and lack rights. But they are protected by the contract none the less because of the sentimental interests of others, most notably their parents. So we have, then, duties involving these children, duties regarding them, but no duties to them. Our duties in their case are indirect duties to other human beings, usually their parents.

As for animals, since they cannot understand contracts, they obviously cannot sign; and since they cannot sign, they have no rights. Like children, however, some animals are the objects of the sentimental interest of others. You, for example, love your dog or cat. So those animals that enough people care about (companion animals, whales, baby seals, the American bald eagle), though they lack rights themselves, will be protected because of the sentimental interests of people. I have, then, according to contractarianism, no duty directly to your dog or any other animal, not even the duty not to cause them pain or suffering; my duty not to hurt them is a duty I have to those people who care about what happens to them. As for other animals, where no or little sentimental interest is present – in the case of farm animals, for example, or laboratory rats – what duties we have grow weaker and weaker, perhaps to vanishing point. The pain and death they endure, though real, are not wrong if no one cares about them.

When it comes to the moral status of animals' contractarianism could be a hard view to refute if it were an adequate theoretical approach to the moral status of human beings. It is not adequate in this latter respect, however, which makes the question of its adequacy in the former case, regarding animals, utterly moot. For consider: morality, according to the (crude) contractarian position before us, consists of rules that people agree to abide by. What people? Well, enough to make a difference – enough, that is, *collectively* to have the power to enforce the rules that are drawn up in the contract. That is very well and good for the signatories but not so good for anyone who is not asked to sign. And there is nothing in contractarianism of the sort we are discussing that guarantees or requires that everyone will have a chance to participate equally in framing the rules of morality. The result is that this approach to ethics could sanction the most blatant forms of social, economic, moral and political injustice, ranging from a repressive caste system to systematic racial or sexual discrimination. Might, according to this theory, does make right. Let those who are the victims of injustice suffer as they will. It matters not so long as no one else – no contractor, or too few of them – cares about it. Such a theory takes one's moral breath away ... as if, for example, there would be nothing wrong with apartheid in South Africa if few white South Africans were upset by it. A theory with so little to recommend it at the level of the ethics of our treatment of our fellow humans cannot have anything more to recommend it when it comes to the ethics of how we treat our fellow animals.

The version of contractarianism just examined is, as I have noted, a crude variety, and in fairness to those of a contractarian persuasion it must be noted that much more refined, subtle and ingenious varieties are possible. For example, John Rawls, in his *A Theory of Justice*, sets forth a version of contractarianism that forces contractors to ignore the accidental features of being a human being – for example, whether one is white or black, male or female, a genius or of modest intellect. Only by ignoring such features, Rawls believes, can we ensure that the principles of justice that contractors would agree upon are not based on bias or prejudice. Despite the improvement a view such as Rawls's represents over the cruder forms of contractarianism, it remains deficient: it systematically denies that we have direct duties to those human beings who do not have a sense of justice – young children, for instance, and many mentally retarded humans. And yet it seems reasonably certain that, were we to torture a young child or a retarded elder, we would be doing something that wronged him or her, not something that would be wrong if (and only if) other humans with a sense of justice were upset. And since this is true in the case of these humans, we cannot rationally deny the same in the case of animals.

Indirect duty views, then, including the best among them, fail to command our rational assent. Whatever ethical theory we should accept rationally, therefore, it must at least recognize that we have some duties directly to animals, just as we have some duties directly to each other. The next two theories I'll sketch attempt to meet this requirement.

The first I call the cruelty-kindness view. Simply stated, this says that we have a direct duty to be kind to animals and a direct duty not to be cruel to them. Despite the familiar, reassuring ring of these ideas, I do not believe that this view offers an adequate theory. To make this clearer, consider kindness. A kind person acts from a certain kind of motive – compassion or concern, for example. And that is a virtue. But there is no guarantee that a kind act is a right act. If I am a generous racist, for example, I will be inclined to act kindly towards members of my own race, favouring their interests above those of others. My kindness would be real and, so far as it goes, good. But I trust it is too obvious to require argument that my kind acts may not be above moral reproach – may, in fact, be positively wrong because rooted in injustice. So kindness, notwithstanding its status as a virtue to be encouraged, simply will not carry the weight of a theory of right action.

Cruelty fares no better. People or their acts are cruel if they display either a lack of sympathy for or, worse, the presence of enjoyment in another's suffering. Cruelty in all its guises is a bad thing, a tragic human failing. But just as a person's being motivated by kindness does not guarantee that he or she does what is right, so the absence of cruelty does not ensure that he or she avoids doing what is wrong. Many people who perform abortions, for example, are not cruel, sadistic people. But that fact alone does not settle the terribly difficult question of the morality of abortion. The case is no different when we examine the ethics of our treatment of animals. So, yes, let us be for kindness and against cruelty. But let us not suppose that being for the one and against the other answers questions about moral right and wrong.

Some people think that the theory we are looking for is utilitarianism. A utilitarian accepts two moral principles. The first is that of equality: everyone's interests count, and similar interests must be counted as having similar weight or importance. White or black, American or Iranian, human or animal – everyone's pain or frustration matter, and matter just as much as the equivalent pain or frustration of anyone else. The second principle a utilitarian accepts is that of utility: do the act that will bring about the best balance between satisfaction and frustration for everyone affected by the outcome.

As a utilitarian, then, here is how I am to approach the task of deciding what I morally ought to do: I must ask who will be affected if I choose to do one thing rather than another, how much each individual will be affected, and where the best results are most likely to lie – which option, in other words, is most likely to bring about the best results, the best balance between satisfaction and frustration. That option, whatever it may be, is the one I ought to choose. That is where my moral duty lies.

The great appeal of utilitarianism rests with its uncompromising *egalitarianism*: everyone's interests count and count as much as the like interests of everyone else. The kind of odious discrimination that some forms of contractarianism can justify – discrimination based on race or sex, for example – seems disallowed in principle by utilitarianism, as is speciesism, systematic discrimination based on species membership.

The equality we find in utilitarianism, however, is not the sort an advocate of animal or human rights should have in mind. Utilitarianism has no room for the equal moral rights of different individuals because it has no room for their equal inherent value or worth. What has value for the utilitarian is the satisfaction of an individual's interests, not the individual whose interests they are. A universe in which you satisfy your desire for water, food and warmth is, other things being equal, better than a universe in which these desires are frustrated. And the same is true in the case of an animal with similar desires. But neither you nor the animal have any value in your own right. Only your feelings do.

Here is an analogy to help make the philosophical point clearer: a cup contains different liquids, sometimes sweet, sometimes bitter, sometimes a mix of the two. What has value are the liquids: the sweeter the better, the bitterer the worse. The cup, the container, has no value. It is what goes into it, not what they go into, that has value. For the utilitarian you and I are like the cup; we have no value as individuals and thus no equal value. What has value is what goes into us, what we serve as receptacles for; our feelings of satisfaction have positive value, our feelings of frustration negative value.

Serious problems arise for utilitarianism when we remind ourselves that it enjoins us to bring about the best consequences. What does this mean? It doesn't mean the best consequences for me alone, or for my family or friends, or any other person taken individually. No, what we must do is, roughly, as follows: we must add up (somehow!) the separate satisfactions and frustrations of everyone likely to be affected by our choice, the satisfactions in one column, the frustrations in the other. We must total each column for each of the options before us. That is what it means to say the theory is aggregative. And then we must choose that option which is most likely to bring about the best balance of totalled satisfactions over totalled frustrations. Whatever act would lead to this outcome is the one we ought morally to perform – it is where our moral duty lies. And that act quite clearly might not be the same one that would bring about the best results for me personally, or for my family or friends, or for a lab animal. The best aggregated consequences for everyone concerned are not necessarily the best for each individual.

That utilitarianism is an aggregative theory – different individuals' satisfactions or frustrations are added, or summed, or totalled – is the key objection to this theory. My Aunt Bea is old, inactive, a cranky, sour person, though not physically ill. She prefers to go on living. She is also rather rich. I could make a fortune if I could get my hands on her money, money she intends to give me in any event, after she dies, but which she refuses to give me now. In order to avoid a huge tax bite, I plan to donate a handsome sum of my profits to a local children's hospital. Many, many children will benefit from my generosity, and much joy will be brought to their parents, relatives and friends. If I don't get the money rather soon, all these ambitions will come to naught. The once-in-a-lifetime opportunity to make a real killing will be gone. Why, then, not kill my Aunt Bea? Oh, of course I *might* get caught. But I'm no fool and, besides, her doctor can be counted on to co-operate (he has an eye for the same investment and I happen to know a good deal about his shady past). The deed can be done . . . professionally, shall we say. There is *very* little chance of getting caught. And as for my conscience being guilt-ridden, I am a resourceful sort of fellow and will take more than sufficient comfort – as I lie on the beach at Acapulco – in contemplating the joy and health I have brought to so many others.

Suppose Aunt Bea is killed and the rest of the story comes out as told. Would I have done anything wrong? Anything immoral? One would have thought that I had. Not according to utilitarianism. Since what I have done has brought about the best balance between totalled satisfaction and frustration for all those affected by the outcome, my action is not wrong. Indeed, in killing Aunt Bea the physician and I did what duty required.

This same kind of argument can be repeated in all sorts of cases, illustrating, time after time, how the utilitarian's position leads to results that impartial people find morally callous. It *is* wrong to kill my Aunt Bea in the name of bringing about the best results for others. A good end does not justify an evil means. Any adequate moral theory will have to explain why this is so. Utilitarianism fails in this respect and so cannot be the theory we seek.

What to do? Where to begin anew? The place to begin, I think, is with the utilitarian's view of the value of the individual – or, rather, lack of value. In its place, suppose we consider that you and I, for example, do have value as individuals – what we'll call *inherent value*. To say we have such value is to say that we are something more than, something different from, mere receptacles. Moreover, to ensure that we do not pave the way for such injustices as slavery or sexual discrimination, we must believe that all who have inherent value have it equally, regardless of their sex, race, religion, birthplace and so on. Similarly to be discarded as irrelevant are one's talents or skills, intelligence and wealth, personality or pathology, whether one is loved and admired or despised and loathed. The genius and the retarded child, the prince and the pauper, the brain surgeon and the fruit vendor, Mother Teresa and the most unscrupulous used-car salesman – all have inherent value, all possess it equally, and all have an equal right to be treated with respect, to be treated in ways that do not reduce them to the status of things, as if they existed as resources for others. My value as an individual is independent of my usefulness to you. Yours is not dependent on your usefulness to me. For either of us to treat the other in ways that fail to show respect for the other's independent value is to act immorally, to violate the individual's rights.

Some of the rational virtues of this view – what I call the rights view – should be evident. Unlike (crude) contractarianism, for example, the rights view *in principle* denies the moral tolerability of any and all forms of racial, sexual or social discrimination; and unlike utilitarianism, this view *in principle* denies that we can justify good results by using evil means that violate an individual's rights –

denies, for example, that it could be moral to kill my Aunt Bea to harvest beneficial consequences for others. That would be to sanction the disrespectful treatment of the individual in the name of the social good, something the rights view will not – categorically will not – ever allow.

The rights view, I believe, is rationally the most satisfactory moral theory. It surpasses all other theories in the degree to which it illuminates and explains the foundation of our duties to one another – the domain of human morality. On this score it has the best reasons, the best arguments, on its side. Of course, if it were possible to show that only human beings are included within its scope, then a person like myself, who believes in animal rights, would be obliged to look elsewhere.

But attempts to limit its scope to humans only can be shown to be rationally defective. Animals, it is true, lack many of the abilities humans possess. They can't read, do higher mathematics, build a bookcase or make *baba ghanoush*. Neither can many human beings, however, and yet we don't (and shouldn't) say that they (these humans) therefore have less inherent value, less of a right to be treated with respect, than do others. It is the *similarities* between those human beings who most clearly, most non-controversially have such value (the people reading this, for example), not our differences, that matter most. And the really crucial, the basic similarity is simply this: we are each of us the experiencing subject of a life, a conscious creature having an individual welfare that has importance to us whatever our usefulness to others. We want and prefer things, believe and feel things, recall and expect things. And all these dimensions of our life, including our pleasure and pain, our enjoyment and suffering, our satisfaction and frustration, our continued existence or our untimely death – all make a difference to the quality of our life as lived, as experienced, by us as individuals. As the same is true of those animals that concern us (the ones that are eaten and trapped, for example), they too must be viewed as the experiencing subjects of a life, with inherent value of their own.

Some there are who resist the idea that animals have inherent value. 'Only humans have such value,' they profess. How might this narrow view be defended? Shall we say that only humans have the requisite intelligence, or autonomy, or reason? But there are many, many humans who fail to meet these standards and yet are reasonably viewed as having value above and beyond their usefulness to others. Shall we claim that only humans belong to the right species, the species *Homo sapiens*? But this is blatant speciesism. Will it be said, then, that all – and only – humans have immortal souls? Then our opponents have their work cut out for them. I am myself not ill-disposed to the proposition that there are immortal souls. Person-ally, I profoundly hope I have one. But I would not want to rest my position on a controversial ethical issue on the even more contro-versial question about who or what has an immortal soul. That is to dig one's hole deeper, not to climb out. Rationally, it is better to resolve moral issues without making more controversial assump-tions than are needed. The question of who has inherent value is such a question, one that is resolved more rationally without the introduction of the idea of immortal souls than by its use.

Well, perhaps some will say that animals have some inherent value, only less than we have. Once again, however, attempts to defend this view can be shown to lack rational justification. What could be the basis of our having more inherent value than animals? Their lack of reason, or autonomy, or intellect? Only if we are willing to make the same judgement in the case of humans who are similarly deficient. But it is not true that such humans – the retarded child, for example, or the mentally deranged – have less inherent value than you or I. Neither, then, can we rationally sustain the view that animals like them in being the experiencing subjects of a life have less inherent value. *All* who have inherent value have it *equally*, whether they be human animals or not.

Inherent value, then, belongs equally to those who are the experiencing subjects of a life. Whether it belongs to others – to rocks and rivers, trees and glaciers, for example – we do not know and may never know. But neither do we need to know, if we are to make the case for animal rights. We do not need to know, for example, how many people are eligible to vote in the next presidential election before we can know whether I am. Similarly, we do not need to know how many individuals have inherent value before we can know that some do. When it comes to the case for animal rights, then, what we need to know is whether the animals that, in our culture, are routinely eaten, hunted and used in our laboratories, for example, are like us in being subjects of a life. And we do know this. We do know that many – literally, billions and billions – of these animals are the subjects of a life in the sense explained and so have inherent value if we do. And since, in order to arrive at the best theory of our duties to one another, we must recognize our equal inherent value as individuals, reason – not sentiment, not emotion – reason compels us to recognize the equal inherent value of these animals and, with this, their equal right to be treated with respect.

That, *very* roughly, is the shape and feel of the case for animal rights. Most of the details of the supporting argument are missing. They are to be found in the book to which I alluded earlier. Here, the details go begging, and I must, in closing, limit myself to four final points.

The first is how the theory that underlies the case for animal rights shows that the animal rights movement is a part of, not antagonistic to, the human rights movement. The theory that rationally grounds the rights of animals also grounds the rights of humans. Thus those involved in the animal rights movement are partners in the struggle to secure respect for human rights – the rights of women, for example, or minorities, or workers. The animal rights movement is cut from the same moral cloth as these.

Second, having set out the broad outlines of the rights view, I can now say why its implications for farming and science, among other fields, are both clear and uncompromising. In the case of the use of animals in science, the rights view is categorically abolitionist. Lab animals are not our tasters; we are not their kings. Because these animals are treated routinely, systematically as if their value were reducible to their usefulness to others, they are routinely, system-atically treated with a lack of respect, and thus are their rights routinely, systematically violated. This is just as true when they are used in trivial, duplicative, unnecessary or unwise research as it is when they are used in studies that hold out real promise of human benefits. We can't justify harming or killing a human being (my Aunt Bea, for example) just for these sorts of reason. Neither can we do so even in the case of so lowly a creature as a laboratory rat. It is not just refinement or reduction that is called for, not just larger, cleaner cages, not just more generous use of anaesthetic or the elimination of multiple surgery, not just tidying up the system. It is complete replacement. The best we can do when it comes to using animals in science is – not to use them. That is where our duty lies, according to the rights view.

As for commercial animal agriculture, the rights view takes a similar abolitionist position. The fundamental moral wrong here is not that animals are kept in stressful close confinement or in isolation, or that their pain and suffering, their needs and prefer-ences are ignored or discounted. All these *are* wrong, of course, but they are not the fundamental wrong. They are symptoms and effects of the deeper, systematic wrong that allows these animals to be viewed and treated as lacking independent value, as resources for us – as, indeed, a renewable resource. Giving farm animals more space, more natural environments, more companions does not right the fundamental wrong, any more than giving lab animals more anaesthesia or bigger, cleaner cages would right the fundamental wrong in their case. Nothing less than the total dissolution of commercial animal agriculture will do this, just as, for similar reasons I won't develop at length here, morality requires nothing less than the total elimination of hunting and trapping for commercial and sporting ends. The rights view's implications, then, as I have said, are clear and uncompromising.

My last two points are about philosophy, my profession. It is, most obviously, no substitute for political action. The words I have written here and in other places by themselves don't change a thing. It is what we do with the thoughts that the words express – our acts, our deeds – that changes things. All that philosophy can do, and all I have attempted, is to offer a vision of what our deeds should aim at. And the why. But not the how.

Finally, I am reminded of my thoughtful critic, the one I mentioned earlier, who chastised me for being too cerebral. Well, cerebral I have been: indirect duty views, utilitarianism, contract-arianism – hardly the stuff deep passions are made of. I am also reminded, however, of the image another friend once set before me – the image of the ballerina as expressive of disciplined passion. Long hours of sweat and toil, of loneliness and practice, of doubt and fatigue: those are the discipline of her craft. But the passion is there too, the fierce drive to excel, to speak through her body, to do it right, to pierce our minds. That is the image of philosophy I would leave with you, not 'too cerebral' but *disciplined passion*. Of the discipline enough has been seen. As for the passion: there are times, and these not infrequent, when tears come to my eyes when I see, or read, or hear of the wretched plight of animals in the hands of humans. Their pain, their suffering, their loneliness, their innocence, their death. Anger. Rage. Pity. Sorrow. Disgust. The whole creation groans under the weight of the evil we humans visit upon these mute, powerless creatures. It *is* our hearts, not just our heads, that call for an end to it all, that demand of us that we overcome, for them, the habits and forces behind their systematic oppression. All great movements, it is written, go through three stages: ridicule, discussion, adoption. It is the realization of this third stage, adoption, that requires both our passion and our discipline, our hearts and our heads. The fate of animals is in our hands. God grant we are equal to the task.

The Scientific Basis for Assessing Suffering in Animals

MARIAN STAMP DAWKINS

'As far as our feelings are concerned, we are locked within our own skins.' I have always found B. F. Skinner's words to be a particularly succinct and dramatic statement of the problem of attributing feelings to anyone but ourselves. I have also been impressed by the fact that although almost everyone acknowledges that this difficulty exists, we go about our daily lives, and particularly our interactions with other people, as though it did not. We all pay lip service to the idea that subjective feelings are private but respond to the people around us as though experiences of pain and pleasure were as public as the fact that it is raining. Thank goodness that we do. Someone who stuck rigidly to the idea that all subjective experiences were essentially private and that there was not, and never could be, evidence that other people experienced anything at all would be frightening indeed. He or she would be without what is, for most of us, perhaps the most important curb on inflicting damage on another person: the belief that the damage would cause pain or suffering and that it is morally wrong to cause those experiences in other people. This is one of the cornerstones of our ideas about what is right and what is wrong. And yet this suffering we are so concerned to avoid is, if we are strictly logical about it, essentially private, an unpleasant subjective state that only we ourselves can know about, experienced by the particular person who inhabits our own skin.

Much of our behaviour towards other people is thus based on the unverifiable belief that they have subjective experiences at least somewhat like our own. It seems a reasonable belief to hold. There is enough common ground between people, despite their obvious differences of taste and upbringing, that we can attempt to put ourselves in other people's shoes and to empathize with their feelings. The fact that we can then often successfully predict what they will do or say next, and above all the fact that they may tell us that we have been successful in understanding them, suggests that the empathy has not been entirely inaccurate. We can begin to unlock them from their skins. We assume that they suffer and decide, largely on this basis, that it is 'wrong' to do certain things to them and 'right' to do other things.

Then we come to the boundary of our own species. No longer do we have words. No longer do we have the high degree of similarity of anatomy, physiology and behaviour. But that is no reason to assume that they are any more locked inside their skins than are members of our species. Even in the case of other people, understanding feelings is not always easy. Different people find pleasure or lack of it in many different ways. It takes an effort to listen and understand and to see the world from their point of view. With other species, we certainly have additional difficulties, such as the fact that some animals live all their lives submerged in water or in the intestines of bigger animals. But those difficulties are not insuperable – merely greater. We know what most humans like to eat, what makes them comfortable, what is frightening, from our own experience. With other species we may have to make an effort to find out. The purpose of this essay is to set down the sorts of things we should be finding out if we really want to know whether other animals are suffering or not. I shall argue that it is possible to build up a reasonably convincing picture of what animals experience if the right facts about them are accumulated. This is not in any sense to deny the essentially private nature of subjective feelings, nor to make any claims about the nature of mental events. It is simply to say that, just as we think we can understand other people's experiences of pleasure, pain, suffering and happiness, so, in some of the same ways, we may begin to understand the feelings of animals – if, that is, we are prepared to make an effort to study their biology. Of course, we cannot *know* what they are feeling, but then nor can we *know* with other people. That lack of absolute certainty does not stop us from making assumptions about feelings in other people. And, suitably equipped with certain biological facts about the particular species we are concerned with, nor should it with other animals either.

A word, first, about what the term 'suffering' actually means. It clearly refers to some kinds of subjective experience which have two distinguishing characteristics. First, they are unpleasant. They are mental states we would rather not experience. Secondly, they carry connotations of being extreme. A mild itch may be unpleasant, but it does not constitute 'suffering' in the way that prolonged, intense electric shocks would do. One of the problems about suffering is that it is not a unique state. We talk about suffering from lack of food, but also about suffering from overeating, as well as from cold, heat, lack of water, lack of exercise, frustration, grief and so on. Each of these states is subjectively different as an experience and has different physiological and behavioural consequences. Suffering from thirst is quite different from suffering from a bereavement, yet the same blanket term 'suffering' is used to cover them both. About the only thing they have in common, in fact, is that they can both be extremely unpleasant, and someone experiencing either of them might feel a desire to be in a different state. For this reason, defining suffering as 'experiencing one of a wide range of extremely unpleasant subjective (mental) states' is about as precise a definition as we are going to be able to devise. If we were dealing with just one sort of experience – that resulting from food deprivation, for example – we would be on much firmer ground. We could study the physiological effects and what the particular species did about it. We could measure hormone levels and brain activity and perhaps come to a precise definition. But no such simplicity exists. Animals in intensive farms have plenty to eat and yet we still worry that they may be suffering from something other than lack of food. Some species may suffer in states that no human has ever dreamed of or experienced. To be on the safe side, we will, for the moment leave the definition deliberately broad, although we will later be in a position to be a bit more precise.

Our task, therefore, is to discover methods of finding out whether and in what circumstances animals of species other than our own experience unpleasant emotional states strong enough to warrant the term 'suffering'. It is the very unpleasant nature of these states that forms the core of the problem. This is what we must look for evidence of – not (to stress the point made earlier) that we can expect direct evidence of unpleasant experiences in another being, but we can expect to gather indirect evidence from various sources and put it together to make a reasonably coherent case that an animal is suffering. There are three main sources of such evidence: its physical health, its physiological signs and its behaviour.

PHYSICAL HEALTH

The first and most obvious symptom of suffering is an animal's state of physical health. If an animal is injured or diseased, then there are very strong grounds for suspecting that it is suffering. All guidebooks and codes on animal care agree on how important it is to see that an animal is kept healthy and to treat any signs of injury or disease at once. For many species the signs of health (bright eyes, sleek coat or feathers) as well as those of illness (listlessness, loss of appetite, etc.) have been listed and in any case are well known to experienced animal keepers. There may be slight problems sometimes. Mammals that are hibernating or birds that are incubating their eggs may refuse food and show considerable loss of weight. These are normally signs of ill-health but in these particular cases seem to be perfectly natural events from which the animals subsequently emerge well and healthy. This simply illustrates that even the 'obvious' signs of suffering, such as physical ill-health, are not infallible and have to be taken in conjunction with other evidence, a point we will return to later.

Another difficulty with using physical health (or the lack of it) to decide whether or not an animal is suffering is that it is not, of course, the disease or injury itself which constitutes the suffering: it is the accompanying mental state. An animal may be injured in the sense of being physically damaged, yet show no apparent signs of pain. The experiences of other people are very revealing here. Soldiers can be wounded in battle but, at the time, report little or no pain. Conversely, people complaining of severe and constant pain can sometimes baffle their doctors because they have no signs of tissue damage or abnormality at all. Damage to the body does not always go with the highly unpleasant experiences we call 'suffering from pain'. Physiology is less help than one might expect in trying to decide when injury gives rise to pain. Although many physiologists believe that the mechanisms of pain perception are roughly similar in humans and other mammals, the physiological basis of the perception of pain is not well understood for any species. It is impossible to say with any certainty that whenever such-and-such a physiological event occurs people always report 'That hurts!' It is known that there are small nerve fibres all over the body which respond to painful stimuli, but it is difficult to interpret the messages they carry. The situation is further complicated by the existence of other nerve fibres which come out from the brain and affect the extent to which the messages in the pain fibres are allowed to travel up the spinal cord into the brain. Sometimes the messages get through and sometimes they do not, and this affects the extent to which pain is actually felt.

While pain continues to be a puzzle to physiologists, it would, however, be a mistake to use this an excuse for ignoring the effect which injury often has on animals. Mild pain may be difficult to pin down, but signs of intense pain in both human and non-human animals are unmistakable (they include squealing, struggling, convulsions, etc.). Uncertainty about whether disease, injury or loss of condition do lead to 'suffering' in a few cases should not be used to dismiss this valuable source of evidence about unpleasant mental states in animals. If animals show gross disturbances of health or injuries with symptoms of pain, it is reasonable to say that they suffer. Experiments or other tests conducted with animals which involve deliberately making them ill, inducing deformities or maiming them in some way can therefore be suspected of causing suffering, unless there are good reasons (such as the fact that an animal uses a deformed limb in an apparently normal fashion) for thinking that it is not experiencing anything unpleasant.

Sometimes the capture and transport of farm animals causes weight loss, injury and physiological deterioration so severe as to lead to death. In such circumstances the case that the animals suffered during the journey becomes very difficult to refute. In fact, the main difficulty with the physical ill-health criterion of suffering lies not so much with the (somewhat remote) possibility that animals may not suffer despite being injured or diseased as with the opposite possibility: that they may appear to be physically healthy and still be undergoing intensely unpleasant mental experiences, perhaps arising from being constantly confined in a small cage. It is this possibility – that not all mental suffering may show itself in gross and obvious disturbance of physical health – that has led people to look for other ways of trying to decide when an animal is suffering.

PHYSIOLOGICAL SIGNS

One of the most important of these methods, which has been gaining ground recently because of advances in the technology now available to it, involves monitoring the physiological processes going on inside an animal's body. As already mentioned, some of the things which are done to animals, such as transporting cattle in certain sorts of trucks, do have such traumatic effects that injury and even death may result. But even before such gross signs of suffering set in, it may be possible to detect physiological changes within the animal – changes in hormone level, for example, or in the ammonia content of muscles. Changes take place within the animal even when, on the surface, all still appears to be well. Changes in brain activity, heart rate and body temperature can also be picked up.

'Stress' is the name given to the whole group of physiological changes (which may also include activation of the sympathetic nervous system and enlargement of the adrenal glands) that take place whenever animals are subjected to a wide range of conditions and situations, such as over-crowding, repeated attacks by a member of their own species and so on. One way of viewing these physiological symptoms of stress is as part of an animal's normal and perfectly adaptive way of responding to conditions which are likely, if they persist, to lead to actual physical damage or death. Thus the heart rates goes up in preparation for an animal's escape from danger, when it will need more oxygen for its muscles in order to do this effectively. The change in heart rate suggested that the animal has recognized possible danger in the form, say, of potential injury caused by the attack of a predator. This leads to a serious difficulty in the interpretation of physiological measurements of stress. It may be perfectly possible to pick up a change in the level of a particular hormone or in heart rate, but what exactly do these changes mean for the animal? There is no justification for concluding that it 'suffers' every time there is a bit more hormone in its blood or its heart rate goes up slightly. On the contrary, these signs may simply indicate that the animal is coping with its environment in an adaptive way. Changes in brain activity may signify nothing more than that the animal is exploring a new object in its environment. We would certainly not want to describe an alert and inquiring animal as 'suffering'. On the other hand, when physiological disturbances become severe (when the adrenal glands are very enlarged, for instance) then they become the precursors of overt disease, and we probably would want to say the animal was suffering.

The problem is to know at precisely what stage physiological changes in the animal stop being part of its usual adaptive response to its environment and start indicating a prolonged or intensely unpleasant state of suffering. The problem lies not so much in detecting the changes as in their interpretation and in relating them to possible mental state. At the moment this remains a major drawback. Physiological measures, although a valuable indication of what is going on beneath the animal's skin, do not tell us everything we want to know about mental states.

A third, and very important, source of information about suffering in animals is their behaviour. Behaviour has the great advantage that it can be studied without interfering with the animal in any way. (Even with today's technology, making physiological measurements may itself impose some sort of hardship on the animal.) Many animals display particular signs which can, with care, be used to infer something about their mental states. Charles Darwin recognized this when he entitled his book about animal communication *The Expression of the Emotions in Man and Animals*. The problem, of course, is to crack the code and to work out which behaviour an animal uses to signal which emotional state.

Various different approaches have been tried. The most direct involves putting an animal in a situation in which it is thought to 'suffer' (usually mildly) and then observing its behaviour. For instance, if we wanted to know how a pig behaved when it was 'suffering from fear' or 'suffering from frustration', we might deliberately expose it briefly to one of its predators (to frighten it) or give it a dish of food covered with glass (to frustrate it). Its behaviour in these circumstances would give some indication of what it does when it is afraid or frustrated. We could then go on to an intensive pig farm and watch the pigs there to see if they showed similar behaviour. If they did, this would give us some grounds for inferring that they too were afraid or frustrated.

This method does have rather severe limitations, however. For one thing, the way a pig expresses frustration at not being able to get at food covered with glass may be quite different from the way it expresses frustration at not having any nest material, so we may simply miss out evidence of frustration through being unfamiliar with its various forms of expression. More seriously, even if we had correctly identified the way in which a pig expressed 'frustration' or 'fear', we would still be left with the same problem of calibration that we encountered with other methods such as the measurement of physiological variables. We would still not know, in other words, *how much* behaviour associated with fear or frustration has to be shown before we are justified in saying that the animal is 'suffering'. A fox temporarily caught in a thicket or unable to get into a henhouse may show agitated movements which are evidence of mild frustration, but we would hardly want to say that it is 'suffering'. But the same animal, confined for long periods of time in a small, bare cage from which there is no way out and performing the same backwards-and-forwards movements over and over again, might justifiably be described as suffering. Somewhere we want to draw the line, but it is difficult, without some further evidence, to know where.

What this method fails to do – indeed, what all the methods we have described so far fail to do – is to come to grips with the really essential issue of what we mean by suffering, to give an indication of how much what is being done to the animal really matters to the animal itself. We may see injury, measure physiological changes or watch behaviour, but what we really want to know is whether the animal is subjectively experiencing a state sufficiently unpleasant to it to deserve the emotive label 'suffering'. Does its injury cause pain? We need, in other words, the animal's opinion of what is being done to it – not just whether it finds it pleasant or unpleasant but *how* unpleasant.

'ASKING' THE ANIMALS

At first sight it may seem quite impossible even to think of trying to obtain any sensible, scientifically based evidence on this point. We cannot ask animals to tell us in so many words what it feels like to be inside their skins. But even with other human beings words are not always our most powerful source of information. We say things like, 'Actions speak louder than words' or 'He put his money where his mouth is.' The word 'mouthing' actually carries an implicit suspicion of 'mere words'. We are, in fact, particularly impressed by someone who does not just say that he dislikes or disapproves of something but shows it by taking some action and 'voting with his feet'. For all our human reliance on words and the complexity of our languages, we are often more impressed by what other human beings do than by what they say. And the things that impress us most about what they do – making choices between difficult alternatives, moving from one place to another, foregoing a desirable commodity for a later, larger reward – are things that many non-human animals do too.

Other animals besides humans can make choices and express their preferences by moving away from or towards one environment or another. They can be taught to operate a mechanism which in some way changes their environment for better or worse. A rat that repeatedly presses a lever to get food or to gain access to a female is certainly 'telling' us something about the desirability, for him, of these things. The rat which crosses an electric grid to get at a female is telling us even more. A. P. Silverman, in an article published in *Animal Behaviour* in 1978, describes an experiment in which rats and hamsters were certainly making their views plain enough. These animals were being used in an experiment to study the effects of cigarette smoke. They were kept in glass cylinders into which a steady stream of smoke was delivered down a small tube. Many of the animals quickly learned to use their own faeces to bung up the tubes and block the smoke stream. It was not completely clear whether it was the smoke itself or the draught of air that they objected to, but it was quite clear that they disliked what was being done to them. Words here would simply have been superfluous.

This 'asking without words' approach has now been used in a wide variety of situations. It is a direct way of finding out, from the animal's point of view, what it finds pleasant or unpleasant. Choice tests, in which animals are offered two or more alternatives, enable them to 'vote with their feet'. For example, as I have described in an article that appeared in *Animal Behaviour* in 1977, chickens which have been kept in battery cages have shown clearly that they prefer an outside run rather than a cage. These two very different environments were presented to hens at the opposite ends of a corridor from the centre of which they could see both simultaneously. They were then free to walk into either one. Most of the hens chose to go into the outside run, not the battery cage, the first time they were given the choice. A few of the hens chose the battery cage at first, probably because that was what they were used to – the run was such a novel experience for them that they did not seem to know what it was. But all they needed was a few minutes' experience of the run, and by the second or third time they were faced with the choice, they too chose the run. This seems to be a fairly objective way of saying that the hens liked the experience of being outside in a run more than they liked being in a battery cage.

While this result is perhaps not particularly unexpected, animals' own preferences do sometimes produce surprises. The Brambell Committee, which produced an important report on intensive farming in the UK in 1965, recommended that fine hexagonal wire should not be used for the floors of battery cages on the grounds that it was thought (by well-meaning humans) to be uncomfortable for the hens' feet. When allowed to choose between different floor types, however, the hens actually preferred the fine mesh to the coarser one which had been recommended by the Committee, as B. O. Hughes and A. J. Black reported in *British Poultry Science* in 1973. Other animals that have been 'asked' their opinion of their surroundings are laboratory mice and rats, which have shown preferences for certain sorts of nest box and cage size; and in 1967 B. A. Baldwin and D. L. Ingram published an article in *Physiology and Behaviour* on pigs which indicated preferences for heat levels and lighting regimes by being provided with switches which they could operate with their snouts to regulate heat and light. Sometimes animals' preferences result in an actual saving for the farmer. In *Farm Animal Housing and Welfare*, edited by S. and M. Baxter and J. MacCormack, Stan Curtis reported a study on a group of young pigs which actually turned their heating down at night, below the level that humans thought should be maintained all the time, which resulted in a considerable saving in fuel. Such a happy coincidence between what animals like and what is best for commercial profit does not, however, always occur.

In any case, just because an animal prefers one set of conditions to another does not neccessarily mean that it suffers if kept in the less preferred ones. In order to establish the link – that is, to make the connection between preference (or lack of it) and suffering – it is necessary to find out how strong the animal's aversion to the less attractive situation is, or how powerfully it is attracted to preferred conditions. If a male rat will cross a live electric grid to get a female or a hen goes without food in order to obtain somewhere to dustbathe, they are demonstrating that these things are not just 'liked' but are very important to them indeed. Many people would agree that animals suffer if kept without food or if given electric shocks. If the animals tell us that other things are as important as or more important to them than food or the avoidance of shock, then we might want to say that they suffer if deprived of these other things as well.

We have, therefore, to get animals to put a 'price' on their preferences. Now, it is obviously something of a problem to decide how to ask animals how they rate one commodity, such as food, against something that may be quite different, such as the opportunity to dustbathe, wallow in mud or fight a rival. But the problem is not insuperable, and one of the easiest ways to determine this is through what psychologists call 'operant conditioning', which simply means giving an animal the chance to learn that by pressing a lever, say, it gets something it likes, such as a piece of food (a reward), or can avoid something it doesn't like (a punishment). Depending on the animal, what it has to do can vary. Birds often find it easier to peck a disc rather than operate a lever, which a rat would do readily, and fish, of course, would have difficulties with either and would have to be given, say, a hoop to swim through. Once the animal has learned to do whatever has been devised for it, the experimenter can then begin to put up the 'price' by making the animal peck the key or press the lever not just once but many times before it gets anything at all. In the Netherlands J. van Rooijen reports, in an article published in *Applied Animal Ethology* in 1983, that he has used this method to measure the strength of the preference of pigs for earth floors by forcing them to make a larger number of responses in order to be allowed access to the earth.

When food is being used as the reward, animals usually appear to be prepared to work harder and harder for the same reward, indicating, not surprisingly, that food is very important to them. Other commodities, however, seem to be less important. Male Siamese fighting fish can readily be trained to do things for the reward of being able to see and display at a rival fish of the same species. But if the number of responses the fish has to make for each opportunity to display at a rival is increased, the fish do not work any harder and so obtain a smaller number of views of their rival, according to J. A. Hogan, S. Kleist and C. S. L. Hutchings, whose findings were published in the *Journal of Comparative and Physiological Psychology* in 1970. A similar result has been reported for cocks pecking at keys for food and for the sight of another cock. When the number of pecks required for each presentation (bit of food or sight of a rival) went up, the birds would work much harder for food than to see their rival. Access to a rival seemed in both these examples to be less important to the animals than food.

AN OBJECTIVE MEASURE OF SUFFERING

There are, then, ways of obtaining measures of how much an animal prefers or dislikes something. Here is the key to discovering the circumstances in which an animal finds things so unpleasant that we want to say that it is suffering. If it will work hard to obtain or to escape from something – as hard as or harder than it will work to obtain food which most people would agree is an essential to health and welfare – then we can begin to compile a list of situations which cause suffering and, indeed, can arrive at a tentative further definition of suffering itself: animals suffer if kept in conditions in which they are without something that they will work hard to obtain, given the opportunity, or in conditions that they will work hard to get away from, also given the opportunity. 'Working hard' can be given precise meaning, as explained earler, by putting up the 'price' of a commodity and seeing how much it is worth to the animal. We have then the animal's view of its environment.

Of course, we have to make one important assumption: that if animals are prepared to work hard in this way, they do experience a mental state which is 'pleasant' if something is rewarding and 'unpleasant' if they are trying to avoid that something. We have, in other words, to make a leap from inside our own skins to the inside of theirs. But this leap is a very bare minimum. It does not assume that other animals find the *same* things pleasant or unpleasant as we do, only that working to obtain or working to avoid something is an indication of the presence of these mental states and that working hard is an indication that they are very pleasant or very unpleasant. Exactly what other animals find very pleasant or very unpleasant is left to experimental tests. In other words, the leap that we have to make from our skins to theirs takes into account the possibility that their suffering or their pleasure may be brought about by events quite different from those that cause them in us. We are not imagining ourselves shut up in a battery cage or dressed up in a bat suit when we try to find out what it is like to be a hen or a bat; we are trying to find out what it is like to *be* them. There is a lot of difference between the two. In the first case we would see animals as just like us, only with fur or feathers. In the second case we acknowledge that their view of the world may be very different from our own, that their requirements and what makes them comfortable or uncomfortable may be nothing like what we ourselves would require. We then have to get down to the business of finding out what their view of the world really is. Operant conditioning may be the key, the window on to their world, but it takes quite a lot of effort to get all the answers we need.

Even then we are not completely home and dry. Preference tests and operant conditioning, though immensely valuable tools, do not provide all the answers. A dog might show very strongly, if 'asked' in this way, that he would rather not go to the vet. One could make out a strong case for saying that he 'suffers' if forced to do so. Cattle, given a free choice, do not always eat what is good for them and may even poison themselves. It would therefore be a mistake to use these methods in isolation from other measures of suffering. A synthetic approach (one, that is, that takes into account all the measures that we have discussed) is probably the safest bet in the long run. Since each of these measures has something to be said against it, some limits to its usefulness, the safest approach is therefore to make as many different sorts of measurement as we can and then to put them together to see what sort of conglomerate picture we get. For example, suppose some hypothetical animals were kept in small cages, in conditions that were very different from those of their wild ancestors. Suppose people had expressed considerable worry that they were suffering. How might we go about evaluating this claim?

We might look first at the physical health of the animals. If we found them to be very healthy, with bright eyes and sleek, glossy coats and no signs of injury or parasites, we might then want to proceed to other measures. If we noticed that the animal showed a number of unusual behaviour patterns not shown by freer animals of the same species, the next step would be to investigate what caused them to behave in this way. In the first case it might be that the unusual behaviour was solely the result of the animals showing positive reactions to their keepers. We might also find that the animals appeared to 'like' their cages and that they would choose them in preference to other conditions which well-meaning humans thought they would prefer. In such circumstances our verdict might be that although the animals were kept in highly unnatural conditions, they did not, on any criteria, appear to be suffering as a result. On the other hand, the conclusions might be very different even for physically healthy animals. If the animals showed evidence of a high degree of frustration, prolonged over much of their lives, with evidence of a build-up of physiological symptoms that were known to be precursors of disease, we might begin to think they were suffering. If, in addition, they showed every sign of trying to escape from their cages, and indeed did so when given the opportunity, our evidence on this point would become even stronger.

The point of these hypothetical examples is to show how, given different sorts of evidence, different conclusions can be reached

The Ideas

about whether or not animals are suffering. We have still not observed their mental states directly. Nor have we escaped altogether from some use of analogy with our own feelings to tell us what a member of another species might be experiencing. In the last analysis, we have to rely on analogy with ourselves to decide that any other being (including another human) experiences anything at all, since our own skin is the only one we have any direct experience of being inside. But analogy with ourselves that relies on seeing animals as just like human beings with fur or feathers is quite different and much more prone to error than analogy which makes full use of our biological knowledge of the animal concerned – the conditions in which it is healthy, what it chooses, its behaviour and its physiology. This second kind of analogy, the piece-by-piece construction of a picture (What does the animal like? What makes it healthy? What are its signs of fear or frustration?), is hard work to construct, as it needs a lot of basic research on each kind of animal with which we might come into contact. But it is the only kind of analogy which, in the end, will give us any real hope of being able to unlock other species from their skins and of beginning to see the world through not just our eyes but theirs as well.

Good Dogs and Other Animals

STEPHEN R. L. CLARK

When sentimental humans call their pet 'good dog', they usually mean only that the dog happens to have done what they wanted him to. We sometimes call babies 'good' for much the same reason, and not because they ought to be imitated by anyone who wants to live a good or an admirable life. Even when we say, 'So-and-so is a good man', we may mean only that the man is a useful worker, to be praised and cosseted and used. But we also know that good men and women ('morally' good men and women) are those who can be counted on to do what they ought, and for the right reasons. They are courageous and kindly, loyal, honest, temperate and just. They have good characters and do what they ought to do because they see they ought.

We usually assume, on the other hand, that animals let nothing stand in the way of their desires. Their wants are simple – like the dog with one thought for each paw (food, food, sex and food) – and anything that satisfies those wants will do. Whereas human beings do not willingly eat everything that is strictly edible (or there would be thriving cockroach farms in every American city), animals will eat anything that their stomachs can digest and that they can capture. Whereas human beings seem to love to make difficulties for themselves in sexual affairs, animals respond to lust as they would to an itch. This is not to say that animals do not have preferences, but they do not seem to have taboos. To live 'like an animal' (especially in the mouths of judges) is to live without any of the acknowledged restraints of decency, good manners or respect for persons. This sounds like a good idea to those romantically inclined to reject civilization, overturn tradition and begin again as noble savages. It usually sounds like a very bad idea to the rest of us. Civilization depends upon our not doing what we immediately and unthinkingly want to do (kill jay-walking pedestrians, steal books, seduce minors).

Those who disapprove of the behaviour of animals naturally feel a similar distaste for alien (presumably savage) human customs. Samuel Johnson, the great moralist and lexicographer who died two centuries ago, could not believe that 'savages', illiterate peoples, could have anything to teach him. According to James Boswell, in his *Life of Samuel Johnson*, he declared, 'Pity is not natural to man . . . but acquired and improved by the cultivation of reason. Savages are always cruel.' 'Natural affection is nothing: but affection from principle and established duty is sometimes wonderfully strong' – so savages have no more affection than do hens. Nor do they marry: 'a savage man and a savage woman meet by chance; and when the man sees another woman that pleases him better, he will leave the first.' Johnson's determined ignorance is now an embarrassment to his admirers (including myself). Why could he not have understood that other human tribes have their own arts and decencies, that they do not merely act out their momentary whims? He spoke from within his tradition, as the Greek philosopher Aristotle did when he declared that the more distant barbarians were beast-like, in that they lived 'only by perception', without – he supposed – being able to give principled reasons for their actions and without any long-term goals.

Every decent moralist is now conscious that all human tribes have inherited cosmologies and political systems. We hope, at least, that there are no 'natural slaves' of the sort Aristotle (unfortunately) taught exploring Europeans to expect, lacking any moral conscience and acting out of immediate desire or fear. But Johnson's attitude to animals – the view that they too are moved only by the prospect of immediate pleasure – is still widely held. 'Anthropomorphism' is the deadly sin of supposing that animals have customs, friends, serious emotions or needs beyond the merely physical. Most commentators recognize that contempt for 'savages' serves ideological and commercial interests, giving us an excuse for disrupting the savages' life, turning them out of their homelands and refusing to accept that they need to be able to control their own lives in accordance with their own traditions. That contempt for animals serves similarly ideological ends is not as widely recognized. To behave 'like an animal' is to have dropped out, to have abandoned cultivated manners and an awareness of one's place in the social universe. To be an animal is to be mere material for the purposes of human beings, whether those purposes are humane or not.

The older habit, and one reason why people now disapprove of anthropomorphism, was to describe animals in entirely human terms. People once believed it literally true that the lion was king of the beasts, that the world of wild things and the world of civilized humanity (which is to say, our kind of human beings) were built according to the same pattern. All animals were members of the kingdom of animals, as though difference of species was no more than a difference of class or profession (and the latter no less than a difference of species). Animals had their own mysterious language, their own law. They did what people did: if one animal killed another, he displayed the same sort of ferocity as would a human warrior. If one looked after another, it was out of maternal or comradely compassion. Moralists took examples from the behaviour of animals even though they also held that animals were really moved by nothing more than desire or fear. For these moralists, the animals were not thinking about what would happen to the creatures they affected and so could not 'really' be compassionate, or soldierly, or loyal.

The older way of thinking about animals was clearly confused, and some scholars were led to attribute far too much human intelligence and moral sensibility to animals. This led others to try to describe animal behaviour without committing themselves to any view about what purposes or perceptions they had. When modern students of animal behaviour say that an animal is 'aggressive', they mean only that the animal goes through certain motions that can usually be expected to result either in a fight or in the withdrawal of the opposing animal. They do not mean to imply that the animal actively wishes to hurt its opponent, or even that it knows it has an opponent. If a stickleback can be made to attack an unrealistic model of a fish with a red belly, we do not need to think that when it fights a real male rival it is 'genuinely' angry, in the way that we sometimes are. When we describe what people are doing we use our knowledge of their motives to distinguish between different acts: when Zachary kills Tamar it is not murder unless he really intended to kill her or hurt her very badly. Orthodox ethologists have abandoned the attempt to say what animals intend or want, and the words they use are not supposed to imply anything about the animals' own feelings. By keeping to what can be measured and recorded on camera or tape, they hope to avoid the perils of anthropomorphism.

This approach is a helpful one when we are dealing with some animals, those that have relatively few options and those with whom we do not readily empathize. If woodlice congregate in damp, dark patches, we need not suppose that they have some idea of what they are looking for, or an internal map of the territory, or any wish to greet their friends and neighbours. It is enough that they move faster when it is dry, and slow down when it is damp. If salmon can find their way back to the stream where they were born, we need not think that they know where they are going, nor do we need to imagine them fighting heroically with the current. They are only swimming towards a stronger concentration of some chemical in the water. If hunting wasps construct nests and supply their future progeny with paralysed caterpillars, it is not because they wish their offspring well but because they are acting out 'fixed action patterns', each one released by the successful completion of its predecessor. If the caterpillar is removed, the wasp will still seal up the nest and move on to the next one.

But though there are good reasons not to read too much of our own experience into the behaviour of animals, and though it is sometimes helpful to attempt as 'objective' a description as possible of what they do, the philosophical assumptions behind this programme are very odd. It is certainly often difficult to know what other people are feeling and thinking. It even makes sense, of a sort, to wonder whether the things we call people are perhaps really cleverly designed robots, whose behaviour is merely physical and who have no subjective life at all. But anyone who seriously concluded that this made it reasonable for him to treat people as if they were indeed nothing but insentient robots would be thought deranged. There are general difficulties about how we can form reasonable beliefs about minds other than our own. There are also general difficulties about how we can be sure that there are real material bodies: it makes sense to suppose that there are none, that all our experiences of closed doors and stubborn boulders are merely mental. Some modern physicists have indeed drawn the conclusion that electrons and photons and the rest of the particles that theory demands are fictitious, that the 'laws of physics' really refer only to the sorts of observation that physicists might make, not to any real world independent of their observations. It is one of the ironies of history that life scientists are much more materialistic than physical scientists. Irony apart, it is at least very peculiar that students of animal behaviour should think that merely 'physical' observations (e.g. how fast a thing is moving) are reliable indicators of the real world, while empathetic understanding of what others might be feeling and thinking can never be relied upon. If we cannot understand each other, all science collapses, since we need to be assured that our colleagues are honest and rational observers. If we refuse to let ourselves understand what animals are doing, if we never let ourselves see things, as it were, with a gull's eye, or a baboon's, how much are we likely to understand? Merely 'physical' description ('And now the chimpanzee's hands have contacted an empty oil can, and the can is rolling around the clearing, and the chimpanzee is emitting sounds') may be an aid to acute observation, but we have a more secure and useful understanding of the event when we know that the chimpanzee is taking advantage of human rubbish to impress his group.

In short: to say that a man has lost his temper is no less an observational statement than to say that he has lost his trousers. The evidence that either is true is, in a sense, compatible with its being false: maybe the man is acting, or maybe there is an optical illusion. Students may devise interesting and useful theories about what is going on at a neurophysiological or chemical level when a man has a tantrum. It may even be that a knowledge of the laws of chemical change would be enough to predict the motions through which his body will go (if only we had enough time to do the calculation). But even such a precise, physical theory would not prove that he was *not* genuinely in a temper, nor would it prove that his being in a temper was not a good explanation for his silence, his tense muscles, his inability to open an envelope tidily, his expressed belief that he has suffered a serious injustice and so on.

Scientists who profess to believe that animals have no accessible inner life are rarely consistent. If this were really their belief, they would consider it a waste of time to try to anaesthetize an animal and would certainly not draw conclusions about the psychology of human beings from the motions of non-human beings. It is perhaps more usual to think that animals do have feelings but that these feelings do not involve any lengthy foresight, nor any concept of the animal's place in the world and in society. This is in essence the traditional view: not that animals are machines, but that they are moved solely by immediate desire or pain. When a rat learns not to run over an electrified floor, this is held to be a mere conditioned reflex, not an intelligent assessment of the situation: although the rat is repelled by the sight or smell of the floor, it does not know why.

Although this view of things is not wholly unbelievable when applied, say, to amoebae, only those who still think that animals and human beings belong to separate kingdoms can easily suppose that chimpanzees are more like amoebae than they are like humans. If no animals except ourselves ever really think (i.e. grasp what is going on and what might be expected to follow, and respond not only to immediate sensations but also to the imagined causes of those sensations), how is it that human beings can think? Are we really alien or supernatural creatures? It seems very much more likely that our minds as well as our bodies resemble those of other animals – some more than others. If hunting wasps do not really care for their young, it is clear that primates do. Vervet monkeys, for example, not only recognize their own cub's cry but recognize too whose responsibility another cub may be (and look towards her). Adult affection for the young may not be genuinely altruistic – young hamadryas baboons must sometimes wish that their elders were not quite as passionate in their pursuit. But the tests that show that wasps do not have any interest in their young are ones that any reasonable higher primate can pass. Monkeys who are reared by human (but in-humane) psychologists in loveless environments, with only imitation 'mothers' to cuddle, themselves make lousy mothers and treat their offspring as they might a rat or an uncomfortable growth. Normal mammals respond appropriately to their offspring's call. Normal primates, in particular, recognize each other as individuals and have clearly personal relations with their fellows.

More generally, to say that animals are 'only' responding to sensory cues, and not to any more global grasp of the situation and their own role in it, is not really a simpler explanation. If an animal is to respond appropriately to a painful stimulus, it must be acting out an innate, fixed action pattern. Even to learn from experience we must already be acting, consciously or not, on the principle 'Do what brought us satisfaction last time.' So there seems no final reason why we should not admit the existence of other general principles of action – dispositions to behave in one way rather than another. Natural virtues are just such dispositions. Moral virtues, indeed, are dispositions that the agent has deliberately acquired. A morally virtuous man has moulded himself to play some part in society that he and others reckon valuable. Maybe non-humans cannot train themselves. It does not follow that they have no natural dispositions or that they have no grasp at all of what goes on.

Even creatures whose behaviour does at first seem to be merely a response to sensory stimuli, in accordance with their natural disposition, may be more complex than we thought. While woodlice need have no internal map of their territory, worms perhaps do: at any rate, they reconstruct their tunnel systems. Many animals, indeed, so far from responding only to present stimuli, operate largely in terms of a learned map of the area, which is why bats sometimes bump into things, and laboratory mice can be induced to leap into empty space with the conviction that there is a safe landing. This is how self-consciousness arises, the capacity to locate oneself within physical and social space (like the vervets), to know where one is and whom one is dealing with and what is expected of one. There is good reason to think that animals may be self-conscious (in differing degrees) and that they can manipulate their companions because they can form an idea of how those companions will respond to their own actions. Witness the young chimpanzee who walks away from a luxury he is too low in the hierarchy to claim, knowing that the others will follow him: a little later he returns secretively to get the treat. Witness also such 'problem dogs' as manipulate their human owners into taking them for walks or never leaving them alone.

The ability to identify others as individuals and to recognize oneself as an object in public space is perhaps connected with the sort of upbringing animals receive. Creatures who produce a lot of young, of whom only a few will survive, are unlikely to recognize or care for them, or for anyone else, as individuals. Creatures who have few, slowly maturing offspring can be expected to care for those offspring. Since such care will require that they be able to provide for them, they will not, in general, wish to do what produces offspring unless they can count on ample provision – unless, that is, they have a territory that will support them (this is not to say that they necessarily think this policy out). This is why birds form couples only when there is territorial space available and may (in some species) be attached precisely to the space rather than to their individual partners. In those species the appearance of marital fidelity is an illusion: what generally keeps the same birds together is that each has an attachment to the territorial space. Those who are unable to make good their claim upon such a territory do not form couples or produce many offspring (except, of course, by 'cheating' –

laying eggs in an established couple's nest or seducing the female). In other species the problem is dealt with by their ability to recognize each other as individuals and their being bound to marital fidelity. Barbary doves, for example, have been shown to be monogamous, to be faithful to their first partners even at unfamiliar nesting sites.

These patterns of preference can be shown to make sense in terms of the needs of the offspring and the nature of the animal's *Umwelt* (which is to say, the environment as it is for an animal of that kind, with those senses, capacities and preferences). Creatures that characteristically produce a few, slowly maturing offspring will not be indifferent to their offspring, or mate promiscuously (which would waste energy), or be unable to distinguish individuals of their own kind (unless they are strongly territorial creatures, which feel about a piece of land as a gander does about his goose).

This conclusion, that mammals, like ourselves, will care for their children as individuals, should not be exaggerated: though human beings have fewer and more slowly maturing offspring than, for example, the domestic cat, it does not follow that human beings cannot treat their young with a comparable sternness. What does seem clear is that some birds and mammals, at least, will be capable of forming personal attachments and will be aware of their own position in the world and in society. Without such attachments, without such awareness, creatures of their kind would not survive long enough to reproduce. Among the natural virtues of the higher mammals, at any rate, will be those of parental care and faithfulness.

We can identify other virtuous dispositions that animals are likely to display. Members of the same species are natural rivals for food and territory and mates. But it does not follow that arrogant individualists will be most successful in propagating their kind. Creatures that always fight to the finish, that will never accept defeat gracefully, that always kill or rob their rivals may win an occasional battle, but they must spend so much time and energy on forcing their will on others that any timid mutant which avoids fights will be able to leave behind more offspring. Rather than fighting directly for the goods they desire, animals are likely to try out their strengths in a way that does not seriously damage anyone. They do not usually use their most dangerous weapons against their rivals, and losers accept their lot. They may even (in disaster areas) let themselves starve to death while the dominant few eat relatively well. This last phenomenon need not be interpreted as a conscious suicide for the good of the tribe. It is more likely to be a byproduct of the usually 'successful' strategy of 'wait and see': better to wait for the dominant's leavings and hope for a return match later on than risk a real fight now. Conversely, it is often better for the dominants (those successful in the contests that define the eating and mating orders) to allow their subordinates lives of their own, sometimes even to assist them, and not to press home their attacks lest their victim turn upon them with the courage of despair.

The rules of 'war' were among the first to be noticed by ethologists: witness the 'merciful wolf', who spares his defeated rival when that rival rolls over and pretends to be a cub again. The assumption made by Konrad Lorenz, one of the few remaining ethologists not to be obsessed by the need to avoid anthropomorphism, that the wolf is 'inhibited' from killing his rival where a human victor would not be is questionable on at least two counts. First, there is good reason to think that human beings are very well able to kill each other but usually do not. There is no clear evidence that their record is much worse than the wolves'. Secondly, Lorenz gives no reason to describe the case as one of 'inhibition'. The wolf does not (generally) kill – but that is evidence that he does not wish to, and perhaps never did wish to. He wishes to establish his superior rank, and that he does. We do not need to suppose that the wolf wants to kill his rival but disapproves of his wanting to do so and accordingly refrains. It is probably better to suppose that any desire he has to kill simply evaporates when his defeated rival resigns the contest. This sort of character is one that we could sensibly commend, but it is not quite as much like human moral virtue as Lorenz implies.

Other forms of animal behaviour might be compared with moral virtue more convincingly. It turns out that incest, or at any rate inbreeding, is much less frequent than we would expect if animals behaved like Johnson's savages. Female chimpanzees resist the advances of their brothers and of any other too familiar males. When Lucy Temerlin, a chimpanzee reared with humans and without experience of her conspecifics, reached puberty she rejected the attentions of her human foster-brother and foster-father while avidly pursuing any other human males. Here the reports do suggest much more strongly that Lucy experienced considerable conflict between her desire and her aversion, a conflict that might plausibly be compared with those of moralizing humanity. In this case an animal was inhibited from doing what she perhaps half-wanted to do. In another, reported by Jane van Lawick-Goodall from her observations of wild chimpanzees in the Gombe National Park, most of the chimpanzees ignored or bullied a companion who was partly paralysed. One chimpanzee, though disliking the smell (and one can reasonably assume) as much 'turned off' by physical weakness and abnormality as his companions (and most humans), did none the less continue to treat the unfortunate and lonely ape as his old friend and companion. The disposition to friendship was stronger in him than the impulse to despise. This character too we would commend, even if we doubted that the altruistic chimpanzee thought he was 'doing his duty' – which some moralists have thought is the most important motive for moral action. He preferred one way of acting to another that he might have preferred.

Moral conscience, as we understand it, reflects on the actions and emotions of others as well as on one's own. To disapprove of oneself is also to disapprove of others similarly placed. Indeed, there is some reason to think that I come to know myself by knowing others who know me; I come to disapprove of myself by knowing, and approving of, others who might. So it is crucial to the existence of conscience (and self-consciousness in general) that there be social groups whose members attempt to regulate each other's behaviour. To do this they must be able to re-identify each other; they must have some grasp of past history; each must attend not merely to what other creatures are doing to him or her but also to what they are doing to each other. Such behaviour is not always found where we might expect it. The cannibalistic pair of chimpanzees discovered in the Gombe, for example, were (understandably) feared and resented by their fellows, but there has apparently been no attempt to ostracize or punish them. Other breaches of tribal discipline perhaps earn greater disapproval, notably (in some species) the attempt to dispossess an established nesting couple (if that is anything more than the mobbing of a supposed predator) or a failure of parental duty. If vervet females can respond to their own cub's cry, and also look (pointedly) at the mother of another crying cub, there is reason to think that they are operating in such a social system and that the roots of conscience are there.

By way of brief conclusion: to be a 'good dog' is to have those virtues of character that must be fairly widespread in a natural population if creatures of that kind are to survive and reproduce. A good dog is discriminating in her choice of mate, faithful to her cubs, prepared to spare her rivals and to accept her place in the social hierarchy of her group with good grace. Those animals that are of a kind that can be expected to identify others as individuals, and to reflect upon their own actions towards those individuals, may show some signs of having preferred the paths of virtue to those of easy gratification. Human animals alone, so far as we can see, have taken the next step, that of trying to assess their own sentiments in the light of reason. When they do, they are easily persuaded that they must not live 'like animals', out of immediate desire or fear. It would perhaps be better to remember that animals themselves do not live 'like animals'. Good animals of any kind (including the human) have some grasp of the physical and social worlds in which they live and prefer the paths of friendship and fidelity to those of war.

Persons and Non-Persons

MARY MIDGLEY

Is a dolphin a person?

This question came up during the trial of the two people who, in May 1977, set free two bottle-nosed dolphins used for experimental purposes by the University of Hawaii's Institute of Marine Biology. It is an interesting question for a number of reasons, and I want to devote most of this chapter to interpreting it and tracing its connection with several others which may already be of concern to us. I shall not go into the details of the actual case but shall rely on the very clear and thoughtful account which Gavin Daws gives in his paper '"Animal Liberation" as Crime', published in *Ethics and Animals*, edited by Harlan B. Miller and William H. Williams.

Kenneth Le Vasseur, the first of the two men to be tried, attempted through his counsel what is called a 'choice of evils' defence. In principle the law allows this in cases where an act, otherwise objectionable, is necessary to avoid a greater evil. For this defence to succeed, the act has to be (as far as the defendant knows) the only way of avoiding an imminent, and more serious, harm or evil to himself or to 'another'. Le Vasseur, who had been involved in the care of the dolphins, believed that their captivity, with the conditions then prevailing in it, actually endangered their lives.

> in his opening statement for the defence, [his counsel] spoke of the exceptional nature of dolphins as animals; bad and rapidly deteriorating physical conditions at the laboratory; a punishing regimen for the dolphins, involving overwork, reductions in their food rations, the total isolation they endured, deprived of the company of other dolphins, even of contact with humans in the tank, deprived of all toys

which they had formerly enjoyed playing with – to the point where Puka, having refused to take part consistently in experimental sessions, developed self-destructive behaviours symptomatic of deep disturbance, and finally became lethargic – 'comatose'. Le Vasseur, seeing this, fearing that death would be the outcome, and knowing that there was no law that he could turn to, believed himself authorized, in the interests of the dolphins' well-being, to release them. The release was not a theft in that Le Vasseur did not intend to gain anything for himself. It was intended to highlight conditions in the laboratory.

But was a dolphin 'another'? The judge thought not. He said that 'another' would have to be another person, and he defined dolphins as property, not as persons, as a matter of law. A dolphin could not be 'another person' under the penal code. The defence tried and failed to get the judge disqualified for prejudice. It then asked leave to go to Federal Court in order to claim that Thirteenth Amendment rights in respect of involuntary servitude might be extended to dolphins. This plea the judge rejected:

> Judge Doi said, 'We get to dolphins, we get to orang-utans, chimpanzees, dogs, cats. I don't know at what level you say intelligence is insufficient to have that animal or thing, or whatever you want to call it, a human being under the penal code. I'm saying that they're not under the penal code and that's my answer.

At this point – which determined the whole outcome of the trial – something seemed perfectly obvious to the judge about the meaning of the words 'other' and 'person'. What was it? And how obvious is it to everybody else? In the answer just given, he raises the possibility that it might be a matter of intelligence, but he rejects it. That consideration, he says, is not needed. The question is quite a simple one; no tests are called for. The word 'person' means a human being.

I think that this is a very natural view but not actually a true one, and the complications which we find when we look into the use of this very interesting word are instructive. In the first place, there are several well-established and venerable precedents for calling non-human beings 'persons'. One concerns the persons of the Trinity and, indeed, the personhood of God. Another is the case of 'legal persons' – corporate bodies such as cities or colleges, which count as persons for various purposes, such as suing and being sued. As Blackstone says, these 'corporations or bodies politic . . . are formed and created by human laws for the purposes of society and government', unlike 'natural persons', who can be created only by God.

The law then can, if it chooses, create persons; it is not merely a passive recorder of their presence (as, indeed, Judge Doi implied in making his ruling a matter of law and not of fact). Thirdly, an instance that seems closer to the case of the dolphins, the word is used by zoologists to describe the individual members of a compound or colonial organism, such as a jellyfish or coral, each having (as the dictionary reasonably puts it) a 'more or less independent life'. (It is also interesting that 'personal identity' is commonly held to belong to continuity of consciousness rather than of bodily form in stories where the two diverge. Science fiction strongly supports this view, which was first mooted by John Locke in his *Essay Concerning Human Understanding*.)

There is nothing stretched or paradoxical about these uses, for the word does not in origin mean 'human being' or anything like it at all. It means 'a mask', and its basic general sense comes from the drama. The 'masks' in a play are the characters who appear in it. Thus, to quote the Oxford Dictionary again, after 'a mask', it means 'a character or personage acted, one who plays or performs any part, a character, relation or capacity in which one acts, a being having legal rights, a juridical person'. The last two meanings throw a clear light on the difference between this notion and that of being human. Not all human beings need be persons. The word *persona* in Latin does not apply to slaves, though it does apply to the state as a corporate person. Slaves have, so to speak, no speaking part in the drama; they do not figure in it; they are extras. There are some similar, and entertaining, examples about women. The following is taken from Susan Möller Okin's book *Women in Western Political Thought*:

> One case, brought before the US Supreme Court in the 1890s, concerned Virginia's exclusion of a woman from the practice of the law, although the pertinent statute was worded in terms of 'persons'. The Court argued that it was indeed up to the State's Supreme Court *'to determine whether the word "person" as used (in the Statute) is confined to males,* and whether women are admitted to practise law in that Commonwealth'. The issue of whether women must be understood as included by the word 'persons' continued even into the twentieth century. . . . In a Massachusetts case in 1931 . . . women were denied eligibility for jury service, although the statute stated that every 'person qualified to vote' was so eligible. The Massachusetts Supreme Court asserted; 'No intention to include women can be deduced from the omission of the word male.' (Emphasis added)

What is going on here? We shall not understand it, I think, unless we grasp how deeply drama is interwoven with our thinking, how intimately its categories shape our ideas. People who talk like this have a clear notion of the drama which they think is going on around them. They know who is supposed to count in it and who is not. Attempts to introduce fresh characters irritate them. They are inclined to dismiss these attempts sharply as obviously absurd and paradoxical. The question of who is and who is not a person seems at this point a quite simple and clear-cut one. Bertie Wooster simply is not a character in Macbeth and that is the end of the matter. It is my main business here to point out that this attitude is too crude. The question is actually a very complex one, much more like 'Who is important?' than 'Who has got two legs?' If we asked 'Who is important?', we would know that we needed to ask further questions, beginning with 'Important for what?' Life does not contain just one purpose or one drama but many interwoven ones. Different charac-ters matter in different ways. Beings figure in some dramas who are absent from others, and we all play different parts in different scripts. Even in ordinary human life it is fatal to ignore this. To insist on reducing all relationships to those prescribed by a single drama – for instance, the social contract – is disastrous. Intellectuals are prone to such errors and need to watch out for them. But when we come to harder cases, where the variation is greater – cases such as abortion, euthanasia or the treatment of other species – this sort of mistake is still more paralysing. That is why these cases are so helpful in illuminating the more central ones.

It is clear that, over women, those who limited the use of the concept 'person' felt this difficulty. They did not want to deny altogether that women were persons, since in the dramas of private life women figured prominently. Public life,however, was a different stage, whose rules and conventions excluded them (queens apart) as completely as elephants or angels. The fact that private life often impinges on public was an informal matter and could not affect this ruling. Similarly in Rome, it is clear that slaves actually played a considerable part in life. In Greek and Roman comedy ingenious slaves, both male and female, often figure as central characters, organizing the intrigue and supplying the brains which the hero and heroine themselves unfortunately lack. This, however, did not confer legal rights on them. The boundaries of particular situations and institutions served to compartmentalize thought and to stop people from raising questions about the rights and status of those who were, for central purposes, currently disregarded.

I think it will be helpful here to follow a little further the accepted lines of usage for the word 'person'. How complete is its link with the human bodily form? What about intelligent alien beings, for instance? Could we call them persons? If not, then contact with them – which is certainly conceivable – would surely require us to coin a new word to do the quite subtle moral job which is done at present by 'person'. The idea of a person in the almost technical sense required by morality today is the one worked out by Kant in his *Foundations of the Metaphysic of Morals*. It is the idea of a rational being, capable of choice and therefore endowed with dignity, worthy of respect, having rights; one that must be regarded always as an end in itself, not only as a means to the ends of others. Because this definition deals solely with rational qualities, it makes no mention of human form or human descent, and the spirit behind it would certainly not license us to exclude intelligent aliens any more than disembodied spirits. The moral implications of the word 'person' would therefore, on our current Kantian principles, surely still have to attach to whatever word we might coin to include aliens. (C. S. Lewis, describing a planet where there are three distinct rational species, has them use the word *hnau* for the condition which they all share, and this term is naturally central to the morality of all of them.)

Now, if intelligence is really so important to the issue, a certain vertigo descends when we ask, 'Where do we draw the line?' because intelligence is a matter of degree. Some inhabitants of our own planet, including whales and dolphins, have turned out to be a lot brighter than was once supposed. Quite how bright they are is not yet really clear. Indeed, it may never become so to us because of the difference in the kind of intelligence appropriate to beings with very different sorts of life. How can we deal with such a situation?

The first thing that is needed is undoubtedly to get away from the single, simple, black-and-white antithesis with which Kant started, that between persons and things. Most of Kant's argument is occupied with this, and while it remains the focus of his concern he does not need to make finer distinctions. *Things* can properly be used as means to human ends in a way in which *people* cannot. Things have no aims of their own; they are not subjects but objects. Thing-treatment given to people is exploitation and oppression. It is an outrage, because, as Kant exclaims, 'A man is not a thing.' Masters sell slaves; rulers deceive and manipulate their subjects; employers treat their secretaries as part of the wallpaper. By dwelling on the simple, stark contrast involved here, Kant was able to make some splendid moral points, which are still vital to us today, about the thorough-going respect which is due to every free and rational human being. But the harsh, bright light which he turned on these situations entirely obscured the intermediate cases. A mouse is not a thing either, before we even start to think about a dolphin.

I find it interesting that, just as the American courts could not quite bring themselves to say that women were not persons, so Kant cannot quite get around to saying what his theory certainly implies – that animals are things. He does say in his lecture on 'Duties Towards Animals and Spirits' that they 'are not self-conscious and are there merely as a means to an end', that end being ours. But he does not actually call them things, nor does he write off their interests. In fact, he emphatically condemns cruel and mean treatment of them. But, like many other humane people who have got stuck with an inadequate moral theory, he gives ingenious but unconvincing reasons for this. He says – and this has gone on being said ever since – that it is only because cruelty to animals may lead to cruelty to humans, or degrade us, or be a sign of a bad moral character, that we have to avoid it. This means that if we can show, for instance, that venting our ill-temper on the dog will prevent our doing it on our families and can produce certificates declaring that we are, in general, people of high moral character, not easily degraded, we can go ahead with a clear conscience. Dog-bashing, properly managed, could count as a legitimate form of therapy, along with gardening, pottery and raffiawork. In no case would the physical materials involved be directly considered because all equally would be only objects, not subjects. And there is nothing degrading about hitting an object.

In spite of the appalling cruelty which human beings show towards animals the world over, it does not seem likely that anyone regards them consistently in this light. Spasms of regard, tenderness, comradeship and even veneration, alternating with unthinking callousness, seem to make up the typical human attitude. Towards fellow human beings too a rather similar alternation is often found. So this cannot really be an attitude confined to things. Even cruelty itself, when it is deliberate, seems to require that its objects should not be mere physical objects but should be capable of responding as separate characters in the drama. More widely, the appeal of hunting, and also of sports such as bull-fighting, seems to depend on the sense of outwitting and defeating a conscious quarry or opponent, 'another' able to be one's opposite in the game or drama. The script distinctly requires non-human characters who can play their parts well or badly. Moby Dick is not an extra. And the degradingness of deliberate cruelty itself surely requires this other-regarding element. 'Another' is not always another human being.

The degradingness of cruelty is, of course, widely admitted, and Le Vasseur's counsel used this admission as the ground of an alternative defence. He drew attention to his client's 'status as a state employee, which conferred authority on him to act as he did in coming to the defense of "another", in this case the United States, whose social values were injured by what was being done to the dolphins'. This argument was rejected on the ground that, in the eyes of the law, cruelty to animals is merely a misdemeanour, whereas theft is a felony. Accordingly, the choice of evils could not properly be resolved in favour of theft, the more serious offence. It is interesting that this argument makes no objection to treating the United States as 'another' or 'another person' – it does not insist that a person simply means a human being – but rests instead on contending that this 'other' finds its values more seriously attacked by theft than by cruelty to dolphins.

This sort of argument is not easy to come to grips with even in the case of an ordinary individual person, still less in that of a nation. How serious an evil is cruelty? Once it is conceded that the victim's point of view does not count, that the injury is done only to the offender or some body of which he is part, we seem to be cut off from the key considerations of the argument and forced to conduct it in a strained manner, on grounds which are not really central. Is cruelty necessarily depraving? On this approach, that seems partly to be a factual question about how easily people are depraved and partly, perhaps, an aesthetic one about how far cruel acts are necessarily disgusting and repellent. These acts seem now to be assimilated to others which are repellent without being clearly immoral, such as eating the bodies of people whom one has not killed or watching atrocities over which one has no control. The topic becomes a neighbour of pornography rather than of abortion and euthanasia. (In the disputes about permissiveness in the 1960s, an overlap actually developed here at times, as when a London art gallery organized a happening in which some fish were to be electrocuted as part of the show, and efforts to ban this were attacked as censorious manifestations of aesthetic narrow-mindedness.)

Something seems to have gone wrong with the thinking here. The distinctive feature of acts censured on purely aesthetic grounds should surely be that their effects are confined to those who actually perform them. No other sentient being is harmed by them. That is why they pose problems for libertarians when bystanders object to them. But cruelty does not pose this kind of problem, since the presence of 'another' who is harmed is essential to it. In our case it is the dolphin, who does seem to be 'another'. Can we avoid thinking of it in this way? Can the central objection to cruelty really be something rather indirect, such as its being in bad taste?

The law seems to rule so here. And in doing this the law shows itself to be in a not uncommon difficulty, one that arises when public opinion is changing. Legal standards are not altogether independent of moral standards. They flow from them and crystallize in ways designed to express certain selected moral insights. When those insights change radically enough, the law changes. But there are often jolts and discrepancies here because the pace of change is different. New moral perceptions require the crystals to be broken up and reformed, and this process takes time. Changes of this kind have repeatedly altered the rules surrounding the central crux which concerns us here: the stark division of the world into persons and property. Changing attitudes to slavery are a central case, to which we will return. But it is worth noticing first that plain, factual discoveries too can make a difference. When our civilization formed the views on the species barrier which it still largely holds, all the most highly developed non-human animals were simply unknown. Legend apart, it was assumed that whales and dolphins were much like fish. The great apes were not even discovered until the eighteenth century, and real knowledge of their way of living has been acquired only within the last few decades. About better-known creatures too there was a very general ignorance and unthinking dismissal of available evidence; their sociality was not noticed or believed in. The central, official intellectual tradition of our culture never expected to be forced to refine its crude, extreme, unshaded dichotomy between man and beast. In spite of the efforts of many concerned thinkers, from Plutarch to Montaigne and from Blake to John Stuart Mill, it did not develop other categories. If alien beings landed tomorrow, lawyers, philosophers and social scientists would certainly have to do some very quick thinking. (I don't expect the aliens myself, but they are part of the imaginative furniture of our age, and it is legitimate to use them to rouse us from our dogmatic slumbers.) Science fiction, though sometimes helpful, has far too often sidetracked the problem by making its aliens just scientists with green antennae, beings whose 'intelligence' is of a kind to be accepted instantly at the Massachusetts Institute of Technology – only, of course, a little greater. Since neither dolphins nor gorillas write doctoral theses, this would still let us out as far as terrestrial non-human creatures were concerned. 'Persons' and their appropriate rights could still go on being defined in terms of this sort of intelligence, and we could quietly continue to poison the pigeons in the park any time that we felt like it.

The question is, why should this kind of intelligence be so important, and why should it determine the limits of our moral concern? It is often assumed that we can owe duties only to beings capable of speech. Why this should be assumed is not altogether clear. At a simple level Bentham surely got it right in his *Introduction to the Principles of Morals and Legislation*: 'The question is not . . . Can they *talk*? but, *Can they suffer*?' With chimps, gorillas and dolphins, however, there is now a further problem because people have been trying, apparently with some degree of success, to teach them certain kinds of speech. This project might have taught us a great deal about just what new categories we need in our attempt to classify beings more subtly. But unluckily it is now becoming obscured by furious opposition from people who still have just the two categories and who see the whole proceedings as an illicit attempt to smuggle contraband from one to the other. This reaction is extremely interesting. What is the threat? Articulate apes and cetaceans are scarcely likely to take over the Government. What might happen, however, is that it would become much harder to exclude them from moral consideration. In particular, their use as experimental subjects might begin to look very different. Can the frontier be defended by a resolute and unbreakable refusal to admit that these animals can talk?

It is understandable that people should have thought so, but this surely cannot really be the issue. What makes creatures our fellow beings, entitled to basic consideration, is surely not intellectual capacity but emotional fellowship. And if we ask what powers can justify a higher claim, bringing some creatures nearer to the degree of consideration which is due to humans, those that seem to be most relevant are sensibility, social and emotional complexity of the kind which is expressed by the formation of deep, subtle and lasting relationships. The gift of imitating certain intellectual skills which are important to humans is no doubt an indicator of this, but it cannot be central. We already know that both apes and dolphins have this kind of social and emotional complexity. If we ask what elements in 'persons' are central in entitling them to moral consideration, we can, I think, cast some light on the point by contrasting the claim of these sensitive social creatures with that of a computer, of the present generation, programmed in a manner which entitles it, according to current controversial usage, to be called 'intelligent'. That computer does not trouble our sleep with any moral claims, and would not do so however much more 'intelligent' it became, unless it eventually seemed to be conscious, sensitive and endowed with emotions. If it did, we should be facing the Frankenstein problem in a very acute form. (The extraordinary eagerness with which Frankenstein drove his researches to this disastrous point is something which contemporary monster-makers might like to ponder.) But those who at present emphasize the intelligence of computers do not see any reason to call them persons or to allow for them as members of the moral community. Speech alone, then, would scarcely do this job for the apes. What is at issue is the already glaring fact, which speech would make it finally impossible to deny, that they are highly sensitive social beings.

These considerations are not, I think, ones confined to cranks or extremists. They seem fairly widespread today and probably occur at times to all of us, however uncertain we may be about what to do with them. If so, and if the law really allows them no possible weight, then we seem to have reached the point at which the law will have to be changed because it shocks morality. There is an obvious precedent, to which the dolphin liberators tried to appeal:

> When the dolphins were taken from the tanks, a message was left behind identifying the releasers as the 'Undersea Railroad', a reference to the Underground Railroad, the Abolitionists' slave-freeing network of pre-Civil War days. Along the Underground Railroad in the 1850s, it sometimes happened that juries refused to convict people charged with smuggling slaves to freedom. That was the kind of vindication Le Vasseur and Sipman were looking for . . . They did not consider themselves to be criminals. In fact they took the view that, if there was a crime, it was the crime of keeping dolphins – intelligent, highly aware creatures with no criminal record of their own – in solitary confinement, in small, concrete tanks, made to do repetitious experiments, for life.

If we go back to the alien beings for a moment and consider whether even the most intelligent of them would have the right to keep visiting human beings, however stupid, in these conditions, even those of us least partial to astronauts may begin to see the point which Le Vasseur and Sipman were making. It surely cannot be dismissed merely by entrenching the law around the definition of the word 'person'. We need new thinking, new concepts and new words, and we are not less capable of providing these than people were in the 1850s.

Images of Death and Life: Food Animal Production and the Vegetarian Option

HARRIET SCHLEIFER

The memories of one Maryland chicken slaughterhouse will always be with me. It was summer, 90 degree heat, humid, no shade, and the chickens were in stacked crates. As we walked in, we were breathing the palpable stench of warm, dying bodies. It soaked through our clothes and skin. We took some birds out of the crates, and they tried to drink melting ice from our hands. They were too weak to keep their heads up. They would have stayed there until the next morning, dying of heat prostration, respiratory failure and so on. We made the security guards call in the manager to finish them off. It's the closest I've ever been to Auschwitz.

> Ingrid Newkirk, unpublished interview

'Enough to turn you vegetarian, places like this,' Quantrill said gloomily into Tait's ear. His work in rural police divisions had taken him often enough into slaughterhouses, but he had never overcome his sense of depression at their sights, their sounds, their smells, their frighteningly casual doing-to-death.

> Sheila Radley, *Death in the Morning*

The heat of the summer city was unbearable. The pigs were waiting, small eyes intent on the men they had learned to fear. Ears and tails flicked with irritation at the tugging pain of scratches, the caked mud clinging to their bodies, and the ever-present insects. One animal lay stretched out, his sides heaving, lost in the agony of a heart attack. Another stood, her head trapped firmly in a gate, moaning with helpless misery. Panting from the heat, several individuals stood near these two sufferers, gently nudging at their bodies to express their sympathy. Waiting.

Presently, a man appeared, equipped with heavy boots and an electric prod. The pigs were overwhelmed with dread. Their screams rose in the open air. The man flayed aimlessly about him, striking legs, heads and backs, as the animals climbed over each other, desperate to escape.

A forced run down the darkened chute; wild thrashing to evade the merciless blows of the captive-bolt pistol; then, unconsciousness. Remorselessly, one by one, human killers stilled the pigs' voices.

> Harriet Schleifer, 'Echoes of a Canadian Stockyard', unpublished

The passages you have just read are imaginative descriptions of reality, not documented scientific facts. Systematic factual accounts of the meat industry's treatment of animals, such as Ruth Harrison's *Animal Machines*, Peter Singer's *Animal Liberation* and Jim Mason's and Peter Singer's *Animal Factories*, are almost numbing in the evidence they present of the needless exploitation and widespread abuse that our diet creates for other sensitive living beings. Surveying the problem on the broadest scale, they distract one's attention from the suffering of each individual and blur its unique significance.

Many people are overwhelmed by the extent of food animals' suffering. The rearing of livestock is commonplace in virtually every society on the planet, and there are billions of deaths every year. Indeed, in *The Hungry Planet* Georg Borgstrom has calculated that the global population of domestic food animals equals our own human population. When the number of fish caught and killed to feed us annually is added to this total, the death toll becomes staggering.

In the USA the meat industry is the second largest manufacturing and processing concern (the largest is the manufacture of cars) and worth approximately $50 billion a year. It plays a prominent role in other countries' economies as well. Large-scale fishing is of primary economic importance in much of the Third World, and significant in developed countries. Related industries, such as steel production and pharmaceutical manufacture, dramatically increase the meat and fish producers' influence and power. The steel industry supplies cages and machinery for factory farms, while more than half the world's production of antibiotics is used in medicated animal feeds.

But these statistics need not be disheartening. However great its size, the farm animal industry is extremely vulnerable to the threat posed to its continued existence by public compassion for the animals it victimizes. Well aware of this fact, meat producers go to extraordinary lengths to conceal and mystify the true nature of their activities. Factory farms and slaughterhouses are hidden from view, located away from urban cores and relatively isolated. Most prohibit all visitors. Our consciousness of what goes on in them is blurred by the way in which meat is typically sold, in neat, bloodless packets. Body parts which would identify meat as animal corpses – feet, tails, fur, eyes – are carefully removed, ostensibly for consumer convenience.

Slick and seductive advertising campaigns reinforce these illusion. Thoughts of living, suffering animals are virtually obliterated. Everyone is familiar with the smiling cows, dancing pigs, and laughing chickens depicted on meat, dairy, and egg industry packaging and vehicles, and which are also frequently used as restaurant logos. Wayne Swanson and George Schultz report in their book *Prime Rip*, which investigates fraud in the meat industry, that 'the industry has always operated strong educational and public-relations programs to keep Americans thinking positive thoughts about meat'. To cite just one example, culled from Dudley Giehl's *Vegetarianism: A Way of Life*, the California Beef Council routinely issues press releases to 'some 500 newspapers and over 300 radio and television stations in California'. Other animal exploiters, such as the dairy and egg industries, use similar tactics. Promotional handouts to supermarkets are common. These banners, posters, and literature are referred to as 'consumer information' despite their industry source. Supermarkets themselves spend the largest proportion of their own advertising budgets on publicity for meat. Meat is a high profit margin product, with a mark-up of about 20 per cent, and they consider it a principal draw for customers.

Aside from their fraudulent use of animals in advertising, some meat industry advocates apparently have no qualms about manipulating public prejudices to sell their products. In *Vegetarianism: A Way of Life* Giehl describes a booklet called 'The Story of Meat', published by the American Meat Institute. It asks the question, 'Why couldn't the North American Indians living in a land teeming with natural resources lift themselves above their primitive stone age culture?' The answer? The Indians 'failed to domesticate livestock for their principal food necessity – meat.' Sexism is also condoned and encouraged. *Prime Rip* mentions a $4.6 million advertising and marketing campaign designed to sell 'sensual beef': '"Sex sells everything else," said a spokesman, 'so why not beef?"'

Special promotional efforts are directed at children, whose open and uninhibited appreciation of living animals presents the most dangerous challenge to a meat-centred diet. Giehl notes that a large proportion of meat industry propaganda is distributed in the public school system. This is confirmed by Swanson and Schultz. According to their research, 'Trade groups are a major provider of educational materials on nutrition (obviously stressing the importance of meat)'. Such material contains not pictures of slaughterhouses but attractive portraits of living animals and commentary on what they 'do for us'. The McDonald hamburger chain is a major producer of children's television commercials. In one of these Ronald McDonald explains that hamburgers 'grow in little hamburger patches'. Star-Kist has developed a series of ads in which Charlie the Tuna tries to be caught so he can be processed by the company. Perhaps the most outrageous example, however, is an Oscar Mayer commercial in which a group of children sing: 'Oh, I wish I was an Oscar Mayer wiener, for that is what I'd really like to be.' As Giehl wryly comments, 'The old maxim that honesty is the best policy does not apply if you expect children to eat meat without compunction'.

The food animal industry has largely succeeded in its attempt to make desirable practices that are inexcusable. A measure of its success is found in *Prime Rip*, whose authors state in all seriousness that 'Many Americans would sooner give up their freedom than give up their meat.' Unfortunately, meat has become a symbol of status. Preferences for specific kinds of meat vary widely, ranging from insects to frogs' legs, from buffalo steaks to pork chops, but it is universally related to wealth, and its absence from the diet is regarded as voluntary or involuntary privation. The problem becomes evident in the marketing of meat analogues, which the status-conscious meat eater rejects as 'imitations', no matter how much they resemble the real thing.

Faced with the onslaught of propaganda and the fact that the consumption of animal products is a respected and entrenched custom in our society, it is little wonder that few people have the temerity to challenge the basis of the entire system. Still, nothing frightens the meat industry more than the idea of vegetarianism. They oppose its spread with aggressive vigour. Frances Moore Lappe's book *Diet for a Small Planet* was criticized as hysterical, unscientific faddism. Of course, significantly, it is the food animal industry that either funds or otherwise supports most research which claims to prove that its products are healthy and nutritionally sound. Its manipulation extends even to the most respected scientific bodies. The 1980 National Academy of Science report exonerating cholesterol as a factor in disease was prepared by paid consultants of the meat, dairy and egg industries. In 1976 intense lobbying by angry meat producers forced the American Government to delete a recommendation in the McGovern report on nutrition, 'Decrease consumption of meat', and to change it to 'Choose meats, poultry and fish which will reduce saturated fat intake'. Such obsessive hostility towards the alternative of a vegetarian diet strongly suggests that its promotion may be a powerful weapon against the habit of meat consumption.

The animal liberation ethic demands a basic shift in moral consciousness, a repudiation of human superiority over other species through force. Our way of viewing the world becomes more compassionate, more respectful of the needs of other living beings. The vegetarian lifestyle is both a fundamental and a personal means of affirming such a shift. Confronting the oppression of food animals through vegetarianism lies at the heart of the animal liberation ethic and offers the greatest potential for the radical transformation of our society.

Killing, unless it is done as a merciful act, must involve a deliberate withholding of sympathy from the victim. Done repeatedly, it results in a hardening of the emotions. Thomas More, although not a vegetarian, recognized this when he wrote *Utopia* in 1518: 'The Utopians feel that slaughtering our fellow creatures gradually destroys the sense of compassion, which is the finest sentiment of which our human nature is capable.' The same theme has reappeared in countless writings, usually with a suggestion that heightened human sensitivity is a desirable goal. Mahatma Gandhi expressed this very clearly in *The Moral Basis of Vegetarianism*, edited by R. P. Prabhu. He commented, 'I do feel that spiritual progress does demand at some stage that we should cease to kill our fellow creatures for the satisfaction of our bodily wants'.

The ethical argument for vegetarianism becomes even more persuasive when one considers the reasons for it that are not related directly to farm animal welfare. (I will not discuss any of the health considerations that make the vegetarian diet an attractive option, since they do not have an essentially moral basis.) Wildlife conservation is a popular concern for many people, though few know the extent to which domestic animals compete with wildlife for space and resources. Ninety per cent of agricultural land in the United States, more than half of the country's total land area, is presently used for meat, dairy and egg operations, making it unavailable as human or wildlife habitat. Nor do people realize that numerous species, among them the dodo and the passenger pigeon, became extinct because we chose to eat them and that other species are currently endangered for the same reason. Furthermore, the men who exploit animals for food do not take kindly to wildlife that interferes with their activities: American ranchers kill predators, antelope and prairie dogs, Australian sheep farmers kill kangaroos, and Japanese fishermen destroy dolphins – in each case because the animals are 'pests'. Other animals are 'incidentally' exterminated; tuna and shrimp nets drown hundreds of porpoises and sea turtles.

Ecologically the production of animal products is wasteful and inefficient. According to Keith Akers' *A Vegetarian Sourcebook*, energy and water requirements are between ten and 1,000 times greater than they would be for an equal amount of plant food. Consequently, most soil erosion (90 per cent), consumptive use of water (80 per cent) and deforestation (70 per cent) is the result of livestock agriculture. It is also responsible for most of our water pollution.

Meat consumption in Western countries is a primary cause of hunger, both at home and in the Third World. Only 42 per cent of an animal's original weight becomes meat. In addition to this wastage, John McFarlane, Executive Director of the Council for Livestock Protection, has calculated that 'The amount of meat lost each year through careless handling and brutality would be enough to feed a million Americans for a year'. Although the unfair distribution which characterizes international trade makes it an unlikely dream, it is also a fact that if everyone in the developed world became a vegetarian, it would be possible to give four tons of edible grain to every starving person.

Many studies have speculated on the connection between meat eating and inter-human violence, although none has been conclusive. Nevertheless, the links are suggestive. In *Fettered Kingdoms*, John Bryant mentions several sources which note that the rate of violent crime in communities is related to the presence of slaughter facilities. Certainly it is true that the slaughterer's occupation is grim and brutalizing. Few people work in stockyards by choice. Most are there because their families have worked in the business; many are illegal immigrants. Workers are forced to become indifferent to the vocal protests and struggling of the animals they kill. It is likely that the callousness they develop in order to endure the realities of their jobs will affect other areas of their lives.

The fact that most consumers try to ignore the horror of meat animals' lives and deny its moral importance suggests an underlying awareness of the unjustified cruelty involved. Human beings do not like to see themselves as killers, notwithstanding the exaggerated glamour we ascribe to the caveman and hunter. We are relieved to have animals killed for us by others, relieved that the distressing sights and sounds of death do not haunt our meals. Some of us repress the facts so well that we can hardly believe that suffering and death are part of meat production. In an interview published in the March/April issue of *Agenda*, Quebec animal rights activist Karen Urtnowski tells of a schoolmate who thought that steaks were surgically removed from cows, who then returned to a peaceful existence in their meadows. If such an example seems farfetched, consider the fact that a large percentage of intelligent, educated adults do not associate cow's milk with the animal's pregnancy. Nor do they realize that the unwanted calves become the raw material of the veal industry.

Whatever their level of awareness, it remains true that people eat meat because they are accustomed to its colour, shape, texture and flavour, and have been conditioned to regard it as a highly desirable food. Their attitudes must be challenged, and changed. As Peter Singer has pointed out in *Animal Liberation*, 'Those who, by their purchases, require animals to be killed have no right to be shielded from this or any other aspect of the production of the meat they buy. If it is distasteful for humans to think about, what can it be like for the animals to experience it?'

The meaning of what we do to meat animals transcends hard statistics. The destructive impulses of the human spirit are grimly revealed in the suffering of these creatures, and most of us naturally recoil from the vision. As with the image of nuclear disaster, knowledge of the meat industry's exploitation of animals confronts us with the unthinkable, and demands a personal response we may feel unable to give. So we reassure ourselves with platitudes about the 'necessity of meat' in human nutrition, arguments about our 'dominion' over nature and the window-dressing provided by regulations designed to ensure humane slaughter.

Sadly, some elements within the animal rights movement itself have accepted these evasions. In despair at the apparent hopelessness of stopping the exploitation, or unwilling to face its reality, they attempt to be 'reasonable' about the issue of food animals. The majority withdraw from the controversy altogether, on the grounds that the public is not ready to deal with it. They offer the myth of the 'attainable goal' as a further rationalization. The idea behind this is to attack less widespread abuses, such as hunting or circuses, in the hope that smaller successes will build up the movement's credibility and popular support and allow the issue of food animals to be dealt with effectively later. The difficulty with this approach is that it tends to involve its proponents in lame excuses about their inaction on the larger problem or, worse, in deceit, actual denial that it has any significance. In effect, they reinforce the food animal industry's messages. The public comes to feel that the use of animals for food is in some way acceptable, since even the animal welfare people say so. This cannot help but make it much more difficult to eliminate the practice in the future. Far better to follow the strategy of union activists, who demand 20 per cent in the hope of receiving at least 10 per cent.

We cannot live in fear of making the public uncomfortable. Change that matters always involves initial doubt and pain, and it is our responsibility to guide that process in a constructive way, to ease the transition from a society that exploits to one that respects other species.

If it is true that once the public understands the immorality of other animal rights issues, it will be easy to convince them to become vegetarians, it is equally true that vegetarianism provides a consistent base for criticizing the lesser wrongs done to animals. Rejecting animal exploitation as ethical vegetarians saves us from the perilous acrobatics involved in dividing animals into two moral categories: animals that it is unequivocally wrong to abuse, and others that it is acceptable to exploit in a benevolent fashion.

Furthermore, the attitude that allows us to raise animals for food colours our treatment of all other creatures, from pets to laboratory animals and wildlife. Once we have accepted that we may utilize animals for so trivial a reason as our enjoyment of the taste of their flesh, it is easy to use them for any purpose which is equally frivolous, such as domesticating them as pets or confining them in zoos to amuse us, or for those which are more serious, such as using them in medical experiments that we believe will save human lives.

Other animal rights activists settle on the 'compromise' solution of humane slaughter to ease their dilemma. The contradictions inherent in adopting such a position are evident. To begin with, sincere concern for living individuals leads such people to become, ironically, experts on the techniques of mass death-dealing. They learn to compare the speed, facility and cost of various devices and systems; the question of whether their use is justifiable at all never arises. The worst aspect of the humane slaughter option is that it focuses discussion on the least important consideration, the method of killing. By doing so, it suggests that the taking of life is not a problem, only the way it is done.

At the very core of the animal liberation philosophy is the idea that we should extend consideration to other species' needs and weigh them against our own. How is it possible to do that while denying, prima facie, that food animals should be free to live out their natural life spans and while killing them not even because it is desirable for them to die, for whatever reason, but simply because we enjoy the taste of their dead bodies? The falseness of advocating humane slaughter, while professing to believe in an animal rights ethic, is patently obvious. As John Bryant declares in *Fettered Kingdoms*, the philosophy behind all food animal farming, whether traditional or intensive, is the same, 'the arrogant stance that we can use animals for whatever purpose we wish'.

To make matters worse, the notion of humane slaughter ignores the fact that the specific moment of death is only a fraction of a larger process. Even were we to agree that the death of food animals is acceptable, humane slaughter's preoccupation with the brief experience of dying is misleading. Some animal rights groups do demand that provisions made for animals prior to slaughter be humane, that they include adequate food, water and shelter. Yet few are willing to discuss regulations to minimize the terror of animals awaiting their deaths in stockyards. In fact such a goal is impossible to achieve. Death for meat animals does not come as a sudden, unexpected shock. Thousands of animals are assembled in a single location, close to a building that all of them must enter to die. They cannot remain unaware of their fate, and intense fear is the natural and inevitable result.

It sometimes seems as if advocates of meat eating understand the nature of the food animal industry better than we do. Adopting the view that killing is an unpleasant necessity, they are often more clear-sighted about their activities than are animal rights campaigners. The comments of Wayne Swanson and George Schultz, authors of *Prime Rip*, are particularly revealing, all the more so because of the complete absence of any empathy with the animals themselves. Evaluating the possibility of reducing corruption in the meat industry, they state:

> No matter how much new technology is developed, and no matter how nicely meat is packaged, the central facts of the meat business cannot be changed. This is an industry built around noisy, foul-smelling animals whose fate is to have an eight-inch-long pin fired into their foreheads at point-blank range. Their blood and guts will spill forth on the killing floor, and their carcasses will be stripped and carved and chopped during a process that, although it is governed by 'humane slaughter' laws, can be nothing other than gross and brutal.

In any event, exploitation is not just killing. It is also the manipulation of animals' genes to make them machines for our use, the denial of freedom, the causing of pain and fear throughout their lifetimes. Death can be a minor evil compared with these. People who believe that the raising of food animals can be made humane are deluding themselves. Meat is murder. If an animal does not have the basic right to exist, any other rights become meaningless. John Bryant says the 'whole concept of "marketing" living individuals is wrong'. It cannot be improved by reforms, however liberal.

The rationale behind much animal abuse, the excuse that an animal is going to die anyway, so it is all right to do X to it, is tempting and convenient and quickly erodes all other considerations. The intensive systems in use today are only the logical and unavoidable outcome of our general attitude towards farm animals as property. The animals' welfare and our desire to have high-quality meat are in direct conflict: well-exercised animals produce stringy meat; their freedom to control their own sex lives makes births too unpredictable and variable.

As long as a farm animal is perceived as an edible object, an 'it' to be put on our dinner plates, he or she will never have any meaningful rights. Domestication itself is an unnatural process, a method of enslaving animals and subjecting their life processes to our will. Animal liberation would return domestic animals to their wild origins, free to pursue their destinies without human interference.

Concrete individual and group action to promote vegetarianism can be both simple and significant. All we need to do is boycott the food animal industry's products. According to my calculations, which are somewhat complicated and which I will not detail here, every person who becomes a vegetarian is directly responsible for saving between forty and ninety-five creatures every year, depending on her or his level of meat consumption. It is the single most effective step one can take to assist individual animals.

Those who choose to take collective action as well increase their impact on the situation proportionally. The possibilities are endless. We can demystify meat through public education and pressure on Governments. Perhaps a law requiring stores to sell only whole, intact animal bodies would be effective in emphasizing what meat is. We could confront those who promote meat directly. Suitable targets for such action might include single stores, restaurants or, for the more ambitious, nationwide chains. In *Big Mac: The Unauthorized Story of McDonald's* Max Boas and Steve Chain estimate that the Corporation, whose hamburgers represent only 1 per cent of the wholesale beef in the United States, accounts for the deaths of over 300,000 cattle annually. Closing them down would be a major triumph. We could publicize the vegetarian alternative, informing people about its potential and preparing meals for them to demonstrate its culinary attractiveness.

George Bernard Shaw wrote in his autobiography: 'eating the scorched corpses of animals – cannibalism with its heroic dish omitted – becomes impossible the moment it becomes conscious instead of thoughtlessly habitual.' As animal rights activists, it is our responsibility to stimulate the necessary thought to make such a transformation possible, both for ourselves and for others. The choice is open to each one of us. Here is one more reminder of what we are trying to stop:

> The young sheep lay dying in the stockyard pen, her broken body filthy with dust and urine, patches of wool torn from her side. A straw thrust painfully at the edge of her nostril, as she drew breath after struggling breath. Flies crawled industriously over her oozing wounds, and tickled her half-closed eyelid. Other sheep milled around by her side, dazed with exhaustion, yet restless with fear. The horror of her memories drifted through her mind: the harsh cries and painful thud of sticks driving her into the truck; the endless, thirsty ride on metal flooring, slippery with blood and dirt; the crush of panicking bodies as she stumbled down the ramp into the straw; the nightmare cycle of mounting fever, nausea and fear.
>
> Two humans drew close, and her terror peaked. But the hands of the animal liberationists lifted her with gentleness. She felt a sharp pain in her leg, and the relief of death was hers.
>
> Harriet Schleifer, 'Echoes of a Canadian Stockyard', unpublished

Part II

The Problems

Speciesism in the Laboratory

RICHARD D. RYDER

The mid-1980s sees the entrenchment of animal experimentation as a political subject. No longer is it a fringe issue, a reform campaign espoused only by eccentrics; it is now a movement which has considerable public support in nearly all Western countries. Like most successful movements, it has a following at all levels in society and embraces a wide range of differing personalities and styles, conservative and radical, old and young, militant and constitutional.

Several factors in the 1970s gave growing weight to the historic anti-vivisection and animal rights movements. Six of these have been identified by Professor Harlan B. Miller, in *Ethics and Animals*, as:

- The momentum of liberation. Once colonialism, racism and sexism have been intellectually (if not practically) vanquished, then the next logical stage in the expansion of the boundaries of the moral in-group is an attack upon speciesism.
- Increasing scientific evidence that non-humans share intellectual and perceptual faculties in common with mankind. Miller emphasizes recent evidence of high intelligence in apes. (But, in addition, the new evidence that all vertebrate classes share with man the biochemical substances associated with the transmission of pain is of equal, or even greater, significance.)
- The ethical debate over abortion. Miller claims that this has moved the 'concept of a person' to the centre of the stage.
- The decline in dualistic views separating mind from body. The greater acceptance that the substance of central nervous systems

(as they exist in many animals) is 'somehow identical with' mental life and consciousness.

• The development of behavioural sciences (such as sociobiology and ethology) which attempt to draw conclusions about human behaviour from observations of other animals. This has spread the view that homo sapiens is one species among other species.

• The rise of the environment and ecology movements, which have indicated an increasing 'awareness of nature' and of 'humanity's interdependence with other species'.

Miller adds a seventh factor in parenthesis. The popularity of science fiction and recent advances in astronomy have widened the view that the universe may contain other alien intelligences.

At a more mundane level, the interest of the media has had a considerable 'positive-feedback' effect, which has magnified the protest movement. Portraying the suffering of laboratory animals on the television screen has shocked the conscience of thousands and has vindicated the vivisectors' opposition to allowing the public to see what they are doing in the public name.

Two further factors have given a new edge to the recent reform campaign. The first has been the emphasis placed upon the search for 'alternative techniques' which are humane. This search has been led by animal welfare groups in America, Britain and Germany. They have not only propagated the idea that humane techniques should be sought but have, in some cases, supplied the funds necessary for research into these new fields. Widespread cynicism among scientists has gradually been dispelled as tissue and organ culture and other techniques have been developed and their relative validities established.

The second factor has been the realization that many experiments on animals are not being performed for strictly medical purposes. To many people it seems logical to argue that deliberately inflicted pain may be justified if the results considerably benefit others. Such pain/benefit analysis usually comes down on the side of the animal when the only benefits from particular experiments are found to be a new cosmetic, soap powder or other inessential product, or greater knowledge of the effects of weapons. Psychological and other behavioural research can also fall into this category. Alan Smith has effectively questioned some of the excessive claims made by those who defend animal experimentation in an article entitled 'The Facts Vivisectionists Get Wrong' and published in the *New Democrat* in 1983.

There are two fundamental, and many subsidiary, objections to research on animals. The first fundamental objection is that it is wrong to kill; the second is that it is wrong to cause pain or suffering. Many people make both objections, but some will give higher value to one or the other. Some objections which are now subsidiary have, in the past, been of greater significance to the movement – for example, the argument that vivisection undermines the character of the vivisector or that its scientific purpose makes it contrary to religion. In our own time the argument has taken on a less religious and a more utilitarian complexion. Likewise it has become less man-centred and more animal-centred. There is less talk of moral *duties* and more of moral *rights*. It is the victim rather than the vivisector who is the object of concern.

Social reformers in Victorian England were often in positions of some influence and came from a relatively small ruling class. Consequently they felt that reforms could be imposed from above and were within their power; accordingly they appealed to the wrongdoer's sense of *duty*. In our own time, however, we see reforms motivated from below by mass movements of the young and the less powerful in society; in such cases the reformers' own sense of relative impotence leads them easily to identify with the oppressed victims and so to champion their *rights*.

THE SIZE OF THE PROBLEM

It has been estimated that between 100 million and 200 million animals die in laboratories around the world each year.

The best statistics have been kept by the Home Office in Britain, where the 1983 figures reveal that 4,221,801 experiments on living animals were licensed in the previous year. Of these, most involved the testing or development of veterinary, medical or dental drugs and other products, but 32,979 were for the testing of pesticides, 15,122 for the testing of herbicides, 66,185 for the testing of substances used in industry, 13,934 for testing household substances, 18,864 for the testing of cosmetics and toiletries, 20,125 for the testing of food additives and 3,214 for testing tobacco and its substitutes. The experiments were performed mainly on rodents (2,442,702 mice, 932,335 rats, 154,740 guinea pigs, 164,993 rabbits) but included 5,654 on primates (monkeys or apes), 13,146 on dogs, 251,818 on birds and 165,833 on fish.

Experiments involving the deliberate induction of psychological stress numbered 43,529; 1,652 involved burning or scalding; 144,322 involved exposure to ionizing irradiation; 14,949 involved the use of aversive stimuli such as electric shock; 19,124 involved the application of substances to the eye; and 86,179 involved interference with the brain or other parts of the central nervous system (other than those areas controlling special senses).

Licences to perform experiments under British law (the Cruelty to Animals Act 1876) were held by 20,800 people, and of these 11,797 reported experiments during the year. Of these active licensees, 2,480 worked in commercial laboratories, 6,545 in universities and medical schools, 471 in National Health Service hospitals, 135 in public health laboratories, 297 in polytechnics, 991 in quasi-autonomous non-governmental organizations, 297 in government departments and 581 in non-profit-making organizations.

Although most experimenters were based at universities and medical schools (55 per cent), these performed only a minority of experiments (19 per cent). The bulk of experiments (52 per cent) were carried out at commercial laboratories.

Overall trends show a peak in animal experiments in Britain (5,607,400) in 1971. The decline in numbers to the latest figure in 1982 (4,221,801) is probably a function of the general economic recession rather than the result of the introduction of non-animal techniques.

Under British law a scientist requires a licence from the Home Office in order to experiment on living vertebrates. The licence provides protection against prosecution for cruelty under the principal animal welfare statute (the Protection of Animals Act 1911). Experiments must be performed on premises registered by the Secretary of State, which are subject to inspection by Home Office Inspectors. Currently there are fifteen inspectors covering 518 registered laboratories (or groups of laboratories), where 4,221,801 experiments were performed in 1982. These inspectors pay about 6,000 visits each year to such laboratories, some without notice.

The Secretary of State is advised in his duties under the law by officials at the Home Office and by an advisory committee chiefly composed of scientists.

THE ELEMENTS OF REFORM

If control is to precede abolition, the licensing of experimenters and the inspection of laboratories are first steps. The reduction of secrecy and the admission of public opinion into the control process must follow. In Sweden experiments are allowed or disallowed by local committees on which lay, animal welfare, animal care (veterinary) and scientific interests are represented. The requirement to use alternative (non-animal) techniques (or lower organisms) wherever possible is the next stage. The control of pain or its prohibition are also key reforms; in Britain experiments may involve 'severe' pain or enduring pain, but not pain which is both severe *and* enduring.

Whether or not an experiment is essential depends upon one's point of view. To the experimenter convinced of the importance of his own research, or to the business man determined to make a profit, almost any procedure may seem justified. Clearly, such decisions ought to be taken more dispassionately, ideally by a panel equally representative of the interests of the animals and the experimenters and arbitrated by a jury of intelligent lay persons. But in certain fields, such as cosmetics testing, behavioural research, agricultural research and weapons testing, the justification for inflicting pain wears thin in the opinion of most people. Here are just a few recent examples of experiments on animals:

- In London British scientists irradiated mice over periods of up to sixty days to cause lung damage. Mice sometimes took six months to die. Death from oesophageal damage can be extremely painful, yet the published report gives no indication that measures were taken to relieve suffering after irradiation.[1]
- In Newcastle castrated mini-pigs were subjected to up to eighty-one periods of compression and decompression. All the pigs suffered attacks of decompression sickness, from which several pigs died.[2]
- In London rabbits were injected in their knee joints to cause chronic inflammation for periods up to seven months, in experiments designed to research rheumatoid arthritis. The reports do not indicate that any pain-killing or anti-inflammatory agents were used to alleviate the animals' suffering.[3]
- In England monkeys were dosed with the weed-killer Paraquat. They became very ill, showing vomiting, anorexia, dyspnoea, hypothermia and acute renal failure. Some took more than a week to die. It is known that paraquat poisoning causes humans to die in extreme agony over a period of days, and it is reasonable to assume that paraquat-poisoned monkeys suffer in a similar way.[4]
- In Hertfordshire electric shocks were repeatedly administered to the tooth pulp of beagle dogs which were injected with various

substances, including in some cases analgesics.[5]

- At the Ministry of Defence research facility at Porton Down monkeys and other animals were repeatedly injected with glutaminase, causing vomiting, palor, spasms, lethargy, diarrhoea, dehydration and death. One monkey survived for twenty-eight days with persistent diarrhoea before being killed.[6]

Pain has become the central issue of the reform movement. In October 1983 the Royal Society for the Prevention of Cruelty to Animals (RSPCA) sent the British Secretary of State for Home Affairs its report, 'Pain and Suffering in Experimental Animals in the United Kingdom', with a foreword by Professor Pat Wall, one of the leading authorities in this subject. The report gave details of thirty-five recent British experiments as proof that the infliction of pain is not an unusual occurrence and concluded that pain is the single most significant issue of the political debate in this field and the main focus of public concern. The difficulty in defining pain was accepted, but the RSPCA pointed out that pain has been a legal concept in British law for more than a century, and difficulties in definition constitute no grounds for resisting reform.

In 1979 the RSPCA's report on shooting and angling, chaired by Lord Medway, had found that certain body chemicals associated with the experience of pain in man were also present in fish and other vertebrate classes. The 1983 report therefore concluded that this new evidence, added to the older neurological and behavioural findings, strongly indicated that all vertebrates share a common capacity to experience pain.

The report went on to recommend that all those experimenting on animals should be required to show competence in modern techniques of anaesthesia, analgesia, tranquillization, euthanasia and animal care, and to use these skills as a matter of course. The physiological effects of analgesia might interfere with some experiments, but so also might the physiological effects of pain itself. Too much was left to the discretion of the experimenter, and there should be constant recourse to independent on-the-spot authority from an expert 'animals' friend' within the laboratory. The absence of certain behavioural or other signs should never be taken as proof of the absence of pain, and as a general rule experimenters should record (and publish) descriptions of all steps taken to assess and maintain an animal's state of well-being.

The RSPCA report concludes by emphasizing the need for public accountability and recommends that experiments should be control-led by central and local ethical committees. These should have a composition balanced by equal representation between those repre-senting the interests of the experimenters and those representing animal welfare, and should assess and balance pain against the probability of benefits.

The RSPCA made clear its total opposition to any suffering in experimentation, and in a meeting with the Minister concerned in February 1984, regretted the Government's proposal to continue to allow the infliction of 'severe' pain.

ALTERNATIVES TO EXPERIMENTATION WITH LIVE ANIMALS

There are at least three definitions of humane alternative techniques:

- those techniques which *replace* experimental animals (the use of sophisticated dummies instead of living animals in car crash studies is but one example of how imaginative scientists have created new techniques which avoid terrible suffering);
- those techniques which *reduce* the use of animals;
- those techniques which reduce or abolish pain or other suffering.

All three definitions have validity.

Using computer models of bodily function, physical models or films for teaching purposes, tissue cultures (i.e. growing living cells in a test tube), organ cultures, gas chromatography and mass spectrometry are all examples of techniques which have had the effect of successfully replacing some animals in research. Many of these techniques are more accurate and less expensive than using animals. Others need further research and development in order to become as good as existing methods. Some, like the simple culturing of human cells, are inexpensive, while others require the purchase of new equipment which can be costly.

One of the great drawbacks of tissue culture has been the need to test new substances on all the systems of the body working together. A substance which is not poisonous to cells alone may become so after it is transformed by the liver, for example, into a new substance. On the other hand, what is poisonous to one species of animal may not affect another species. Rats and mice can react quite differently to the same substance. So can the human animal.

In 1980 Professor George Teeling-Smith wrote on the subject of statutory toxicity (poison) testing on animals in a paper entitled *A Question of Balance* (published by the Association of the British Pharmaceutical Industry):

> The statutory bodies such as the Committee on Safety of Medicines which require these tests do so largely as an act of faith rather than on hard scientific grounds.
>
> With thalidomide, for example, it is only possible to produce the specific deformities in a very small number of species of animal. In this particular case, therefore, it is unlikely that specific tests in pregnant animals would have given the necessary warning: the right species would probably never have been used. Even more strikingly, the practolol adverse reactions have not been reproducible in any species of animal except man. Conversely, penicillin in very small doses is fatal to guinea pigs. If it had been tested in those animals before being given to man, its systemic use in humans might well have been considered too hazardous and unethical.
>
> Hence the first problem in minimizing risks with new medicines is the difficulty inherent in trying to predict adverse reactions in man from studies in experimental animals. The present tendency is to ask for more and longer animal tests merely in the hope that they may somehow make medicines safer. It has to be remembered that in addition they do three things. First, they will in some cases rule out the human use of medicines which would in fact be safe and valuable. Second, more predictably, they delay the introduction of all new medicines. Third, they add enormously to their cost.

The undoubted advantage of the tissue-culture approach is that it can use *human* cells cultured in the test tube. Moreover, it can use different types of living human cell and even diseased cells, such as human cancer cells removed during routine surgery.

Some of the heaviest users of animals are the firms which carry out routine toxicity testing of new products. The cruel and clumsy LD50 test involves dosing animals with large doses of cosmetics or drugs, weed-killers or consumer products, in order to see what dose kills 50 per cent of the animals within a certain time (for example, fourteen days). Scientists attach little importance to the results of such crude procedures, yet bureaucracies still obstinately and cruelly refuse to channel research funds into developing better alternative and humane techniques. The Draize test (applying substances to the eyes of animals) is a similarly primitive procedure.

Another case is the testing of products for their carcinogenic (cancer-forming) potential. Thousands of animals perish miserably each year despite the fact that *human* cancer tumours cannot satisfactorily be produced in other species.

In 1976 some ICI scientists reported important evidence in *Nature*, 16 December, to show that several cheap and humane procedures constitute an accurate method of screening substances for carcinogenicity. They concluded that their results 'clearly establish that the Ames Test and the Cell Transformation Assay are both able to detect a high percentage of a wide range of carcinogens while also generating an acceptably low level of false positives'. In plain words, the safety of products (that is, concerning carcinogenicity) can be tested by using humane test-tube methods.

In 1978 the late Professor D. H. Smyth published the results of his survey of humane alternatives carried out for the Research Defence Society, *Alternatives to Animal Experiments*. He widened his definition of 'alternatives' to cover 'experiments on animals not causing pain or distress'. Smyth called for a body to be set up to collate reliable information on the subject and recommended that industry and Government should spend money on investigating the literature, particularly with regard to toxicity testing; projects should be funded to find an alternative to the Draize test, and to encourage the development of Immunoassay, which Smyth described as 'one potentially very useful alternative'.

In 1979 a workshop was held in Montreal under the auspices of the Canadian Society for Prevention of Cruelty to Animals, which published its findings the following year. This workshop reviewed the field of *in vitro* methods, concluded that many offered great potential and urged Governments and research organizations to devote more funds towards the development and validation of these techniques.

While it would be wise not to exaggerate the applicability of non-sentient alternative techniques as they exist at the present time, it cannot be denied that the twentieth century has seen many instances of the rapid development of technologies from small beginnings. Within a lifetime human beings have learned to fly and have reached the moon. In the matter of alternatives to laboratory animals we are at the beginning, but the potential is surely there – all that is needed is the political, commercial, legal or moral incentive. If scientists cannot mend their morals, then the laws may have to provide that final impetus to oblige experimenters to develop humane methods. Necessity has, after all, so often found herself pregnant with invention.

DEBATES ON TACTICS

The growth of direct tactics in animal liberation has caused disputes within the movement about the morality and effectiveness of sabotage to laboratories, the freeing of animals and attacks upon the personal property of experimenters. In most countries the animal liberation hard-liners have observed a self-imposed moral code, which has meant that they have purposefully harmed no living creature, human or non-human. Some, however, have had no qualms about attacking property, especially that associated with vivisection.

The frequently voiced objection to such tactics from the traditional animal welfarist is that they are 'counter-productive'. Yet any historian knows that in some earlier reform movements little progress was made until illegal and sometimes violent acts occurred. Whether reforms would have been achieved without the direct action of the suffragists, for example, or whether they would have been achieved more slowly, are matters for conjecture.

There is no doubt that experimenters have felt directly threatened by the militants, though they may sometimes have exaggerated the physical dangers posed by such groups. Admittedly, in 1982 and 1983 a series of small-scale letter bombs were sent to political leaders in Britain, allegedly from an animal rights organization. But the reaction of every genuine animal rights group in the country was one of outrage and condemnation. Indeed, many suggested that the bombs were sent by fanatics on the other side of the argument as an attempt to discredit the movement at a crucial juncture in the campaign to ban Canadian baby seal imports into the European Community.

Various right-wing commentators have seen the animal liberation movement as some sort of left-wing conspiracy. Yet no evidence has appeared of any ulterior political motivation. Few in the movement have had prior experience as political activists in any party. Certainly, however, the British movement has been associated in recent years with the parties of the centre and the left – the Labour, Social Democrat and Liberal parties. This has marked a change from the animal welfare movement of previous decades which had become very middle-class and conservative, a phenomenon deriving from the highly respectable position attained by the promotion of animal welfare in late Victorian society. Prior to the 1970s in Britain, centre and left-wing politicians tended to scorn animal welfare, and some viewed it as middle-class sentimentality – a preference for pets over people. This outlook was gradually changed by the new campaigns of the 1970s, the spate of serious publications on the subject and the deliberate attempt to 'put animals into politics'.

These successful campaigns were won by neither the political nor the militant action approaches on their own. Both techniques played their part. It remains true that mass movements for change benefit from a full range of positions (from reform to abolition) and from a full spectrum of tactics (from political debate to direct action).

The question has also arisen of when, if ever, it is right for a campaigner to compromise with the forces of the status quo. The answer is complex, and although dialogue with Governments, and even with opposing forces, is usually desirable, it is wrong to confuse the role of the campaigner with that of a sovereign state in international diplomacy. It is probable that, unlike a sovereign state, the pressure group can only gain and has nothing much to lose. The job of a pressure group therefore is to press and not to negotiate.

This does not rule out of the pressure process rational argument, expressions of gratitude, civilized behaviour or even a graduated approach to reform. But it means that the making of concessions by animal protection groups in discussions with a Government is irrelevant except to the latter, which can then portray the agreement as support for its actions or lack of them.

The pressure group, unlike a foreign Government, cannot make a trade deal or treaty which is of any real consequence in national terms. Thus it is an unfortunate reality that in pressure-group politics (far more than in business or diplomacy) the stick counts for more than the carrot. Compromise by a pressure group, especially premature compromise when the tide of public opinion is flowing strongly in favour of the aims of the pressure group, is an unnecessary waste of effort at best and at worst will be seized upon and exploited by the Government for its own ends.

Governments move only when pressed; when the pressure is released they cease to move. In the case of modern pressure-group politics the principal tools of the trade are media attention, the arousal and targeting of public opinion and direct approaches to Government and politicians.

The classical example of this in animal politics was the stopping of the slaughter of grey and common seals in Scotland in 1978. First, Greenpeace boats confronted the sealers and thus caught the attention of the media. The International Fund for Animal Welfare made the next major move by placing whole-page advertisements in the British press telling members of the public to 'Write to the Prime Minister'. (This caused Mr Callaghan to receive some 17,000 letters on this topic in one week – the most ever received on one subject by any Prime Minister in such a short period.) Finally, I led an RSPCA deputation to the Secretary of State bearing some scientific findings which cast an element of doubt upon the scientific research of the Government; this duly helped to provide the Government with the excuse it by then needed to call off the seal slaughter. In this campaign the three elements (direct action attracting the media, the channelling of already aroused public feeling and high-level political contact providing a face-saver for the Government) all worked perfectly together. Furthermore, the refusal of the RSPCA to condone the seal slaughter, even in the slightest degree, helped to make the Government's position untenable.

The old argument has also raged about whether half a loaf of progress today is better than waiting for the full loaf at some uncertain time in the future. This argument has been complicated by doubt as to whether legislative half-measures should be regarded as paving the way for more sweeping reforms or whether they merely take the wind out of the sails of the campaign and give Governments the excuse to do nothing for a few years. On an issue like animal experimentation, where publicity invariably rouses public opinion on the side of the animals, the former point of view is probably more correct, especially as moderate (as opposed to extreme) reforms may not provoke strong and effective opposition.

However, although legislative half-measures are probably better than nothing, this does not mean that they should be quietly accepted by reformers as the end of the road. Instead, campaigners should see them as stepping stones on the way and should maintain their pressure for further progress.

NOTES

[1] *Br. J. Radiol.* 1976, 49 and *Eur. J. Cancer* 1979, 15.
[2] *Br. J. Exp. Path.* 1980, 61, 39.
[3] *Br. J. Exp. Path.* 1981, 62.
[4] *Toxicology* 1979, 15/1.
[5] *Br. J. Pharmac.* 1980, 70.
[6] *Br. J. Exp. Path.* 1980, 61.

Brave New Farm?

JIM MASON

In our mind's eye the farm is a peaceful, pleasant place where calves nuzzle their mothers in a shady field, pigs loaf in the mudhole and chickens scratch and scramble about the barnyard. We comfort ourselves with these bucolic images – images that are implanted by calendars, colouring books and the countrified labelling and advertising of animal products.

The reality of modern animal production, however, is starkly different from these scenes. Now, virtually all of our poultry products and about half of our milk and red meat come from animals mass-produced in huge factory-like systems. In some of the more intensively managed 'confinement' operations, animals are crowded in pens and cages stacked up like so many shipping crates. On these factory farms there are no pastures, no streams, no seasons, not even day and night. Health and productivity come not from frolics in sunny meadows but from syringes and additive-laced feed.

The new factory systems allow operators (not all farmers operate them and not all who operate them are farmers) to maintain a larger number of animals in a given space, but they have created serious problems for consumers, farmers and the environment, and they raise disturbing questions about the degree of animal exploitation that our society should accept. The factory farm is one of the more inappropriate technologies of this century: it requires high inputs of capital and energy to carry out a simple, natural process; it causes a costly chain of problems and risks; and it does not in fact produce the results claimed by its proponents. Moreover, the animal factory pulls our society one long, dark step backward from the desirable goal of a sane, ethical relationship with other beings and the natural world.

FACTORIES COME . . . FARMS GO

Right under our noses agribusiness has wrought a sweeping revolution in the ways in which animals are kept to produce meat, milk and eggs. It began in the years before World War II, when farmers near large cities began to specialize in the production of chickens to meet the constant demand for eggs and meat. These first mass-producers were able to turn out large flocks all the year round once poultry experts discovered the role of vitamins A and D. When these were added to the feed, chickens could be raised indoors because they no longer needed sunlight and exercise for proper growth and bone development.

Large-scale indoor production caught on fast around the urban market centres, but the new methods created a host of problems. Nightmarish scenes began to occur in the crowded sheds. Birds pecked others to death and ate their remains. In the poorly ventilated poultry sheds contagious diseases were rampant, and losses multiplied throughout the budding commercial poultry industry. But during the war years demand for poultry was high, and the boom in the chicken business attracted the attention of the largest feed and pharmaceutical companies, which put their scientists to work on the problems of mass-production. Breakthroughs began to come thick and fast. Someone found that losses from pecking and cannibalism could be reduced by burning off the tips of chickens' beaks with a blowtorch. Within another year or two an automatic debeaking machine was patented, and its use became routine. The development of a new strain of hybrid corn made for richer feeds, faster-gaining birds and a greater number of 'crops' of chickens each year for farmers. Foremost of the developments, however, was the discovery that sulfa drugs and antibiotics could be added to feed to help hold down diseases in the crowded sheds.

The chicken itself was not entirely ready for mass-production, and the poultry industry set about looking for a better commercial bird. In 1946 the Great Atlantic and Pacific Tea Company (now A&P) launched the 'Chicken of Tomorrow' contest to find a strain of chicken that could produce a broad-breasted carcass at low feed cost. Within a few years poultry breeders had developed the prototype for today's fast-flesh broiler, a chicken that grows to market weight in about seven weeks. The pre-war ancestor of this bird took twice as long to grow to market weight.

News of the successes on the meat side of poultry production rapidly spread to egg producers. They too went to work on engineering their own specialized chicken, the 'layer' hen, which would turn out eggs and more eggs. Today's model lays about 25 per cent more eggs per year than did the all-purpose backyard chickens of the 1940s.

Egg producers tried to follow broiler producers' factory ways, but they were faced with one major problem: confined layer hens produced tons of manure each week. Broiler producers had had the manure problem in their large flocks too, but their birds were in and out within twelve weeks, and accumulations could be cleaned out between 'crops'. Egg producers, however, kept their birds indoors for a year or more, and they needed a means of manure removal that would not disturb the hens or interfere with egg production. Unfortunately for the layer hen, they found it: producers discovered that they could confine their chickens in wire-mesh cages suspended over a trench to collect droppings. At first they placed their hens one to each cage, but when they found that birds were cheaper than wire and buildings, crowded cages became the rule. Although crowding caused the deaths of more layer hens, this cost was slight against the increased total egg output. Evidently profits were being made, for ever-larger cage systems rapidly took over the egg industry. Articles in the May and July 1978 issues of *Poultry Management* report that between 1955 and 1975 flock size in a typical egg factory rose from 20,000 to 80,000 birds per house, and that in 1967 44 per cent of the nation's 300 million layer hens are caged in automated factory buildings. The typical cage in today's egg factory holds four or five hens on a 12- by 18-inch floor area.

Having proven that the chicken could be reduced to an animal machine, husbandry experts began looking about for ways to extend factory technology to the other farm animal species. In the 1960s they began developing systems for pigs, cattle and sheep that incorporated the principles of confinement, mass-production and automated feeding, watering, ventilation and waste removal. The wire cage, which made everything possible for the egg industry, would not work for these heavier, hoofed animals. But an innovation was found: it was the slatted floor – rails of metal or concrete spaced slightly apart and built over gutters or holding pits. Now large numbers of animals could be confined indoors and held to rigid production schedules, for the hard work of providing bedding and hauling manure had been eliminated.

The basics of factory husbandry had been established. Now the job of refining mass-production systems and methods fell to husbandry experts, and it opened up a great new field for them. It opened up, as well, great new markets for the agribusiness companies that could profit from the expanded sales of feed, equipment, drugs and the other products required by the new capital-intensive technology. Humanity and concern retreated further as animal scientists, funded by grants from these companies, worked out the 'bugs' in the new systems.

THE FACTORY FORMULA

Factory methods and equipment vary from species to species, but the principles are the same: to keep costs down and to manipulate animals' productivity upward. These principles ensure that factory animals are crowded, restricted, stressed, frustrated, held in barren environments and maintained on additive-laced, unnatural diets. Although factories exist, or are in development, for each species of farm animal, pigs, chickens and veal calves suffer the most under the new husbandry and, for that reason, their plight should be examined in more detail.

The modern chicken is a business creation; it comes from the sterile laboratories of a handful of 'primary breeders'. These companies sell breeding animals to a few hundred 'multiplier' firms, which in turn produce the chicks that go to egg and broiler farms. At the multipliers birds have the run of the floors in the breeding houses, for freedom and exercise produce a higher percentage of fertile eggs. The eggs are usually hand-gathered and placed in giant incubators.

If the hatchery is turning out birds for egg factories, the first order of business is the destruction of half the 'crop' of chicks. Males don't lay eggs, and the flesh of these specialized layer breeds is of poor quality – 'not fit to feed', as one hatchery worker put it. At some hatcheries 'egg-type' males are thrown into plastic bags and allowed to suffocate. Females of the strain are debeaked, vaccinated and sent to 'grow-out' houses until, at about twenty weeks of age, they are ready to start laying eggs. At this point they are installed in the automated cage layer house. After a year or two in the cages their egg productivity wanes and it becomes unprofitable to feed and house them. The factory farmer may decide to use 'force moulting', a procedure which shocks the birds into renewed egg productivity for another few months by leaving them in the dark for several days without food or water. After a force moult or two the hens are spent, and they are delivered to the processors to be turned into soup stock, frozen pies and other convenience foods.

With broiler strains males are kept and raised for markets, although they are separated from females on many farms. Debeaked and toe-clipped, day-old chicks are ganged up under heaters at one end of the long broiler shed. As they grow, the partition is moved down the building until the young birds take over the entire floor. On most farms the floor is covered with wood shavings or other absorbent litter material. Here the broilers have it a bit better than their cousins in the layer cages. Nor are they confined as long, for they reach market weight (about 3½lb) in approximately eight weeks. But their numbers are huge: over four *billion* broiler birds go through these systems each year in the USA alone.

Pigs are raised in a variety of systems, but there has been a trend towards larger farms with factory facilities. Some of these farms have 'total-confinement' systems in which the pigs never see the light of day until they go to market; they are conceived, born, weaned, and 'finished' (fattened) in specialized buildings similar to those used in the poultry industries. These farms typically keep a few boars and a few hundred breeding sows to turn out the pigs raised for market, but an increasing number of farms don't bother with boars, relying instead on artificial insemination.

Shortly after conception the factory sow's misery begins when she is moved to a 'gestation' building. On some farms she may share a small pen with other sows, but in the more intensive factories she is restricted to a narrow stall in which she can only stand or lie down. In either event, she remains in her pen or stall for about four months, during which she may be kept in darkness and fed only once every two or three days.

A week or so before her pigs are due, she is moved to a 'farrowing' building and restricted again to a narrow stall. This stall permits her to lie and stand, but she cannot walk or turn around; its purpose is to keep her in position only to eat, drink and keep her teats exposed to the baby pigs. Soon after birth the pigs receive a battery of injections; their 'needle' teeth are clipped; their tails are cut off; and their ears are notched for identification. Near weaning time, in a couple of weeks or so, the males are castrated without anaesthetic. At this point the sow goes back to the breeding area, and the pigs are moved to pens in the finishing buildings, where they spend about twenty weeks until they reach a market weight of about 220 lb.

Veal factories are perhaps the harshest of all the confinement systems. Newly born calves are taken from their mothers and turned into anaemic, neurotic animals to provide the luxury-grade 'milk-fed' veal preferred by gourmet cooks and fancy restaurants. The young calves, stressed by separation from their mothers, are placed in narrow wooden stalls, lined up row on row in the confinement building. For between fourteen and sixteen weeks each calf is confined to a space scarcely larger than its own body and is often tied at the neck to restrict movement further. The calf is fed only 'milk replacer', a liquid mixture of dried milk products, starch, fats, sugar, antibiotics and other additives. The milk replacer is deficient in iron to induce anaemia – a necessary condition if the producer's calves are to have flesh white enough to fetch the market price for 'prime' veal. No hay or other roughage is permitted, for that too might darken the flesh. Even the wooden stalls and neck chains are part of the plan, as these restrictions keep the calf from licking its own urine and faeces to satisfy its craving for iron.

Other species are now being exposed to factory methods. Sheep experts are perfecting confinement systems in the USA, Europe and Australia. Domestic rabbits are being raised in cage systems similar to those used by the egg industry, and the budding rabbit industry is working hard to increase public demand for rabbit meat. In beef cattle feedlots stress from crowding and an unnatural diet adversely affect the animals' health. Liver abscesses are common in these animals because their digestive tracts are geared more to roughage than to the steady diet of high-energy grain and growth promotants that they receive.

FACTORY PROBLEMS, FACTORY SOLUTIONS

The industrialization of farm animals has provided farmers with tighter controls over their herds and flocks and it has eliminated much of the labour of feeding, waste removal and other chores, but it has also created a whole new set of problems for producers. These problems are seen as challenges by an ever-growing army of experts who churn out increasingly elaborate management schemes to keep the system working. Constant manipulations of animals' anatomy, physiology, heredity and environment are required to keep health problems in check so that mass commodity production can be maintained at a profitable level. Chief among these factory-related health problems are stress and disease.

In confinement animals are subjected to a variety of stresses. When birds are debeaked or when calves or pigs are weaned prematurely or castrated, some die from the shock. These causes of stress are occasional, however, and after a few days of adjustment most of the animals return to 'normal'. But other causes of stress in the factory farm are continuous. The animals have no relief from crowding and monotony. In a less restrictive environment they would relieve boredom by moving; confined animals cannot. Nor have they relief from social disturbances caused by factory conditions. When animals are crowded and annoyed, the likelihood and frequency of aggressive encounters increases. When growing pigs are moved to larger pens, outbreaks of fighting can occur, leaving pigs dead or injured. In the restricted space of confinement pens less agressive animals cannot get away to make the show of submission dictated by instinct. Some animals may become so fearful that they dare not move, even to eat or drink, and they become runts and die. Others remain in constant, panicky motion, a neurotic perversion of their instinct to escape.

Under socially stressful conditions cannibalism can occur, especially among poultry and swine. Cannibalism in poultry results from a distortion of the birds' instinct to establish a social hierarchy or 'pecking order'. Birds that have evolved over millions of years, socializing in flocks of about a hundred members, cannot establish a pecking order among the thousands on the floor of a modern broiler or turkey house. In these superflocks birds would peck each other relentlessly if controls were not used. Caged birds have the opposite problem: each cage contains a small 'flock', and one member has to fall at the bottom of the social ladder. This unfortunate bird cannot escape its tormentors. In pigs cannibalism takes the form of tail biting, described by one expert, in an article published in the March 1976 issue of *Hog Farm Management*, as follows:

> Acute tail biting is often called cannibalism and frequently results in crippling, mutilation and death . . . Many times the tail is bitten first and then the attacking pig or pigs continue to eat further into the back. If the situation is not attended to, the pig will die and be eaten.

For the factory farmer management of these stress-related problems calls for manipulation of both animal and environment but not relief of crowded conditions – the primary underlying cause. Stress and related health problems can be reduced by keeping animals in darkness or under very low-intensity lights. Many total-confinement veal and pig operations keep their animals in total darkness around the clock except for brief inspection and feeding periods. For the factory farmer, on the other hand, cannibalism calls for direct animal engineering: if the factory cannot be modified to suit the animal, the animal is modified to suit the factory. To ensure that stressed pigs cannot tail-bite, farmers routinely cut off ('dock') the tails of young pigs a few days after birth. Cannibalism among poultry is controlled by debeaking, an operation that removes the front one-third of the bird's beak. Broiler chicks require only one debeaking because they are sent to market before their beaks grow back. Most egg producers debeak their birds twice, once at about one week of age and again during the growing period when the birds are between twelve and twenty weeks of age.

In large flocks labour costs are high, and the debeaking procedure is carried out as quickly as possible; experts recommend a speed of about fifteen birds a minute. Patience and precision tend to give way in monotonous work, and the beaks of many birds are sloppily cut. According to F. D. Thornberry, W. O. Crawley and W. F. Krueger, whose article on debeaking appeared in *Poultry Digest* in May 1975:

> An excessively hot blade causes blisters in the mouth. A cold and or dull blade may cause the development of a fleshy, bulb-like growth on the end of the mandible. Such growths are very sensitive and will cause below-average performance . . . Incomplete severance causes torn tissue in the roof of the mouth. The bird's tongue must be held away from the blade. Burned or severed tongues result in cull (worthless) hens.

Even if debeaking is properly done, it is painful and can affect birds' health later. Some debeaked birds do poorly during the production cycle and do not grow to full size because 'beak tenderness' makes it difficult for them to eat and drink.

On some farms at the same time as birds are debeaked their toes are clipped just behind the claw by the same hot-knife machine. This operation is said to keep the birds quieter, as it prevents 'back ripping' and fighting. To hold down pecking and fighting among males on breeding farms producers usually cut off their wattles and combs.

Heightened levels of aggression and activity take their toll of stressed animals in a more direct way. Like any over-worked machine, they simply wear out. Pigs in particular are prone to a reaction that we would probably call 'shock' if it occurred in humans; the pork industry calls it porcine stress syndrome (PSS). Pigs may literally drop dead from stress when they are weaned, moved to a new pen, mixed with strange pigs or shipped to market. A condition common in layer operations is termed caged layer fatigue (CLF). The fatigued birds have brittle or broken bones and a pale, washed-out appearance in their eyes, combs, beaks and feet. It is thought that they somehow withdraw minerals from their bones and muscles, and eventually these birds are unable to stand. In broiler operations, some birds suddenly jump into the air, give off a loud squawk and fall over dead. This 'flipover syndrome' is usually seen in the larger, faster-growing birds, yet poultry experts say its cause is not known. One southern broiler farmer told me that he had been losing several birds a day from this condition, which he called 'heart attack'. He told me that the problem is 'in the birds – they grow too fast these days'.

Stress leads to a string of reproductive problems as well. Reproductive functions are not essential to survival at the moment of stress, and so the animal's system puts them 'on the back burner' until the stress is gone. Under constant stress reproductive functions are *always* on the back burner. Hence male pigs lose their sex drive, females fail to conceive and the offspring of these animals may have incompletely developed reproductive organs and may be slower to reach puberty.

In attempts to compensate for these problems, factory operators resort to manipulation of animals' reproductive systems. In some of the more intensively managed factory pig and cattle operations, females are dosed with hormones to synchronize their oestral cycles or to tune in their labour contractions and delivery times to the factory schedule. Although these procedures can cause shock or death, artificial control of oestrus, ovulation, gestation and birth provides greater control over the entire factory operation. Oestrus control decreases time between pregnancies, aids assembly-line artificial inseminations, increases the chance of conception and makes planning and record keeping easier. Use of prostaglandins to induce labour contractions makes calving and farrowing more convenient and predictable for the farmer. Injections of progestins or steroids bring on twin calves, larger litters of pigs and bigger lamb crops.

Even without the use of drugs, farmers speed up reproductive cycles by separating calves, lambs and pigs from their mothers much earlier than nature would. In nature a calf might nurse and run with its mother for about a year; on a dairy farm it is lucky to spend more than a day with its mother. Although most factory pig farmers leave their sows and pigs together for about three weeks before separation and weaning, a few are trying to wean only a few days after birth in order to rebreed the sow sooner.

In addition to the manipulation of sex and reproduction, factory experts control growth rates to increase production. The poultry industry has known for some time that birds' rates of growth and egg laying depend on the daily change in the ratio of light to dark. In the spring, when days grow longer and nights become shorter, birds' body cycles pick up and their rates of egg laying increase. It didn't take poultry producers long to figure out that control over light meant control over production. They began to experiment with various light schedules. Some broiler producers have total control over light in their windowless houses; others take advantage of sunlight during the day and use artificial lights after dark. Egg producers try to create the illusion of eternal spring by keeping the lights on a little longer each day. After about a year of this the flock's productivity drops, and many producers use 'force moulting' to revive it. A few birds die in the process, but most come through and begin producing all over again on a renewed pseudo-spring light schedule.

Under the stresses of factory life an animal's defences are down, and it is more prone to the infectious diseases that easily spread throughout crowded buildings, since the controlled environment of an animal factory can be a hothouse of air pollution and airborne germs. Even with powerful ventilators working properly, the air of pig and poultry factories contains dust raised by mechanical feeders and excited animals, and it is often laden with ammonia and other irritating gases from the manure pits. Because factory buildings are usually in use all the year round and are isolated from the cleansing effects of sunlight and rain, many develop what producers call 'bacteria build-up'. A producer may have relatively few health problems in a new factory building during the first year or two, but eventually the interior can become infested with a variety of disease-causing organisms. Farming magazines indicate that both pig and dairy factories are plagued with diseases, many of which are brought on by factory conditions.

This battle against bacteria calls for strict measures throughout the factory. Everyone – animals, managers and visitors – must follow a one-way route from building to building to avoid bringing germs back to younger animals. Between 'crops' of animals farmers sterilize practically everything inside with an arsenal of hot water, high-pressure hoses, acids, cleansers and disinfectant chemicals. Animal disease experts recommend 'health programs' – routine doses of sulfa, antibiotics, vitamins and other medications at regular intervals throughout the production cycle – to help hold down disease losses. Producers must also use pesticides to get rid of the mites, ticks, fleas and other insects that tend to build up around concentrations of animals.

The factory operator, if he or she is a good manager, tries to control temperature, humidity, light, ventilation, drafts, dust, odours, noise, fighting, disease, waste removal, the supply of food and water and everything else that makes up an animal's environment. But when hundreds or thousands of animals are confined in a single room, it is not likely that every element of the environment will be satisfactory to every individual animal. Thus the health of some animals fails, and the causes are so diffuse that they are difficult to trace. Because of this, and because the mass-production schedule does not allow for precise, individualized treatment of animals, many producers use a shotgun approach to disease: they reach for a syringe full of broad-spectrum antibiotics when any symptoms appear.

Throughout the factory, then, constant manipulation of animals is necessary to maintain a profitable flow of meat, milk and eggs. The factory process provides a prime example of the disparity in the way we view technology (our own works) and the way we view animals and natural processes: we worship technology; we despise animals and nature. Animals have been reduced to mere things for our use, and all of their complex and wonderful life processes – growth, mating, birth, death – have been subjected to human design and control. We are simply unable to accept animals – especially food animals – as beings in their own right. Until we do, we will not be able to achieve sane and ethical relations with the rest of the natural world.

DRUG DEPENDENCE IN THE FACTORY

It's hardly an overstatement to claim that today's factory animals are drug-dependent. The US Office of Technology Assessment reported in *Drugs in Livestock Feed* that nearly all poultry, most pigs and veal calves and 60 per cent of cattle get antibiotic additives in their feed, and according the US Department of Agriculture's *Northeast Regional Newsletter* of June 1978, 75 per cent of pigs eat feed laced with sulfa drugs.

Although farmers receive instructions to withdraw additives from the feed before shipping their animals, sometimes slip-ups occur, and residues can show up in the products. A few years ago the General Accounting Office monitored the US Department of Agriculture's meat and poultry inspection programme and published its findings in a 1979 report entitled *Problems in Preventing the Marketing of Raw Meat and Poultry Containing Potentially Harmful Residues*. According to the report, 14 per cent of meat and poultry produces sampled by the Department between 1974 and 1976 contained illegally high levels of drugs and pesticides. The report stated: 'Of the 143 drugs and pesticides identified as likely to leave residues in raw meat and poultry, forty-two are known to cause or are suspected of causing cancer; twenty of causing birth defects and six of causing mutations.'

More recently the US Food and Drug Administration has expressed concern that as many as 500 or 600 toxic chemicals may be present in the country's meat supply, yet no adequate testing and monitoring programme exists to check for them. In an article published in the *New York Times* on 15 March 1983, Marian Burros noted that at present the Department of Agriculture monitors residues of only sixty chemicals. Despite calls by the General Accounting Office in its 1979 report and by the Carter Administration in 1980 for expanded residue testing, the Department of Agriculture continues to take random samples at the rate of only one per 220,000 animals slaughtered. Many scientists and government officials believe this residue monitoring programme is inadequate considering the extent to which the livestock and poultry industries rely on drugs and chemicals today. 'There is a good chance that the American public consumes meat with violative levels of carcinogenic and teratogenic chemical residues with some regularity,' according to Carol Tucker Foreman, Assistant Secretary of Agriculture from 1977 to 1980, whom Marian Burros cites in her article. Because of the rising concern over consumer health and safety, Representative James J. Howard of New Jersey has introduced the Farm Animal Practices bill (HR 3170) before Congress. If enacted, it would establish a special commission to investigate the ramifications of the use of drugs and chemicals in modern farm production.

More subtle but potentially more dangerous, perhaps, is a

shocking new kind of pollution created by drug-dependent husbandry methods. Animal agriculture's extensive use of antibiotics since World War II has unloaded these substances into the environment and has exposed them to a wide range of microorganisms. As a result, a number of common disease-causing germs – for example, the bacteria that cause diarrhoea, septicaemia, psittacosis, salmonella, gonorrhoea, pneumonia, typhoid and childhood meningitis – have now had long-standing exposure to antibiotics and have developed drug-resistant strains. This means that if you come down with a disease from one of these strains, a shot of antibiotics will not help as it might have a decade or so ago.

FARMERS (AND THE REST OF US) ARE VICTIMS TOO

Ironically, the trend toward complex, expensive husbandry systems is hurting farmers and rural communities. Those huge buildings full of specialized floors and feeding equipment don't come cheap. A modern, family-sized pig factory can cost from a quarter to a half a million dollars and a modest dairy facility about the same – not counting the cost of the land and animals. These financial burdens are so great the factory farmers must keep their buildings at capacity twelve months of the year, working longer and harder than ever just to meet their loan payments. So much for the 'labour efficiency' of the modern factory farm!

Moreover, the high capital investments required are a lure for agribusiness companies, urban investors and other non-farm interests looking for tax relief. US tax laws allow them to deduct from taxes due up to 10 per cent of money invested in factory buildings, and many obtain other tax advantages through transactions involving breeding animals. Some of these investors (and some of the largest farmers) may be more interested in the tax breaks than in profits, and they tend to keep producing even when prices are down. This tendency to operate at capacity in order to cover capital costs has created chronic overproduction in the poultry, pork and dairy industries. Constant overproduction keeps markets depressed, and small non-factory producers have a hard time breaking even on their small herds and flocks. When this happens the small farmers tend to quit raising animals altogether, and more and more production falls into the hands of the largest, most intensive operations.

The poultry industry, the originator of factory systems, offers a clear example of how the trend towards capital intensification affects farmers. Chickens and eggs, along with hogs, used to be the mainstay of the small, independent family farm before the poultry scientists and agribusiness companies got involved. As Harrison Wellford has pointed out in *Sowing the Wind*, as late as 1959 nearly 60 per cent of broilers and most turkeys were grown by independent farmers and sold on the open market. Today some fifty agribusiness corporations produce over 90 per cent of poultry meat. The farm family has been reduced to the status of 'poultry peons' who turn out company birds on company feed according to company schedules and specifications.

Despite these problems associated with the trend towards factory methods, agribusiness experts keep looking for solutions, keep tinkering with animals to get gains in productivity. Too much, they feel, has been invested to think of turning back. Yet animals' efficiency as commodity producers has biological limits, and not even factory methods can continue to squeeze greater and greater productivity from them. 'Sounding the Alarm for Ag Research', an article by R. L. Kohls in the June 1977 issue of *Confinement*, notes, for example, that increases in milk production per cow have levelled off since 1972; egg production per hen has levelled off at about 230 eggs per year; and pigs saved per sow have actually decreased since 1969. Now that data like these are coming in, factory methods are beginning to look less and less attractive. Farming magazines report that high energy costs and production problems are causing a few farmers to go back to less intensive methods. Because of his unpleasant experiences with factory systems, one farmer complained to *Hog Farm Management* in March 1979 that 'ten years of confinement raises more questions than answers'.

There are many, many costs in the new factory methods and systems for raising animals, although agribusiness experts would have us hear only their talk of benefits. They are fond of using cost-benefit analyses to justify the use of antibiotics in feed, chemical growth promotants or nitrites to cure meats. They assert that the benefits to consumers from these uses outweigh the risks involved. But if this sort of test is to have any validity in agricultural affairs, it must take into account all the costs of factory methods, which include threats to:

● the health of consumers, who dine on fatty, chemically dosed, antibiotic-fed animals;

- the environment, as a result of the accumulation of huge quantities of noxious animal wastes;
- our limited stores of fossil fuels;
- starving people, whose lives might be saved by the food and agricultural resources we are wasting;
- the land, which is forced to produce more and more grain to be turned into meat;
- wildlife, whose habitat is destroyed to grow grain;
- farm families and rural communities, whose livelihood and economic vitality have been undermined by the headlong rush toward high-tech factory systems;
- the animals themselves, who are restricted, mutilated, manipulated and reduced to mechanized production units;
- human dignity and self-respect, as a result of carrying on all of the above on such a massive scale.

Factory methods of animal production are not, as some agriculture experts claim, the inevitable result of a 'natural tide of history'. They are the product of decades of government policy and corporate profiteering. Although the trend is reversible, the forces behind it are well entrenched. Therefore there can be no *immediate* end to factory methods; it will take patient struggle to bring sanity and humanity back to farming.

THE NEW MOVEMENT AGAINST FACTORY FARMING

In Europe during the past two decades there has been rising concern about animal welfare, food quality and the other problems associated with factory farming. As a result, government is beginning to be involved in action against the worst abuses of animals in livestock systems. In Britain the publication of Ruth Harrison's book *Animal Machines* in 1964 stirred up a controversy that led to the appointment of a parliamentary committee to investigate the new husbandry methods. The Brambell Committee – nine scientists, agricultural experts and others – reported in 1965 to the Ministry of Agriculture, Fisheries and Food (MAFF). Among other things, it recommended the passage of a new law to safeguard animals that would set maximum stocking densities for various systems, prohibit the debeaking of poultry and the docking of pigs' tails, prohibit the close tethering of veal calves and gestating sows and require the provision of iron supplements and roughage for veal calves.

No such law was ever passed, but in 1971 the MAFF established voluntary codes for various species that largely ignored the substance of the Brambell recommendations. The few recommendations made were couched in terms such as 'may be necessary' and 'should preferably have', and some of these recommendations have been ignored in practice.

In 1981 the House of Commons Agriculture Committee published a report on the welfare of animals in poultry, pig and veal calf systems which made recommendations similar to those of the Brambell Committee, though more cautious in tone. Again, the report was critical of the MAFF and the Government's enforcement of farm animal protection provisions. Among other things, the Agriculture Committee recommended more research into animal behaviour under intensive conditions, a change in taxation policy to discourage undesirable methods and to encourage alternative systems, an 'early end' to veal calf crates, the phasing out of close confinement of gestating sows and tighter controls on tail docking and debeaking. In response, the MAFF has indicated that these recommendations will be ignored once again.

On the Continent a West German appellate court has ruled that the battery caging of chickens amounts to cruelty under that country's animal protection laws because the birds are permanently unable to act out their inherited behaviour patterns. Enforcement of the decision is being stayed until the German Agriculture Ministry can study the economic impacts.

The Council of Europe Convention for the Protection of Animals Kept for Farming Purposes underwrites the principle that farm animals must be housed, fed, watered and cared for in ways appropriate to their physiological and ethological needs. Most EEC countries have ratified this Convention, as has the European Commission itself. More recently, the Convention published a draft proposal that would establish minimum standards with respect to cage size, floor space, lighting, beak trimming and other factors to safeguard the welfare of laying hens.

Progress against intensive systems has moved beyond the study/recommendation stage in Switzerland, where a 1978 law and subsequent regulations have outlawed many factory farming practices. These provisions will, in effect, make battery cages for laying hens illegal by 1991. Switzerland's veal calves must receive iron in their feed and roughage in some form. Pigs must be allowed rooting time with straw, roughage or other suitable material, and restricted sows must be allowed exercise time periodically. Other provisions establish standards for lighting, flooring materials, space and other environmental factors.

In the United States efforts to stop intensive practices lag behind Europe's because until quite recently public awareness was low. Now major broadcast and print media are reporting the issues, and a number of animal protection organizations are campaigning more actively against factory methods. The Animal Welfare Institute, the Food Animal Concerns Trust and the Humane Society of the United States all have staff specialists in intensive farming, who regularly publish up-to-date information about farm animal welfare issues. The Farm Animal Reform Movement also publishes valuable material, although this grassroots group's main concern is picketing, demonstrations and other forms of activism to increase public awareness of farm animal welfare issues.

WHAT CAN BE DONE

The surest way to start working against factory farming is to stop consuming its products. You can refuse to eat 'milk-fed' veal, factory eggs, feedlot beef and other factory-farmed animal products. Of course, you can stop consuming animal products altogether, as is recommended by an increasing number of health experts. In either event, consumer demand can make a difference in that it will encourage independent farmers to seek the safest, most humane methods in animal production lest they destroy their markets.

Individual dietary changes will not be enough, however. While you get your food shopping, preparation and eating habits under control, you should work actively toward broader changes in agriculture and food policy. Since consumer demand affects food production, we should begin by making the following demands:

- Demand the prohibition of the use of antibiotics, growth promotants and other feed additives in animal agriculture. The Food and Drug Administration's efforts to ban or regulate these drugs are under way, but they are being stymied by drug and agri-business corporations. Without these shortcuts to genuine animal care and health, animal losses in crowded factories would be so great that factory systems and methods would not be profitable.

- Demand an end to the public subsidies that prop up factory farming. If society is to subsidize agriculture, it could make much better choices about the kinds of production to be supported and the kinds of food to be produced.
- Demand an end to tax-supported research and technological development of factory systems. The present funding scheme is one big boondoggle for drug and equipment manufacturers. Demand that this money and expertise be directed instead to work on farming methods that farmers can afford and manage, and ones that give consumers safe, wholesome food.
- Demand local markets and food co-operatives where farmers and consumers can trade directly. Every community has a square or park where space could be set aside for outdoor markets. Find the food co-operative in your community; if there is none, start one.
- Demand meatless meals and non-factory farm products from restaurants, hotels, airlines, caterers, school lunch services and all other public food outlets. Let them know that you are aware of where food comes from and that you are worried about food produced by factory methods.
- Demand labelling laws that will ensure the marking of all factory-produced animal products. (Don't settle for a statement to the effect that the farming systems have been approved by an animal welfare organization; there are some that will rubber-stamp anything just to get their names around.)
- Demand that supermarkets and other food outlets separate factory and non-factory foods. (In the USA there is a precedent for this in state laws regulating the labelling and display of kosher foods and, in some states, 'organic' or chemical-free foods.)
- Demand a tax on meat and animal products that would provide funding to subsidize the production of other crops. This would be no more absurd than our present policy of subsidizing the production of what are essentially luxury foods. If people want to continue to prop up costly, risky animal production, they should have to pay a premium, and the premium could be channelled towards the support of better foods and production methods.
- Demand an end to meat industry propaganda in local schools; demand to know how nutrition is being taught to your children.
- Demand a change of government policy so that it puts good food and farm livelihood first. The present prevailing pro-agribusiness bias is a scandal that has driven millions of farmers from the land and has saturated consumers with junk food.

- Demand land reforms and zoning laws that would bring small, diversified farms closer to populated areas. Too large a proportion of the cost of food is attributable to transport, handling and profiteering as food moves from the farm to the consumer.
- Demand that food products be labelled to carry the name of the corporation that owns the brand line. This would expose the monopolism behind the myth of a competitive food industry – and the lie that your ham, eggs, milk, etc., come from good old Farmer Jones down on the farm.
- Demand an end to the animal products industries' 'check-offs', which charge consumers and small farmers for advertising that props up our diet which is wasteful and weighted towards animal products.

Against Zoos

DALE JAMIESON

ZOOS AND THEIR HISTORY

We can start with a rough-and-ready definition of zoos: they are public parks which display animals, primarily for the purposes of recreation or education. Although large collections of animals were maintained in antiquity, they were not zoos in this sense. Typically these ancient collections were not exhibited in public parks, or they were maintained for purposes other than recreation or education.

The Romans, for example, kept animals in order to have living fodder for the games. Their enthusiasm for the games was so great that even the first tigers brought to Rome, gifts to Caesar Augustus from an Indian ruler, wound up in the arena. The emperor Trajan staged 123 consecutive days of games in order to celebrate his conquest of Dacia. Eleven thousand animals were slaughtered, including lions, tigers, elephants, rhinoceroses, hippopotami, giraffes, bulls, stags, crocodiles and serpents. The games were popular in all parts of the Empire. Nearly every city had an arena and a collection of animals to stock it. In fifth-century France there were twenty-six such arenas, and they continued to thrive until at least the eighth century.

In antiquity rulers also kept large collections of animals as a sign of their power, which they would demonstrate on occasion by destroying their entire collections. This happened as late as 1719 when Elector Augustus II of Dresden personally slaughtered his entire menagerie, which included tigers, lions, bulls, bears and boars.

The first modern zoos were founded in Vienna, Madrid and Paris in the eighteenth century and in London and Berlin in the nineteenth. The first American zoos were established in Philadelphia and Cincinnati in the 1870s. Today in the United States alone there are hundreds of zoos, and they are visited by millions of people every year. They range from roadside menageries run by hucksters, to elaborate zoological parks staffed by trained scientists.

The Roman games no longer exist, though bullfights and rodeos follow in their tradition. Nowadays the power of our leaders is amply demonstrated by their command of nuclear weapons. Yet we still have zoos. Why?

ANIMALS AND LIBERTY

Before we consider the reasons that are usually given for the survival of zoos, we should see that there is a moral presumption against keeping wild animals in captivity. What this involves, after all, is taking animals out of their native habitats, transporting them great distances and keeping them in alien environments in which their liberty is severely restricted. It is surely true that in being taken from the wild and confined in zoos, animals are deprived of a great many goods. For the most part they are prevented from gathering their own food, developing their own social orders and generally behaving in ways that are natural to them. These activities all require significantly more liberty than most animals are permitted in zoos. If we are justified in keeping animals in zoos, it must be because there are some important benefits that can be obtained only by doing so.

This conclusion is not the property of some particular moral theory; it follows from most reasonable moral theories. Either we have duties to animals or we do not. If we do have duties to animals, surely they include respecting those interests which are most important to them, so long as this does not conflict with other, more stringent duties that we may have. Since an interest in not being taken from the wild and kept confined is very important for most animals, it follows that if everything else is equal, we should respect this interest.

Suppose, on the other hand, that we do not have duties to animals. There are two further possibilities: either we have duties to people that sometimes concern animals, or what we do to animals is utterly

without moral import. The latter view is quite implausible, and I
shall not consider it further. People who have held the former view,
that we have duties to people that concern animals, have sometimes
thought that such duties arise because we can 'judge the heart of a
man by his treatment of animals', as Kant remarked in 'Duties to
Animals'. It is for this reason that he condemns the man who shoots
a faithful dog who has become too old to serve. If we accept Kant's
premise, it is surely plausible to say that someone who, for no good
reason, removes wild animals from their natural habitats and denies
them liberty is someone whose heart deserves to be judged harshly.
If this is so, then even if we believe that we do not have duties to
animals but only duties concerning them, we may still hold that
there is a presumption against keeping wild animals in captivity. If
this presumption is to be overcome, it must be shown that there are
important benefits that can be obtained only by keeping animals in
zoos.

ARGUMENTS FOR ZOOS

What might some of these important benefits be? Four are commonly cited: amusement, education, opportunities for scientific
research, and help in preserving species.

Amusement was certainly an important reason for the establishment of the early zoos, and it remains an important function of
contemporary zoos as well. Most people visit zoos in order to be
entertained, and any zoo that wishes to remain financially sound
must cater to this desire. Even highly regarded zoos, like the San
Diego Zoo, have their share of dancing bears and trained birds of
prey. But although providing amusement for people is viewed by the
general public as a very important function of zoos, it is hard to see
how providing such amusement could possibly justify keeping wild
animals in captivity.

Most curators and administrators reject the idea that the primary
purpose of zoos is to provide entertainment. Indeed, many agree that
the pleasure we take in viewing wild animals is not in itself a good
enough reason to keep them in captivity. Some curators see baby
elephant walks, for example, as a necessary evil, or defend such
amusements because of their role in educating people, especially
children, about animals. It is sometimes said that people must be
interested in what they are seeing if they are to be educated about it,

and entertainments keep people interested, thus making education possible.

This brings us to a second reason for having zoos: their role in education. This reason has been cited as long as zoos have existed. For example, in 1898 the New York Zoological Society resolved to take 'measures to inform the public of the great decrease in animal life, to stimulate sentiment in favor of better protection, and to cooperate with other scientific bodies . . . [in] efforts calculated to secure the perpetual preservation of our higher vertebrates'. Despite the pious platitudes that are often uttered about the educational efforts of zoos, however, there is little evidence that zoos are very successful in educating people about animals. Stephen Kellert's paper 'Zoological Parks in American Society', delivered at the annual meeting of the American Association of Zoological Parks and Aquariums in 1979, indicates that zoo-goers are much less knowledgeable about animals than backpackers, hunters, fishermen and others who claim an interest in animals, and only slightly more knowledgeable than those who claim no interest in animals at all. Even more disturbing, zoo-goers express the usual prejudices about animals; 73 per cent say they dislike rattlesnakes, 52 per cent vultures and only 4 per cent elephants. One reason why some zoos have not done a better job in educating people is that many of them make no real effort at education. In the case of others the problem is an apathetic and unappreciative public.

Edward G. Ludwig's study of the zoo in Buffalo, New York, in the *International Journal for the Study of Animal Problems* for 1981, revealed a surprising amount of dissatisfaction on the part of young, scientifically inclined zoo employees. Much of this dissatisfaction stemmed from the almost complete indifference of the public to the zoo's educational efforts. Ludwig's study indicated that most animals are viewed only briefly as people move quickly past cages. The typical zoo-goer stops only to watch baby animals or those who are begging, feeding or making sounds. Ludwig reported that the most common expressions used to describe animals are 'cute', 'funny-looking', 'lazy', 'dirty', 'weird' and 'strange'.

Of course, it is undeniable that some education occurs in some zoos. But this very fact raises other issues. What is it that we want people to learn from visiting zoos? Facts about the physiology and behaviour of various animals? Attitudes towards the survival of endangered species? Compassion for the fate of all animals? To what degree does education require keeping wild animals in captivity?

Couldn't most of the educational benefits of zoos be obtained by presenting films, slides, lectures and so forth? Indeed, couldn't most of the important educational objectives better be achieved by exhibiting empty cages with explanations of why they are empty?

A third reason for having zoos is that they support scientific research. This too, is a benefit that was pointed out long ago. Sir Humphrey Davy, one of the founders of the Zoological Society of London, wrote in 1825: 'It would become Britain to offer another, and a very different series of exhibitions to the population of her metropolis; namely, animals brought from every part of the globe to be applied either to some useful purpose, or as objects of scientific research – not of vulgar admiration!' Zoos support scientific research in at least three ways: they fund field research by scientists not affiliated with zoos; they employ other scientists as members of zoo staffs; and they make otherwise inaccessible animals available for study.

The first point we should note is that very few zoos support any real scientific research. Fewer still have staff scientists with full-time research appointments. Among those that do, it is common for their scientists to study animals in the wild rather than those in zoo collections. Much of this research, as well as other field research that is supported by zoos, could just as well be funded in a different way – say, by a government agency. The question of whether there should be zoos does not turn on the funding for field research which zoos currently provide. The significance of the research that is actually conducted in zoos is a more important consideration.

Research that is conducted in zoos can be divided into two categories: studies in behaviour and studies in anatomy and pathology.

Behavioural research conducted on zoo animals is very controversial. Some have argued that nothing can be learned by studying animals that are kept in the unnatural conditions that obtain in most zoos. Others have argued that captive animals are more interesting research subjects than are wild animals: since captive animals are free from predation, they exhibit a wider range of physical and behavioural traits than animals in the wild, thus permitting researchers to view the full range of their genetic possibilities. Both of these positions are surely extreme. Conditions in some zoos are natural enough to permit some interesting research possibilities. But the claim that captive animals are more interesting research subjects than those in the wild is not very plausible. Environments trigger

behaviours. No doubt a predation-free environment triggers behaviours different from those of an animal's natural habitat, but
there is no reason to believe that better, fuller or more accurate data
can be obtained in predation-free environments than in natural
habitats.

Studies in anatomy and pathology are the most common forms of
zoo research. Such research has three main purposes: to improve zoo
conditions so that captive animals will live longer, be happier and
breed more frequently; to contribute to human health by providing
animal models for human ailments; and to increase our knowledge of
wild animals for its own sake.

The first of these aims is surely laudable, if we concede that there
should be zoos in the first place. But the fact that zoo research
contributes to improving conditions in zoos is not a reason for having
them. If there were no zoos, there would be no need to improve them.

The second aim, to contribute to human health by providing
animal models for human ailments, appears to justify zoos to some
extent, but in practice this consideration is not as important as one
might think. There are very severe constraints on the experiments
that may be conducted on zoo animals. In an article entitled 'A
Search for Animal Models at Zoos', published in *ILAR News* in 1982,
Richard Montali and Mitchell Bush drew the following conclusion:

> Despite the great potential of a zoo as a resource for models, there are
> many limitations and, of necessity, some restrictions for use. There is
> little opportunity to conduct overly manipulative or invasive research
> procedures – probably less than would be allowed in clinical research
> trials involving human beings. Many of the species are difficult to
> work with or are difficult to breed, so that the numbers of animals
> available for study are limited. In fact, it is safe to say that over the
> past years, humans have served more as 'animal models' for zoo
> species than is true of the reverse.

Whether for this reason or others, much of what has been done in
using zoo animals as models for humans seems redundant or trivial.
For example, the article cited above reports that zoo animals provide
good models for studying lead toxicity in humans, since it is common
for zoo animals to develop lead poisoning from chewing paint and
inhaling polluted city air. There are available for study plenty of
humans who suffer from lead poisoning for the same reasons. That
zoos make available some additional non-human subjects for this
kind of research seems at best unimportant and at worst deplorable.

Finally, there is the goal of obtaining knowledge about animals for its own sake. Knowledge is certainly something which is good and, everything being equal, we should encourage people to seek it for its own sake. But everything is not equal in this case. There is a moral presumption against keeping animals in captivity. This presumption can be overcome only by demonstrating that there are important benefits that must be obtained in this way if they are to be obtained at all. It is clear that this is not the case with knowledge for its own sake. There are other channels for our intellectual curiosity, ones that do not exact such a high moral price. Although our quest for knowledge for its own sake is important, it is not important enough to overcome the moral presumption against keeping animals in captivity.

In assessing the significance of research as a reason for having zoos, it is important to remember that very few zoos do any research at all. Whatever benefits result from zoo research could just as well be obtained by having a few zoos instead of the hundreds which now exist. The most this argument could establish is that we are justified in having a few very good zoos. It does not provide a defence of the vast majority of zoos which now exist.

A fourth reason for having zoos is that they preserve species that would otherwise become extinct. As the destruction of habitat accelerates and as breeding programmes become increasingly successful, this rationale for zoos gains in popularity. There is some reason for questioning the commitment of zoos to preservation: it can be argued that they continue to remove more animals from the wild than they return. Still, zoo breeding programmes have had some notable successes: without them the Père David Deer, the Mongolian Wild Horse and the European Bison would all now be extinct. Recently, however, some problems have begun to be noticed.

A 1979 study by Katherine Ralls, Kristin Brugger and Jonathan Ballou, which was reported in *Science*, convincingly argues that lack of genetic diversity among captive animals is a serious problem for zoo breeding programmes. In some species the infant mortality rate among inbred animals is six or seven times that among non-inbred animals. In other species the infant mortality rate among inbred animals is 100 per cent. What is most disturbing is that zoo curators have been largely unaware of the problems caused by inbreeding because adequate breeding and health records have not been kept. It is hard to believe that zoos are serious about their role in preserving endangered species when all too often they do not take even this minimal step.

In addition to these problems, the lack of genetic diversity among captive animals also means that surviving members of endangered species have traits very different from their conspecifics in the wild. This should make us wonder what is really being preserved in zoos. Are captive Mongolian Wild Horses really Mongolian Wild Horses in any but the thinnest biological sense?

There is another problem with zoo breeding programmes: they create many unwanted animals. In some species (lions, tigers and zebras, for example) a few males can service an entire herd. Extra males are unnecessary to the programme and are a financial burden. Some of these animals are sold and wind up in the hands of individuals and institutions which lack proper facilities. Others are shot and killed by Great White Hunters in private hunting camps. In order to avoid these problems, some zoos have been considering proposals to 'recycle' excess animals: a euphemism for killing them and feeding their bodies to other zoo animals. Many people are surprised when they hear of zoos killing animals. They should not be. Zoos have limited capacities. They want to maintain diverse collections. This can be done only by careful management of their 'stock'.

Even if breeding programmes were run in the best possible way, there are limits to what can be done to save endangered species. For many large mammals a breeding herd of at least a hundred animals, half of them born in captivity, is required if they are to survive in zoos. As of 1971 only eight mammal species satisfied these conditions. Paul and Anne Ehrlich estimate in their book *Extinction* that under the best possible conditions American zoos could preserve only about a hundred species of mammals – and only at a very high price: maintaining a breeding herd of herbivores costs between $75,000 and $250,000 per year.

There are further questions one might ask about preserving endangered species in zoos. Is it really better to confine a few hapless Mountain Gorillas in a zoo than to permit the species to become extinct? To most environmentalists the answer is obvious: the species must be preserved at all costs. But this smacks of sacrificing the lower-case gorilla for the upper-case Gorilla. In doing this, aren't we using animals as mere vehicles for their genes? Aren't we preserving genetic material at the expense of the animals themselves? If it is true that we are inevitably moving towards a world in which Mountain Gorillas can survive only in zoos, then we must ask whether it is really better for them to live in artificial environments of our design than not to be born at all.

Even if all of these difficulties are overlooked, the importance of preserving endangered species does not provide much support for the existing system of zoos. Most zoos do very little breeding or breed only species which are not endangered. Many of the major breeding programmes are run in special facilities which have been established for that purpose. They are often located in remote places, far from the attention of zoo-goers. (For example, the Bronx Zoo operates its Rare Animal Survival Center on St Catherine's Island off the coast of Georgia, and the National Zoo runs its Conservation and Research Center in the Shenandoah Valley of Virginia.) If our main concern is to do what we can to preserve endangered species, we should support such large-scale breeding centres rather than conventional zoos, most of which have neither the staff nor the facilities to run successful breeding programmes.

The four reasons for having zoos which I have surveyed carry some weight. But different reasons provide support for different kinds of zoo. Preservation and perhaps research are better carried out in large-scale animal preserves, but these provide few opportunities for amusement and education. Amusement and perhaps education are better provided in urban zoos, but they offer few opportunities for research and preservation. Moreover, whatever benefits are obtained from any kind of zoo must confront the moral presumption against keeping wild animals in captivity. Which way do the scales tip? There are two further considerations which, in my view, tip the scales against zoos.

First, captivity does not just deny animals liberty but is often detrimental to them in other respects as well. The history of chimpanzees in the zoos of Europe and America is a good example.

Chimpanzees first entered the zoo world in about 1640 when a Dutch prince, Frederick Henry of Nassau, obtained one for his castle menagerie. The chimpanzee didn't last very long. In 1835 the London Zoo obtained its first chimpanzee; he died immediately. Another was obtained in 1845; she lived six months. All through the nineteenth and early twentieth centuries zoos obtained chimpanzees who promptly died within nine months. It wasn't until the 1930s that it was discovered that chimpanzees are extremely vulnerable to human respiratory diseases, and that special steps must be taken to protect them. But for nearly a century zoos removed them from the wild and subjected them to almost certain death. Problems remain today. When chimpanzees are taken from the wild the usual procedure is to shoot the mother and kidnap the child. The rule of thumb among trappers is that ten chimpanzees die for every one that is delivered alive to the United States or Europe. On arrival many of these animals are confined under abysmal conditions.

Chimpanzees are not the only animals to suffer in zoos. In 1974 Peter Batten, former director of the San Jose Zoological Gardens, undertook an exhaustive study of two hundred American zoos. In his book *Living Trophies* he documented large numbers of neurotic, overweight animals kept in cramped, cold cells and fed unpalatable synthetic food. Many had deformed feet and appendages caused by unsuitable floor surfaces. Almost every zoo studied had excessive mortality rates, resulting from preventable factors ranging from vandalism to inadequate husbandry practices. Battan's conclusion was: 'The majority of American zoos are badly run, their direction incompetent, and animal husbandry inept and in some cases non-existent.'

Many of these same conditions and others are documented in *Pathology of Zoo Animals*, a review of necropsies conducted by Lynn Griner over the last fourteen years at the San Diego Zoo. This zoo may well be the best in the country, and its staff is clearly well-trained and well-intentioned. Yet this study documents widespread malnutrition among zoo animals; high mortality rates from the use of anaesthetics and tranquillizers; serious injuries and deaths sustained in transport; and frequent occurrences of cannibalism, infanticide and fighting almost certainly caused by overcrowded conditions. Although the zoo has learned from its mistakes, it is still unable to keep many wild animals in captivity without killing or injuring them, directly or indirectly. If this is true of the San Diego Zoo, it is certainly true, to an even greater extent, at most other zoos.

The second consideration is more difficult to articulate but is, to my mind, even more important. Zoos teach us a false sense of our place in the natural order. The means of confinement mark a difference between humans and animals. They are there at our pleasure, to be used for our purposes. Morality and perhaps our very survival require that we learn to live as one species among many rather than as one species over many. To do this, we must forget what we learn at zoos. Because what zoos teach us is false and dangerous, both humans and animals will be better off when they are abolished.

Animal Rights, Endangered Species and Human Survival

LEWIS REGENSTEIN

> Between half a million and 2 million species – 15 to 20 per cent of all species on earth – could be extinguished by the year 2000. . . . Extinction of species on this scale is without precedent in human history.
>
> *The Global 2000 Report to the President*, 1980

Since the year 1600, when records of this sort first began to be kept, over 350 known species and subspecies of birds and mammals have vanished from the face of the earth. Although a few animals have become extinct because of natural factors such as climatic changes, the vast majority of recent extinctions have been the result of human cruelty, greed and foolishness.

Humans have, in the last 2,000 years, exterminated about 3 per cent of the world's known mammal species. But over half these losses have occurred since 1900, and several times that percentage may now be endangered. Thus, the annihilation of wildlife has accelerated in modern, 'civilized' times, as more sophisticated methods of destruction have come into use.

During the last of the great geological eras – the Pleistocene, or Ice Age, which began about 1 million or 1½ million years ago and officially ended about 10,000 years ago – an incredible array of animal life evolved. But unfortunately for many of these life forms, a super-predator, *Homo sapiens*, also appeared during this period.

British zoologist James Fisher, in *Wildlife in Danger*, gives a detailed account of the devastating effect of humans on the world's Pleistocene animals and their role in completely wiping out many of the earth's giants. Throughout the world there were incredible arrays of giant birds, some so big that they could not fly and, indeed, did not need to. In North America there was the teratorn, the biggest bird of prey that is known to have lived. Europe had a giant flightless 'superswan' as well as the giant Maltese vulture, the last example of which is thought to have occurred at Monte Carlo 100,000 years ago. Until the seventeenth century Madagascar had the 10 ft tall, half-ton elephant bird, whose eggs had a fluid capacity of over two imperial gallons, the equivalent of 200 chicken eggs. And the Indian Ocean islands of Mauritius, Reunion and Rodriguez had the famous dodo (extinct *c.* 1680) and other strange, flightless birds. In New Zealand flourished the giant, 12 ft tall moas, the tallest birds the world has ever known, until they became extinct between 1500 and 1850.

Giant animals also roamed the earth. In North America there were giant bison, camels, beavers, elephants and even lions. South America had giant armadillos called glyptodons and mammoth ground sloths. In Europe forest elephants, hippopotami and huge bison and deer lumbered over the land.

In many cases the extinction of these animals appears generally to have coincided with the arrival of humans on the scene. Early humans are known to have been in Europe some 250,000 years ago, and as their hunting skills improved the Pleistocene giants were inevitably destroyed.

The impact of the arrival in North America of *Homo sapiens* was even more devastating for the wildlife paradise that once flourished there. According to a growing body of scientific theory, primitive tribesmen, perhaps from Siberia, first invaded North America about 12,000 years ago, crossing the Bering land bridge linking Siberia and Alaska and moving south through Canada. They discovered a population of large mammals which, having evolved in the absence of humans, were 'innocent' and unafraid of them, much as Antarctic animals are today. These animals were thus unable to cope with the new threat. It is theorized that these hunters, marching from Alaska through South America, exterminated most of these species of large mammals in about 1,000 years.

Many of these extinct animals are preserved in remarkably good condition in the famous La Brea asphalt tar pits of Los Angeles, California, and these 'specimens' give us a good idea of the fantastic variety of wildlife that flourished during this period. According to James Fisher's account in *Wildlife in Danger*, the La Brea tar pits have yielded fifty-four different species of Pleistocene or prehistoric mammals, twenty-four of which are now extinct, as well as 113 birds, twenty-two of which are gone. Extinct species found at La Brea include the huge short-faced bear and short-faced coyote; the tremendous dire wolf; the fabled saber-toothed cat, *Smilodon*; the giant long-necked camel or giant llama, *Camelops*, which measured 7 ft wide; the giant lion, *Panthera atrox*, which was a full one quarter larger than modern African lions; 20 ft long ground sloths; and bison 7 ft high at the hump, with a 6 ft spread between their giant horns. Other giant mammals of that era included the elephant-like mastodon; the huge-tusked mammoth with shaggy, red hair; and the giant beaver, weighing over 400 lbs. It has been estimated that the extinction of these great herds of giant herbivores – bison, horse, mammoth – may have reduced the total weight of large mammals on the North American continent by an incredible 90 per cent!

The first extinction that was actually recorded appears to have been the European lion around AD 80. But it is since 1600 that the most accelerated rate of extinction has occurred. Since that time, according to James Fisher, thirty-six species of mammals and at least sixty-four races or subspecies have become extinct. Ninety-four separate species of birds have also been obliterated, along with 164 different races. In addition to the approximately 350 identified species and subspecies of birds or mammals that are known to have disappeared, numerous other life forms have perished but gone unrecorded.

One of the best-known of all extinct species is the great auk, a large, flightless bird that was found on the rocky islands of the North Atlantic Ocean. Jacques Cartier, the first man to land on its breeding grounds in 1534, quickly slaughtered enough of these helpless, unresisting birds to fill two boats. Subsequent expeditions killed enormous numbers of these birds for food and oil, and as the species became rare museum collectors and scientists rushed in to obtain specimens and eggs before they were all gone. Carl Siemson, a collector's agent from Reykjavik, Iceland, offered a sizeable reward for skins of remaining birds. As a result, the last two auks known to have existed were killed on Eldey Island, off Iceland, in 1844 by an Icelandic fisherman, Vilhjalmur Hakonarsson, who collected 100 crowns for the world's last members of this species.

At least two species of marine mammals have recently become extinct, Steller's sea cow and the sea mink. Steller's sea cow *(Hydrodamalis stelleri)*, also called the giant sea cow, was first discovered in 1741 by a German naturalist Georg Wilhelm Steller on the Aleutian Islands, off the coast of Alaska. This giant mammal attained a length of 30 ft and weighed as much as 4 tons. In the 1700s whale, seal and sea otter hunters begin to kill the sea cows in large numbers for their meat, an easy task since these slow-moving creatures were virtually helpless and unable to defend themselves, and appeared to have little fear of humans. They seemed to be highly intelligent and affectionate towards one another. In his journals Steller described the sea cow as showing 'signs of a wonderful intelligence, indeed, an uncommon love for one another, which extended so far that when one of them was hooked, all the others were intent upon saving it'. The sea cows would surround and circle the one being killed or would jostle the attacking boat. One male spent two days swimming into shore near its mate, which was lying dead on the beach. By 1768, only twenty-seven years after the first human sighted this remarkable species, it had been completely obliterated.

The sea mink *(Mustela vison macrodon)* has also been extinct since about 1880. Formerly found along the coast and islands of Maine, it was hunted for its fur until none remained.

The Caribbean monk seal *(Monachus tropicalis)*, or West Indian seal, also appears to be extinct, as no sightings of it have been reported for several years. A contributing factor in its decline was its friendliness and seeming affection for people, which greatly facilitated its killing. This seal once occurred throughout the Caribbean and the Gulf of Mexico. It may have been the first New World animal to be recorded, and Columbus' crew killed eight of them for food on his second voyage in 1494. The Caribbean monk seal was intensively hunted in the 1600s and 1700s, and by 1850 it was almost gone. It continued to be shot and clubbed by fishermen, and in 1911 a group of Mexican fishermen wiped out what may have been the last large herd of these seals off the coast of Yucatan. The last reported sighting of a monk seal thought to be valid occurred in 1962; although there have been rumours of seals seen off British Honduras and the Caribbean coast of Mexico, intensive searches of possible habitats have failed to turn up even a trace. (The other two species of monk seals, the Mediterranean *(Monachus monachus)* and the Hawaiian *(Monachus schauinlandis)* are seriously endangered, with the latter numbering only a few hundred.)

The status of many other animals is unknown; several of these too may be extinct. The unique dog-like marsupial, the Thylacine or Tasmanian wolf, which carries its young in a pouch, has not been seen for two decades, although it is thought that one or two lonely pairs may exist on the Australian island state of Tasmania. The mysterious laughing owl of New Zealand, which makes its presence known through hoots, barks and shrieks, has not been seen or heard since 1900.

BRINGING CIVILIZATION – AND CARNAGE – TO THE NEW WORLD

The 'discovery' of America by 'civilized' Europeans also doomed much of its wildlife. When the American colonists arrived in South Carolina they found a land, as one of them wrote in 1709, filled with 'endless Numbers of Panthers, Tigers, Wolves and other Beasts of Prey' that filled the night with 'the dismall'st and most hideous Noise'. But the settlers wasted little time in wiping out the native wildlife, including elk, buffalo, deer and wild pigeons 'in flocks so dense they blotted out the sun'. The 'great flocks of parakeets' that filled the air were completely extirpated, and the Carolina parakeet is now extinct. And even the prolific deer were eliminated, with over 64,000 deerskins being shipped to England by the Carolina Colony in 1699 alone. (The deer found today in South Carolina were transplanted from elsewhere to provide targets for hunters.)

In the North and West fur traders moved across the country wiping out the beavers in their path until very few were left in most areas. And in the South the beautiful and stately egrets, great white herons and roseate spoonbills were mercilessly slaughtered for their feathers, which were shipped to New York and used for plumage by the women's fashion industry. Fortunately, laws were passed in time to save these birds, and today remnant flocks of them still survive.

One of the most remarkable feats of the early American settlers was the wiping out of the passenger pigeon, among the most prolific species in North America and one of the most plentiful bird species the world has ever known. Accounts by naturalist John James Audubon in the early 1800s describe seemingly endless flocks of these birds blackening the sky for days at a time as they passed overhead, only to be shot down by the thousands (many by Audubon himself). In the 1860s and 1870s tens of millions of these birds were slaughtered annually. This massive hunting, combined with the destruction of nesting areas, led to the demise of the bird; the last passenger pigeon left in the world died in the Cincinnati Zoo in 1914.

It soon became apparent that no animal, no matter how powerful or abundant, was safe from the White Man's destructiveness. The 'winning of the West' involved the destruction of the buffalo, which was so abundant as to be considered virtually inexhaustible (as many animals are today). The buffalo was one of the most populous mammals ever to exist – one herd seen in 1870 in Arkansas was described as stretching 'from six to ten miles in almost every direction'. In the Far West the herds were even larger and stretched for as far as the eye could see. In 1871 a cavalry troop rode for six days through a herd of buffalo, but fifteen years later a survey counted only 541 in the entire West. In a few years the buffalo population had been reduced from an estimated 60 million to a low of about 22 individuals according to some estimates. Often white hunters would shoot them for the 'fun' or 'sport' of it, and leave the carcasses behind to rot. Moreover, US government policy encouraged the destruction of the buffalo herds so as to deny the Indians an important source of food and hides. Inevitably, the extirpation of the buffalo helped to eliminate other animals dependent upon it for food, such as the plains wolf and, eventually, the Indians.

The pioneers who settled the West also succeeded in wiping out sixteen separate races of grizzly bear (in the traditional taxonomy), six of wolves, one fox and one cougar. Since the Puritans landed at Plymouth Rock in 1620 over 500 types of native American animals and plants have disappeared from the United States.

THE WAITING LIST FOR EXTINCTION

Today many animals stand on the very abyss of oblivion. Most species of our biological cousins, the primates, are threatened to some degree, including our closest living relatives, the Great Apes: chimpanzees, gorillas, and orang-utans. No more than 240 mountain gorillas are thought to survive in the wild, facing a constant threat from poachers, 'collectors' and habitat-destroying humans who continue to encroach on their last refuges in the mountain rain forests of Rwanda, Uganda and Zaïre. The wild population of California condors were down to about seventeen, as of mid-1984. And in 1983 only five dusky seaside sparrows could be found in their only known habitat, a National Wildlife Refuge in Florida; unfortunately, they were all males.

As David Day observes in his 1981 book *The Doomsday Book of Animals*, many species classified as endangered are 'merely [on] a waiting list for extinction'. He reports: 'It is estimated that there are today one Abingdon Galapagos tortoise, two Kauai O–O honey-eaters, five Mauritian ring-necked parakeets, five Javan tigers, six Mauritian kestrels, twelve Chatham Island robins, eighteen Mauritian pink pigeons, about fifty Javan rhinoceroses.' Obviously, by the time a species is reduced to such a precarious level recovery is difficult, if not impossible, to achieve. Yet many species of once-abundant wildlife continue to be subjected to slaughter so massive as to threaten their survival.

Despite worldwide campaigns waged for over a decade to save the whales, their commercial slaughter continues apace, albeit at a much reduced rate. For almost as long as humans have known about whales, they have hunted them. One of the first to organize commercial whaling expeditions was King Alfred of England in about AD 890. In the eleventh century the Basques were hunting North Atlantic right whales in the Bay of Biscay and, by the fifteenth century, had nearly wiped out this population stock. Beginning in the 1600s whalers took about a hundred years to decimate the whale population of the Arctic, and the Greenland right whale was reduced to the verge of extinction. In the late 1700s whalers successively moved through the Pacific, Indian, and Atlantic oceans, destroying these whale populations by the 1920s. By this time the oceans of the northern hemisphere contained so few whales that most of the hunting shifted to the southern hemisphere, where the Antarctic Ocean made up for the whale shortage elsewhere.

The history of whaling in the recent decades up to the 1970s records the exploitation of the most valuable species until they have become virtually extinct; then they have been declared 'protected', and whalers have moved on to the next largest species until they too have disappeared. In the last fifty years more than 2 million whales have been killed, with a record 67,000 'taken' in 1962. The quota for the 1973–74 season was 37,500; current annual quotas have fortunately been reduced to between 10,000 and 12,000. The quota for the 1984–85 season has been set at about 6,800. In 1982 the International Whaling Commission (IWC) voted a general moratorium on commercial whaling to begin in the 1985–86 whaling season. But the major whaling nations, including Japan, the Soviet Union and Norway,have formally objected to the measure, so it remains to be seen whether or not it will be implemented.

As a result of this carnage at least one species of whale, the Atlantic grey *(Eschrichtius gibosus)*, once found in the North Atlantic, has been totally wiped out. Several other species, such as the bowhead and the humpback, are seriously endangered, as both are still being reduced by aboriginal hunting.

One of the most gravely threatened of the Great Whales is also the most spectacular: the mighty blue whale *(Balaenoptera musculus)*, the largest creature ever to inhabit the earth and, judging by the size and convolutions of its huge brain, certainly one of the most intelligent. Its newborn calf can weigh more than an adult elephant and nurses for seven months, taking in up to 1,000 lb of milk a day! Writer John Barbour has described this leviathan:

> Nothing on earth has ever matched its size. It is larger than 30 elephants; larger than the combined size of three of the largest dinosaurs that ever lived. It weighs more than 2,000 people, a small town. Its heart weighs 1,200 lbs, its liver a ton, its tongue more than one-third of a ton.

The precarious state to which these mammals have been reduced can clearly be seen in the catch figures for the Antarctic in recent decades, as compiled by the IWC. In the 1930–31 winter whaling season almost 30,000 blue whales were taken. By 1945–46 fewer than 10,000 were caught, and the catch in the late 1950s averaged fewer than 1,500 a year. In 1962–63, for the first time, fewer than 1,000 blue whales were available for 'harvesting': only 944 could be found and killed. The stocks of blue whales were now clearly on the verge of collapse, but the slaughter continued. The following year, 1963–64, the take dropped to 112 blue whales, and by 1964–65 only twenty could be found and killed by the whalers.

Finally, in 1965, when the whaling industry (primarily Japan, the Soviet Union and Norway) was unable to locate enough blue whales for which to set quotas, the IWC declared the Antarctic stocks to be 'protected', and a nominal 'ban' on their killing was announced. By this time over 325,000 blue whales had been killed since the turn of the century. In December 1970, when the US Department of the Interior placed the blue whale on its list of endangered species, it estimated that only between 600 and 3,000 remained worldwide. More recently, purported sightings by Japanese whalers have pushed some estimates as high as 10,000–20,000, but these appear to be grossly inflated.

Even if the illegal and unreported killing of blue whales were to be completely halted, there is serious doubt about whether enough males and females, scattered throughout the vast expanse of the world's oceans, will be able to find each other and breed in sufficient numbers to perpetuate the species.

Other whales, such as the humpback, bowhead, right, fin, sei and sperm, have similarly been severely depleted by commercial whaling (and, in the case of the bowhead, also by continued hunting by Alaskan Eskimos). All of these whales, along with the blue and California grey, are listed by the US Government as endangered species. The fate of the whales may depend on whether or not the whaling nations agree to accept the general moratorium on commercial whaling voted by the IWC.

THE MASSIVE EXTINCTION OF 'LOWER' LIFE FORMS

The remorseless and well-documented annihilation of 'higher' life forms, cruel, senseless and destructive as it is, pales by comparison with the much vaster yet less well-known, extirpation of the more obscure species, such as plants, molluscs and crustaceans. As the rate of extinction of these life forms accelerates, we are beginning to learn that many creatures which may now seem most 'expendable' may turn out to be fundamental to the well-being and survival of many other species, including humans.

As pointed out in the 1978 report published by the President's Council on Environmental Quality (CEQ), *The Global Environment and Basic Human Needs*:

> the total number of plant and animal species on earth may be as high as 10 million – only about 15 per cent of which have been identified in scientific literature, let alone been well studied. If current trends continue, a good share of the unrecorded majority of species will vanish for ever before their existence, or their biological importance, is known.

Over the next decade or two, warns CEQ, 'unique ecosystems populated by thousands of unrecorded plant and animal species face rapid destruction – irreversible genetic losses that will profoundly alter the course of evolution.'

Because of the ever-increasing exploitation and destruction of the tropical rain forests, most of the forthcoming extinctions of foreign plants will occur in these regions. Rain forests receive extraordinary amounts of warmth, moisture and sunlight and thus provide an ideal habitat for an amazing variety of species. The Amazon Basin, probably the richest biological community on earth, alone may house 1 million species (in addition to various unique and endangered tribes of Indians that are also threatened there). More types of woody plant species are found on the slopes of a single Philippine volcano than in the entire United States.

In the last thirty years half of the world's rain forests have been destroyed, and the remainder are being cut at a rate of between 27 and 50 million acres a year – one or two acres a second! Worldwide there are thought to be at least 5 million species of plants and animals (many of which are yet to be 'discovered' by man) that inhabit tropical forests, are dependent on them for survival and are found nowhere else in the world. At the present rate of deforestation, experts fear that at least several hundred thousand such species are candidates for extinction over the next two decades. The destruction of the rain forests is dooming not only such creatures as orang-utans and other primates, jaguars, parrots and various crocodilians but also numerous lesser-known life forms. In his book *The Sinking Ark* wildlife specialist Norman Myers estimates that at least one species *a day* is already being wiped out in the tropical forests and that given the increasing rate of timber exploitation, one species *an hour* may soon be lost in the years ahead.

THE LOSS TO HUMANITY

These losses will deprive the world not only of countless beautiful and diverse life forms, but also of future sources of food, drugs and medicines of incalculable value.

The United Nations Environment Programme in its *World Conservation Strategy* report of March 1980, describing the immense potential value of these plants.

> Penicillin, digitalis, quinine, rubber, pectin, resins, gums, insecticides – these and other medicines and products come from plants. One out of two prescriptions filled in the US each day is for a drug based on an ingredient in a plant. . . . The wheat we know today began as wild plants – and some humans some unknown number of years ago may well have considered those wild plants worthless seeds.

As the 1978 CEQ report observes, the extinction of these species will also entail the loss of many useful products:

> Perhaps the greatest industrial, agricultural and medical costs of species reduction will stem from future opportunities unknowingly

128 *The Problems*

lost. Only about 5 per cent of the world's plant species have yet been screened for pharmacologically active ingredients. Ninety per cent of the food that humans eat comes from just twelve crops, but scores of thousands of plants are edible, and some will undoubtedly prove useful in meeting human food needs.

Tropical forests are today the main source of drugs made from plants, and up to half of our prescription drugs come from such flora. In addition, these forests have been the original source of such important food items as bananas, pineapples, rice, millet, sugar cane, cassava, yams and taro. Such valuable products as rubber and quinine come from plants, and it is possible – even probable – that plants of comparable significance are being wiped out. Thus in destroying the rain forests our generation is not only wiping out numerous life forms that have the right to exist but is also depriving itself and future generations of plants that could provide cures for dread diseases and could become important food items for an increasingly hungry and overpopulated planet.

Other types of species of great potential value to mankind are the obscure and little-known snails, clams, scuds, and other molluscs and crustaceans, thousands of which are in serious peril because of water pollution, dredging, stream channelling, the building of highways, dams, housing developments and other destruction of habitat, carried out mainly by the Federal Government. As Dr Marc Imlay, formerly a biologist with the Interior Department's Office of Endangered Species, has pointed out:

Though they seem inconsequential in size, mussels and crustaceans are an indispensable part of the living world. Besides fitting into the food chain, these creatures have recently been recognized as being able to produce poisons, antibiotics, tranquilizers, antispasmodics, and antiseptic chemicals in their systems. Scientists believe these unique abilities can be used as models for the development of synthetic drugs.

It is not possible to quantify or predict the consequences and magnitude of these losses or the impact they will have on the earth and future generations. What is clear is that the results will be profound and could be catastrophic. As Eric Eckholm of the World-watch Institute has observed in *Disappearing Species: The Social Challenge*:

Should this biological massacre take place, evolution will no doubt continue, but in a grossly distorted manner. Such a multitude of species losses would constitute a basic and irreversible alteration in the nature of the biosphere even before we understand its workings – an evolutionary Rubicon whose crossing *Homo sapiens* would do well to avoid. . . . humans appoint themselves as the ultimate arbiters of evolution and determine its future course on the basis of short-term considerations and a great deal of ignorance. . . . Scientists cannot yet say where the critical thresholds lie, at what level of species extermination the web of life will be seriously disrupted. .. .

Eckholm further notes that when a plant species is wiped out, between ten and thirty dependent species, such as insects and even other plants, can also be jeopardized. 'Crushed by the march of civilization, one species can take many others with it, and the ecological repercussions and rearrangements that follow may well endanger people.'

DESTROYING OUR FELLOW CREATURES – AND OURSELVES

As human beings are part of nature, we are bound by its laws. We ignore this fact at great risk to ourselves, for eventually we will certainly destroy a species or ecosystem that is essential to our own survival. For example, whales, dolphins and porpoises, slaughtered by the tens of thousands each year, play a vital, though little understood, role in maintaining the health and stability of the world's oceans. By eliminating these intelligent cetaceans we further upset the delicate balance of life in the seas and imperil oxygen and food-producing ecosystems that are necessary for the survival of all life forms – including humans.

Every species plays some role in the environment that may be necessary for the proper functioning of the ecosystem. (For people who do not accept the concept of 'animal rights' such arguments on behalf of wildlife can be persuasive.) Even such 'ugly', dangerous and unpopular creatures as alligators and crocodiles are useful. Alligators kill and eat water moccasins and other poisonous snakes, and during times of drought – which occur periodically in the southeastern US – they dig water holes, thus providing water, food and habitat for fish, birds and the other creatures of the swamp, allowing them to survive these difficult periods. When crocodiles were eliminated from lakes and river systems in areas of Africa and Australia, many of the food fish also declined or disappeared. It is now thought that this occurred because the crocodiles had been feeding on scavenging or predatory species of fish not eaten by the natives, which, left unchecked, multiplied out of control and preyed on or crowded out many of the food fish. Thus those reptiles serve a function that is much more valuable than providing hides for shoes, wallets, belts and other fashion accessories, the demand for which has driven most of these reptile species to the verge of extinction.

If we are to save the world's wildlife, we must adopt an ethic that recognizes the right of all animals to exist, places equal value on the grotesque and the spectacular and shows as much concern for the crocodile as for the cheetah, as much for the condor as the eagle. We must realize that it is just as important to save a species of butterfly as the elephant, that the extinction of a species of mollusc is as great a tragedy as the loss of a bird or mammal. Even endangered plants should merit our concern, for not only do they have the right to live but also the well-being of a host of higher animals, including humans, may depend on their survival. As Dr George Small observes in his book *The Blue Whale*:

> The tragedy of the blue whale is in the reflection of an even greater one, that of man himself. What is the nature of a species that knowingly and without good reason exterminates another? When will man learn that he is but one form of life among countless thousands, each of which is in some way related to and dependent on all others? How long will man persist in the belief that he is the master of the Earth rather than one of its guests?

Fortunately, in connection with the question of whether or not to preserve the world's wildlife the morally right consideration happens also to be the one that it is in our own selfish interest to choose. Cleveland Amory, president of the Fund for Animals, once wrote that humans have an infinite capacity to rationalize their own cruelty. But while cruelty to animals may be easy for some to accept, it is far more difficult for policy makers to defend such actions when they clearly have adverse consequences for humans. Our failure adequately to protect other species and their natural environment is already having grave consequences for much of humanity. Throughout Asia, for example, the clear-cutting of forests and the resulting flooding have caused massive loss of life, homes and farmlands. Such degradation of the environment is helping to condemn literally millions of people to lives of misery and desperation.

We have done more ecological damage to the world in the last few decades than in the entire preceding period of recorded history. If we continue at the current rate, or even at a greatly reduced level, our planet will soon be unfit for habitation by most higher life forms, including our own. In wiping out the natural heritage over which we were given dominion and stewardship responsibilities, we are engaging in nothing less than the wholesale destruction of our planet and are endangering most of the living creatures on it. As Ecclesiastes points out so wisely: 'For that which befalleth the sons of men befalleth beasts; even one thing befalleth them: as the one dieth, so dieth the other; yea, they have all one breath; so that a man hath no pre-eminence above a beast; for all is vanity.'

There are thus many reasons to preserve threatened wildlife. Most important, animals have a right to live and fulfil their given roles as nature intended; they add beauty and diversity to the world; they are interesting to observe and study in the wild; and they have non-consumptive economic value (as with tourism and photography). But there is one more reason that should not be overlooked. In taking action to save wildlife we may well be saving ourselves, a fact that animal protection advocates should never cease to stress.

Few conservationists and animal rights advocates need to be convinced that an animal species is of value to humans to be persuaded that it should be protected from destruction. In the last decade a significant evolution in public sentiment has become apparent as increasingly large numbers of people around the world have adopted the view that animals themselves have rights wholly apart from any value they may have for humans. It has become 'respectable' – indeed, common – for people to appreciate that animals have rights and that they should not be needlessly killed or abused.

Fortunately, a significant proportion of the public has come to view in this light many highly evolved imperilled mammals, such as primates (monkeys and apes), elephants, wolves, bears, kangaroos, tigers, cheetahs and leopards and marine mammals (whales, dolphins, porpoises, seals, and sea otters). These creatures are easy to identify with, and many are seen as highly intelligent, family-oriented animals with thoughts and emotions not unlike ours, living in social groups comparable with those of humans.

Unfortunately, this strong identification with, and sympathy for, some of the 'highest' species of wildlife has not yet been adequately extended to the more obscure, less glamorous species, creatures that also have innate rights and may, ironically, be more important to us than those with complex brains, large eyes, soft fur and appealing beauty. Moreover, by stressing the legitimate right of animals to live and survive free of fear and suffering, and thereby understating the value of such creatures to the ecosystem and therefore to humans, animal rights advocates sometimes to fail to raise some of the most compelling arguments in favour of wildlife preservation, ignoring points that may appeal to many otherwise unconcerned people.

If our wildlife is to be saved, every valid argument must be raised in order to ensure this; pointing out a species' value to humanity (as a non-consumptive resource) in no way diminishes its intrinsic rights. Indeed, as the world becomes more and more overpopulated with humans, crowding out other creatures and destroying their habitats, human-centred arguments for wildlife and wilderness preservation may be the only ones that will be effective in some situations. Above all, we must make people aware of a single, overriding consideration; if we are to succeed in saving our planet – and ourselves – we must make it a safe world for all of the creatures of the earth. Only then will our own future be secure.

Part III

The Activists and their Strategies

The Silver Spring Monkeys

ALEX PACHECO with ANNA FRANCIONE

I discovered animal rights in 1978, when I first entered a slaughter-house and witnessed the violent deaths of terrified dairy cows, pigs and chickens. What I saw changed my life. Shaken by the slaughter-ing, I sought and joined the animal protection community. As a newcomer to the movement, anxious to learn what others could teach me, I could not have been more fortunate than to find two brilliant activists, Nellie Shriver, founder of American Vegetarians, and Constantine Salamone, an artist, feminist and animal rights activist. They became my teachers. Over the next few years my animal-related experiences increased as I joined the Hunt Saboteurs' outings in Britain, sailed on the *Sea Shepherd* in the Atlantic, studied endangered humpback whales in Alaska aboard the RV *Jingur* and learned all I could about mankind's exploitation of other species.

Upon moving to Washington, DC in 1980, I joined forces with Ingrid Newkirk who had accomplished major victories for animals in her eleven years as an animal law-enforcement officer. By the spring of that year we had formed People for the Ethical Treatment of Animals (PETA), both believing that this young movement needed a grassroots group in the USA that could spur people to use their time and talents to help animals gain liberation. Our emphasis was to be on animals used in experimentation and food production, while at the same time being out on the streets, bringing as many animal issues to the public's attention as we could.

In the summer of 1981, after my third year as a political science and environmental studies major at George Washington University,

I discussed with Ingrid the need to gain some first-hand experience in a laboratory. It now shocks me to think how easily we fell upon the atrocities at the Institute for Behavioral Research (IBR), because it suggests that such conditions are common to many other facilities. I simply found IBR listed in the US Department of Agriculture directory of registered animal research facilities and chose it because it was a stone's throw from where I lived.

I was greeted at IBR by a research assistant. I told him that I was seeking employment, and he referred me to Dr Taub. Taub took me into his office and explained that research was being conducted on surgically crippled primates to monitor the rehabilitation of impaired limbs. There were no paid positions available, he said, but he offered to check to see if they could use a volunteer. I called the next day, as he suggested, and was offered the opportunity to help Georgette Yakalis, his student protégé. On 11 May 1981 I began work and was given a tour by Taub himself.

The Institute was divided into two areas. The rooms near the front were used for work with humans. They appeared unremarkable. The animals were kept in the back. As we went through the doors to that section, I had my first indication that something was wrong. The smell was incredible, intensifying as we entered the colony room where the monkeys were kept. I was astonished as I began to comprehend the conditions before me. I saw filth caked on the wires of the cages, faeces piled in the bottom of the cages, urine and rust encrusting every surface. There, amid this rotting stench, sat sixteen crab-eating macaques and one rhesus monkey, their lives limited to metal boxes just 17¾ inches wide. In their desperation to assuage their hunger, they were picking forlornly at scraps and fragments of broken biscuits that had fallen through the wire into the sodden accumulations in the waste collection trays below. The cages had clearly not been cleaned properly for months. There were no dishes to keep the food away from the faeces, nothing for the animals to sit on but the jagged wires of the old cages, nothing for them to see but the filthy, faeces-splattered walls of that windowless room, only 15 ft square.

In the following days the true nature of the monkeys' sad existence became apparent. Twelve of the seventeen monkeys had disabled limbs as a result of surgical interference (deafferentation) when they were juveniles. Sarah, then eight years old, had been alone in her cage since she was one day old, when she was purchased from Litton Laboratories and then forgotten. According to a later count, thirty-nine of the fingers on the monkeys' deafferented hands were severely deformed or missing, having been either torn or bitten off.

Many of the monkeys were neurotic, particularly Chester, Sarah and Domition. Like a maniac, Sarah would attack her foot and spin around incessantly, calling out like an infant. Domitian attacked his arm mercilessly and masturbated constantly. Chester saw himself as the troupe leader, powerless to defend his fellows, enraged at the world. It was astounding that Taub and the other researchers expected to gain any reproducible, let alone reliable, data from these animals, considering the condition of the animals themselves and of the colony and surgery rooms. The surgery room had to be seen to be believed. Records, human and monkey, were strewn everywhere, even under the operating table. Soiled, discarded clothes, old shoes and other personal items were scattered about the room. Because of a massive and long-standing rodent problem, rat droppings and urine covered everything, and live and dead cockroaches were in the drawers, on the floor and around the filthy scrub sink.

No one bothered to bandage the monkeys' injuries properly (on the few occasions when bandages were used at all), and antibiotics were administered only once; no lacerations or self-amputation injuries were ever cleaned. Whenever a bandage was applied, it was never changed, no matter how filthy or soiled it became. They were left on until they deteriorated to the point where they fell off the injured limb. Old, rotted fragments of bandage were stuck to the cage floors where they collected urine and faeces. The monkeys also suffered from a variety of wounds that were self-inflicted or inflicted by monkeys grabbing at them from adjoining cages. I saw discoloured, exposed muscle tissue on their arms. Two monkeys had bones protruding through their flesh. Several had bitten off their own fingers and had festering stubs, which they extended towards me as I discreetly took fruit from my pockets. With these pitiful limbs they searched through the foul mess of their waste pans for something to eat. I began to understand the size of the problem and the opportunity that had been presented to me. When I came home in the evenings Ingrid and I agonized about the problem and together considered how best to use the information. We knew that I must document everything carefully and that months would have to elapse to show the consistent pattern of behaviour and neglect that I was witnessing. If I blew the whistle now or after a few weeks, it would be too easy for Taub to discredit me.

Soon I had a chance I had not expected. Even though I had made it plain to Taub that I had no laboratory experience, within a week of starting work I was put in charge of a pilot study. With the opportunity to work alone, I could better document the operation of the facility and the life the monkeys lived there. Taub called the study a 'displacement experiment'. I was given two monkeys and told to put them in separate cages in a room. The monkeys, Augustus and Hayden, were deprived of food for two to three days, and I was to go alone into their room, set up video equipment to record events and feed them about fifty raisins each. After some weeks I was to withhold their food for three days and then, instead of giving them the raisins, I was just to show them the raisins but not allow them to eat, and then record their frustrated reactions.

Perhaps I was too recently initiated into this scientific environment, but I asked Taub and Yakalis three times what the purpose of the experiment was and what I should keep my eyes open for. On each occasion they responded that they hoped to find something 'interesting', in which case they 'could get [grant] funding'. It made me wonder if this typified scientific method. Working at IBR was becoming more and more of a strain. I was beginning to appreciate the monkeys as individuals and had especially close relationships with Billy, Sarah, and Domitian. Night after night, I agonized over what to do.

The stench of the laboratory permeated everything. When I got home I would have to strip, stand under the shower and scrub to get the smell out of my skin and hair. I could see the evidence of IBR's filth and decomposition under my nails and in the lines of my skin. If only I could have scrubbed the image of the monkeys out of my mind. It became increasingly difficult to go back to IBR every day, yet I knew that I would have to continue if I was to succeed in helping these monkeys and other animals in similar situations.

Meanwhile I had begun to keep a log of my observations. After about a month I was put in charge of yet another experiment: the 'acute noxious stimuli test'. I was to take a monkey from the colony and strap him into a homemade immobilizing chair, where he would be held at the waist, ankles, wrists and neck. The acute noxious stimuli were to be applied with a pair of haemostats (surgical pliers) clamped and fastened on to the animal, and locked to the tightest notch. I was to observe which parts of the monkey's body felt pain. (The noxious stimuli used to be administered by using an 'open flame' – a cigarette lighter.) Taub's protocol (*Mechanisms Mediating Biofeedback Learning*, 1980, App. E, p. 77) stated that the stimuli were to be applied to the monkeys every four months. The work was conducted in such a haphazard way that this schedule was never adhered to. As I was working alone, I was able to fabricate data to avoid hurting them.

Before beginning the test on my own I was instructed in how to apply the haemostats. Domitian was unfortunate enough to be chosen as the 'example' animal and was placed in the chair and the haemostat clamps were latched as tightly as possible on to his testicles. Terrified, he thrashed violently and screamed. This was repeated three times over a forty-five minute period so that I could witness a 'positive' reaction: an enraged creature, desperately thrashing against the restraints to escape the pain. That same day the surgical pliers were twice thrust into Domitian's mouth and raked against his teeth and gums. Such was my introduction to the acute noxious stimuli test.

By the time I was put in charge of administering the test on my own, I had requested (and received) a set of keys on the pretext of doing more work on the weekends and in the evenings. I was now freer to explore the entire laboratory and take photographs of the monkeys, the cages, the rodent droppings, the dried blood on the floors, the restraining chairs and so on.

Inside an ice-choked freezer I found two plastic bags labelled 'Herbie' and 'Caligula'. I asked Yakalis what had happened to these monkeys. She said that she did not know Herbie had died but that Caligula had developed gangrene from a filthy, unchanged bandage. She told me that Caligula had been in such bad shape that he had begun to multilate his own chest cavity, and she then confided that putting him in a restraining device, and administering the noxious stimuli test, with his chest ripped open, and having to experience the stench of his rotting body, was the most disgusting thing she had ever done. After the acute pain test, she said, he was destroyed.

As time went on I discovered that I was not the only one who came in late at night. Several times, while taking pictures around midnight, my heart would jump as one of the two caretakers came in to pick up a paycheck or to 'clean' the colony room. The caretakers took turns coming into the laboratory at any time of the night, and as no schedules were assigned to them, they often did not come in at all. I also found that they were paid not by the number of hours they worked, nor by the number of cages they were supposed to clean, but simply by the number of rooms in their charge. They were paid $10 a day. The colony room, with seventeen monkeys, was only damp-mopped, because there was no drain in the floor to take any water away. Every few days the faecal trays, sometimes filled to the top, were emptied but never cleaned. To feed the monkeys, the caretakers would simply open the cage doors and throw in half a scoop of monkey chow – when and if they fed them at all. The markers I put in the chow cans indicated there were many days, often several at a time, when the monkeys went without food. When they were fed, the food would fall through the wire mesh into the faecal trays below, as no bowls or food receptacles were ever used. The employees usually worked carelessly and as fast as they could, getting out as soon as possible.

I soon began to take more photographs, hiding my camera and risking discovery by photographing the monkeys in the restraining chair during the day. At that point I was still under the impression that all animal experimentation was exempt from anti-cruelty code enforcement, so I still hadn't determined what action I would be able to initiate. There were many times when I felt very alone, unsure of whom I could approach with the evidence or of what recourse would be available to prevent Taub from continuing his practices.

Then, after about two months, I found out that a revision of the Maryland statute had excluded language designed to exempt animal experimenters. Elated, I began to prepare my criminal case against Taub. One of the first things I had to do was to stop giving the monkeys the fresh fruit I was smuggling in for them. The food sacks which were clearly marked with an expiry date (after which the food is nutritionally deficient) had all expired four months before I started work at IBR. I realized that Taub would use any improvement in their health brought about by my independent feeding of them to defend his treatment of the animals. I also discovered that virtually all the medication in the laboratory had expired, some in 1979, others as far back as 1969. The broken and the intact containers were kept in a filthy refrigerator, strewn about next to a bag of putrified apples that were actually covered with cobwebs. Near this refrigerator was the shell of another. This one had been converted into a chamber containing a plexiglass immobilizing chair. A monkey would be placed in the chamber, and electrodes attached to his body. The monkey would be forced to try to squeeze a bottle of fluid with his surgically crippled arm in order to stop the painful electric shock that coursed through his body. The ceiling and walls of the chamber were covered with blood. I remembered Taub's assistant, John Kunz, telling me that some monkeys would break their arms in desperate attempts to escape the chair and the intense electric shocks.

On several occasions things were so bad that I risked appearing suspiciously concerned about the primates and suggested that a veterinarian be called in to treat the most serious injuries. At one point Billy's arm was broken in two places and I repeatedly asked that a veterinarian be called. Then, it was finally openly admitted to me that they did not use a veterinarian. Billy's extremely swollen, broken arm was left untreated.

Conditions were so bad that it was clear that it would be crucial to bring in some expert witnesses who could vouch for the conditions I was witnessing. I cautiously approached five people with expertise in various related fields. They were Dr Geza Teleki, an ethologist and global expert in primatology; Dr Michael Fox, a writer, veterinarian and ethologist; Dr Ronnie Hawkins, a physician who had worked with laboratory primates; Dr John McArdle, a primate anatomist and former primate researcher; and Donald Barnes, a lay psychologist who had radiated monkeys for seventeen years in the military before rejecting such practices. These people accompanied me through the laboratory at night, signing affidavits afterwards. I was grateful for their support because their professional assessments of the state of the animals and the laboratory would lend credence to my testimony in any future legal proceedings.

On 8 September I took my affidavit and those of the five expert witnesses, as well as my notes and photographs, to the Silver Spring, Maryland, police. After their preliminary investigations Detective Sergeant Rick Swain obtained the precedent-setting search and seizure warrant from Circuit Court Judge John McAuliffe. The first raid of a research facility in the United States took place at IBR on 11 September. Swain and a search team of six confiscated the monkeys and the files.

We had considered carefully the problem of where we could house seventeen traumatized, fragile monkeys. The National Zoo, the facility most capable of assisting, refused to help. Local animal shelters, although sympathetic, were not equipped. We were finally forced to adapt the basement of a local activist's home. After the installation of drains in the floor, new windows, a ventilation system, insulation, etc., their refuge was ready.

A devoted PETA volunteer built new cages that were more than twice the size of those at IBR. For the first time since their capture in the jungle, our refugees had something to sit on comfortably and enough room to extend their cramped and pitiful limbs. They even had food containers and objects to handle and explore. Our delight at seeing them relish even these minor improvements was shadowed by our anxiety about what might follow. We were on an uncharted course, and the future of the animals was to be tested as their case passed through the courts.

The events of the next few days did not augur well. Taub's attorneys swung into action, demanding the return of their client's property. We were shocked to hear them introduce two recent US Department of Agriculture reports of inspections of IBR, marked 'Minor deficiencies' and 'No deficiencies noted'. Judge David Cahoon listened to the assurances of improvements given by a veterinarian who had worked earlier for Taub, yet refused to hear from our experts, who were prepared to swear that a return to IBR would jeopardize the monkeys' safety and well-being. Taub's motion to have the monkeys returned was granted. The abused were to be returned to their abuser the next day.

That night the monkeys disappeared. Bench warrants were issued for the arrest of Ingrid, Jean Goldenberg, director of the Washington Humane Society/SPCA, and Lori Lehner, whose home had been the monkeys' temporary resting place. Lori spent a night in jail before it was decided that there was insufficient evidence against any of the women.

Taub then held a press conference, demanding the return of the monkeys, which he now valued at between $60 and $90,000 each (a total value, according to Taub's arithmetic, of between $1,020,000 and $1,530,000 for an experiment costing a total of $221,000). Taub then offered only a $200 reward for their return.

The problem now was that without the monkeys there could be no criminal prosecution of Taub. Yet to return the monkeys would most likely mean their further suffering and death at Taub's hands. Negotiations began between the police and the monkeys' new guardians, through an intermediary. Secret conditions were agreed upon – mainly that if the monkeys were returned, they would not be returned to IBR. But the guardians' trust was betrayed, not by the police but by the court. No sooner were the monkeys back in Maryland than Judge Cahoon cancelled a full hearing without ever allowing any of the State's witnesses to testify. He immediately ordered the monkeys back to IBR. A crowd gathered at Lori's home, and people stood in the street and cried as the monkeys were loaded into Taub's rented truck. Wellwishers and those who had come to love the monkeys then stood vigil outside IBR, hoping for new developments to save the monkeys.

Taub was now charged with seventeen counts of cruelty to animals: one count for each monkey. Meanwhile the national Institutes of Health (NIH) announced its suspension of Taub's grant after conducting its own investigation and set a date for Taub to account for his expenditures and research results. At later hearings of the US House Subcommittee on Science, Research, and Technology, at which I testified on the conditions at IBR, the NIH admitted that in the IBR case, their system had failed.

Five days after the monkeys were sent to IBR, one of them was injured and another, Charlie, died of what Taub described as a 'heart attack'. These two wild male macaques had been placed together in a cage just $17\frac{3}{4}$ inches wide, while a commercial steam cleaner was operated in the room – resulting in a fight, as even a novice could have predicted. The police demanded Charlie's body, which was sent to Cornell University for a necropsy. The examiner reported back that the cause of death could not be determined because some important parts were missing, namely Charlie's heart, lungs, kidneys, a testicle and several glands. Judge Cahoon, finally realizing his mistake, reversed his earlier order and shipped the monkeys out of IBR and into safekeeping at NIH's Poolesville, Maryland, primate quarantine centre. There they joined almost 1,000 other unfortunate primates. The NIH was ordered not to take any 'extraordinary measures' unless authorized by the court. None the less, Hard Times had to be destroyed after being in great pain and paralysed from the waist down for two days. Taub's surgery had caught up with Hard Times. Taub fought to deny this monkey even his final release, arguing that he wanted to keep Hard Times alive to complete his experiments. Next Nero's arm had to be amputated when a chronic bone infection that had originated months earlier in Taub's laboratory threatened his life. Again Taub fought the action. Today Nero is in much better shape, without his mutilated arm.

As for the criminal trials, the first one lasted a week, during which time Taub was defended by two of Washington's most prestigious law firms, Arnold and Porter, and Miller, Miller, and Steinberg.

The animal experimentation community didn't know what to do; it could take the risky step of ostracizing one of its own, or clutch Taub to its bosom and blame the whole incident on 'lay ignorance'. For the most part it chose the latter course. We had cogent testimony from experts, but clearly we presented a threat to others in the animal experimentation industry. Taub's defence fund grew. He sat flanked by six attorneys, his public relations representatives behind him, while Roger Galvin, the Assistant State's Attorney, stood alone, presenting the case for the State of Maryland.

Taub was vociferous in his own defence, even appearing to frustrate his counsel by his loquaciousness. The *Washington Post* viewed his stance as that of 'a professor lecturing a class full of students'. He had nothing but contempt for our concerns and went so far as to charge that photographs introduced by the prosecution were 'staged' and to insinuate that someone had bribed the care-takers into doing a sloppy job.

It soon became clear that psychological suffering, a lack of cage space and critical sanitation problems would not be considered violations of the law by the courts. We knew we were in for an uphill fight.

On 23 November 1981 Taub was found guilty of six counts of cruelty for failing to provide proper veterinary care to six of the monkeys. It is hard to describe our feelings when the verdict was announced, but at last now, whatever might happen to the monkeys as we continued to fight for their safety, the public would know that something was definitely wrong with the way in which some segments of the scientific community operated. The criminal con-viction had chipped a hole in the wall that protects animal experi-menters from public scrutiny.

As we had expected, Taub appealed his conviction. The second trial was even more difficult. This time the new judge required that the prosecution present only evidence relating to the six monkeys who had figured in the conviction – no matter what the other monkeys had been through, the jury would not be allowed to know. The twelve jurors were instructed that they must find Taub not guilty if they could not unanimously determine that the monkeys had suffered physical pain extending beyond their deafferant limbs. Again, we were pleased to have the support of our original experts, joined now by Colonel Simmonds, DVM, of the Uniformed Services University of the Health Sciences, Dr Robinson and Dr Ott of the San Diego and Brookfield zoos, and Dr Roberts of the US Army. Their testimony countered statements from Taub's associates – defence statements that could only be considered outrageous.

Two researchers, friends of Taub from the University of Penn-sylvania, testified that monkeys were nothing more than 'defecating machines', that it was acceptable not to administer veterinary care for a broken arm and that an infestation of cockroaches provided a 'good source of ambient protein' for laboratory primates. To testimony by one of Taub's expert witnesses that there were 'no data' to suggest that heavy accumulations of excrement were a health hazard, Mr Galvin rebutted that if this were true, the American public had been fooled into thinking they needed sewage systems.

Unfortunately, there were many things that the jury was never allowed to consider in making its decision, things it was never allowed to hear, know about or see. For example, the jury was not permitted to hear about the discovery of two 55-gallon barrels filled with the corpses of monkeys and weighted down with used auto parts and wood. The jury could not ask, 'What became of them? How did they die?' The jury was never allowed to hear that Taub was denied a grant application because between 80 and 90 per cent of his animal subjects died before the end of his experiments. It could not see the 1979 US Department of Agriculture inspection report that read: 'Floors were dirty with blood stains all over them.' It was never allowed to know that Taub operated illegally, in violation of federal law, for seven years, while receiving hundreds of thousands of federal tax dollars. The jury did not know that Caligula suffered from gangrene and mutilated his own chest cavity, that blood splattered the wall and ceiling of the converted refrigerator chamber, that the NIH had investigated Taub and found him in violation of its own guidelines, that Charlie had died of an unexplained 'heart attack'. It was never allowed to see or hear of the surgically severed monkey hand or the skull that Taub used as paperweights in his office. And, perhaps most unfortunately, the jury was never allowed to see the living evidence, the monkeys themselves.

With all the new restrictions and limitations, four of the jury members felt there was insufficient evidence left to convict Taub without doubt, while eight of the jurors wanted a guilty verdict on all six counts. The verdict, of course, had to be unanimous. After two and a half days of deliberation the jurors reached agreement. The jurors unanimously found Taub guilty on one count. Later conversations with members of the jury showed how hopelessly restricted they had felt. A local newspaper report described the jurors' 'unprecedented' interest in following through on the case and their concern for the fate of the monkeys.

Taub was not to be stopped. He appealed this conviction to the

Maryland Court of Appeals in Baltimore and this time succeeded. The court, after months of waiting, ruled that animal experimenters who receive federal tax funding do not have to obey the State anti-cruelty laws. No matter how heinous the deeds committed by an animal experimenter in Maryland, the court held that the experimenter could not be prosecuted. Sadly, the court did not consider whether or not Taub had treated the monkeys cruelly. The court made it clear that it was not interested in resolving this question. Rather, as stated in its decision, 'The issue in this case is whether the animal cruelty statute . . . is applicable to research pursuant to a federal program . . . we do not believe the legislature intended [the cruelty statute] to apply to this type of research activity under a federal program. We shall, therefore, reverse Dr Taub's conviction . . .' (*Taub* v. *State*, 296 Md 439 (1983)). The court's opinion enraged not only the Maryland State's Attorneys Office but also the many scientists and supporters who saw Taub slip through a crack in the criminal justice system.

At the time of writing, the fate of the monkeys is undetermined. Taub, encouraged by the reversal of his conviction, appealed against the NIH's decision to terminate his grant. The appeal was rejected, but Taub has now applied for a new grant. If this application is successful, he has pledged to continue his experiment, which involves surgically crippling the monkeys' remaining normal arms and, ten days later, 'sacrificing' them. This would probably take place at the University of Pennsylvania, where some of his closest colleagues are employed. We have vowed never to let this happen.

The Taub case has been an intense, consuming battle, accompanied by many small battles. It devoured our time and resources, taught us some new values and confirmed some old ones. It renewed our resolve to research our targets carefully and thoroughly before 'going public'. It made us understand how valuable persistence is.

After working for animal protection at the grassroots level, with demonstrations, letter-writing campaigns and boycotts, and lobbying at the state and federal levels, conducting investigations, bringing criminal and civil cases to court, testifying before state and federal legislative hearings, participating in conferences and federal regulatory enforcement agency hearings and meetings, several things have become clear. First, the animal protection movement has not been aggressive enough or persistent enough. It has often taken a simplistic approach in attempting to solve problems. Second, organizations and individuals have allowed tactical and other differences to prevent them from co-operating with each other on mutually agreeable projects. There is a dire need to agree to disagree and get on with the work. Third, we will not make meaningful changes for animals on a large scale until we have effectively harnessed the widespread support that exists in this country. Without doubt, the potential is there. I believe our job must be to alert people to the severity of animal exploitation and abuse and to the needlessness of it all. This educational process can be accelerated by getting public leaders and popular figures to speak out for animal protection and by working with the mass media. Animal rights must fill the air.

I believe that it is best to take a strong ethical stand and to be strategically assertive, never forgetting – not even for a minute – our ultimate goal. Realizing that total abolition of some aspects of animal exploitation may never come, we should not simply demand 'total abolition or nothing at all', as that often ensures that those suffering today will continue to suffer. Nor should we hold a conservative line, which will also make tomorrow's suffering assured and accepted. Difficult as it may be, I believe that tactfully and strategically we must combine parts of both approaches: we must fight for today's reforms while aiming for and advocating abolition.

The Island of the Dragon

DEXTER L. CATE

It is called Tatsunoshima, the Island of the Dragon. It lies curled in a 'C', with its back to the rough Japan Sea and its feet stretched towards Iki Island across a mile-wide channel. Its moods are changeable . . . and sometimes deadly.

During the summer months the Dragon is warm and friendly; vacationers flock by the hundreds to nestle up to its white sand belly and row boats in the clear, quiet waters of the protected bay. Katsumoto village, a community on the northern coast of Iki Island, makes most of its summer money catering to these visitors and tourists.

During the winter months of February through April, however, the Dragon shows its grim side. Amid human shouts, high-pitched whistles of dolphins in distress and sounds of frantic splashing, the crystal water turns a brilliant red. The dragon bloods its kill: the annual dolphin slaughter has begun.

It hasn't always been thus. Until just a few years ago Tatsunoshima was used only by vacationers and other visitors who sought contact with their Shinto past; the small, uninhabited island is designated a national park. Its serene beauty summons up an image of ancient Japan. This image changed abruptly in 1978, when the fishermen of Iki Island thrust Tatsunoshima into world prominence by slaughtering over 1,000 dolphins, drawing cries of anger and protest from around the globe.

I caught my first glimpse of Tatsunoshima in August on 1978, through the forest of masts in Katsumoto harbour. I was there to talk with Niichiro Kashii, head of the Katsumoto Fishermen's Co-

operative, in order to understand the fishermen's position concerning the slaughter of dolphins. I found Kashii-san to be a gentle,
gracious host who made a genuine attempt to understand the furore
the dolphin slaughter had caused abroad. He made every effort to
explain to me the fishermen's viewpoint.

I was already aware of the extent of dolphin killing in Japan. In
1975 I had toured Japan as part of a marine studies course. My
particular interests were Japan's whaling industry and marine
pollution. I learned of the extensive dolphin 'fishery' while talking to
dolphin researchers at Tokyo University. At that time the primary
reason for dolphin slaughters was food and, to a lesser extent,
fertilizer and oil. The situation in Iki was rather different: the main
issue was competition for limited resources.

For over ten years local fishermen had complained of dolphins
scaring away the *buri* (yellowtail tuna) and squid. After asking for,
and being denied, help from their Government, they took matters
into their own hands. Dolphins were herded into the deep cove of
Tatsunoshima, barricaded by nets at the bay's mouth, and method-
ically slaughtered. To the fishermen, who saw their profits dropping
yearly, there seemed no alternative.

When I told Mr Kashii of my interest in finding an alternative to
the slaughter he was receptive to the idea, although sceptical about
whether it could succeed.

I returned in December of 1978, financed by the Fund for Animals
and Greenpeace. I took with me Jim Nollman, a specialist in
interspecies music. In addition, I also took along a Jacques Cousteau
film which showed the fishermen of Mauritania co-operating with
dolphins to catch fish, which, I hoped, would illustrate to the local
fishermen that co-operation was possible. Accomplishing this, we
would journey to the fishing area and use Nollman and his instruments to attempt to attract dolphins to our boat. Jim had been
successful at this very thing before in both California and Mexico,
and we hoped that a successful demonstration here would convince
the fishermen that co-operation with dolphins, as opposed to
competition, was worth exploring further. The film was a great
success, sparking the interest not only of Kashii but of the village
children as well. Unfortunately, the attempt to attract dolphins drew
a blank. There were no dolphins in the area at that time.

We did, however, attract considerable media attention. Our
attempts to communicate with the dolphins in the hope of finding a
solution to the Iki 'dolphin problem' received nationwide, and quite

sympathetic, coverage on two of the three top television networks in Japan.

My next visit to Iki and the Dragon Island came the following March. This time I took along Frank Robson from New Zealand. Robson, author of the book *Thinking Dolphins, Talking Whales*, had demonstrated amazing success in communicating empathetically with dolphins. While head of the dolphin-training programme at Marineland in New Zealand, he did all training by communicating directly with the dolphins, eschewing both whistle and food rewards. The performances of his dolphins remain unexcelled to this day.

The plan this time was for Frank to try to communicate to the dolphins that they should stay on the periphery of the fishing banks, leaving the centre to the fishermen; thus any fish trying to escape the dolphins would head straight for the fishing boats. The dolphins would be able to catch the fish they needed while acting as a sort of living net to help the fishermen. It was much like the method of the fishermen and dolphins in Mauritania.

Again the media showed considerable interest in the project. Frank was shown on NHK, the national TV network, as he talked to dolphins at an oceanarium near Tokyo. The dolphins took an obvious interest in him, appearing to understand what he was saying. Frank, a grandfatherly figure, has been a fisherman for forty years. He understands the problems of that way of life. We headed for Iki with high hopes of bridging the gap between the fishermen and the dolphins.

We were too late. The dragon had spread its claws. The week before we arrived fishermen had conducted a dolphin round-up and had slaughtered some 400 dolphins. For the duration of our week-long visit, the only dolphins to be seen at Tatsunoshima were dead ones.

It wasn't, however, an entirely wasted trip. We made several trips to the fishing banks with the fishermen and saw, at first hand, the methods used to catch the *buri* and squid. Hardy Jones, of the Breach Foundation, recorded it all on film. At these fishing banks the truth of the situation became apparent: the problem was, very clearly, not one of too many dolphins but of too many fishermen. The fishing banks were literally packed with boats, giving fishermen little room to manoeuvre. We learned that as other fishing grounds around Japan became fished out, more and more fishermen were converging upon these banks. In the last three years alone the number of boats fishing this small area had increased by more than 200. It was an obvious case of overfishing, and the dolphins were being made the scapegoats.

The dolphins migrate through these waters annually on their way north in the Japan Sea. They are in the area for only two or three months. The fishing banks the Iki fishermen claim as their own have undoubtedly been dolphin feeding stops for thousands, possibly millions, of years. Despite the fact that the dolphins obviously have prior claim to fish resources here, any solution to the conflict would have to be agreeable to the fishermen.

The closer we looked at the situation, the more clearly we could see the problems the fishermen were facing. I visited a *buri* farm on the island. I learned that the culture of *buri*, a quality fish that fetches a premium price in Japan, is a booming business – so successful, in fact, that it is undercutting the *buri* fisheries. The bulk of *buri* sold in Japanese markets is cultured. To make matters worse, the *buri* farms obtain their *buri* fry, called *mojako*, from the spawning areas near Kyushu. Hundreds of tons of the tiny fish are netted with small-mesh nets, some to be sold directly as food in the markets nationwide, the rest to be sold to the *buri* farms. Thus fewer *mojako* survive to become adult *buri* and migrate up the coast to the Iki fishing banks. Along their path up the Kyushu coast the *mojako*, who hug the shoreline, pass numerous industrial centres, including Minamata, the 'home' of mercury poisoning, or Minimata disease. The *mojako* are very susceptible to chemical pollution, especially mercury. It became apparent that overfishing was only part of the problem.

In one respect the fishermen were probably correct: there *weren't* enough fish left for both humans and dolphins. Yet, as a human problem, it had to have a human solution. Punishing the dolphins was as unfair as it was ecologically foolish.

Fortunately, a number of potentially workable human solutions presented themselves during my subsequent research, and in November of 1979 a telephone petition urging the implementation of these dolphin-saving alternatives was directed to the US (because of the tuna–dolphin problem) and Japanese Governments. As a part of that campaign, a proposal I had drawn up was delivered to various Japanese government agencies. This proposal included: a dolphin-damage insurance plan, designed to reimburse Iki fishermen for any financial losses caused by dolphin intervention, with the dolphins remaining unmolested; government assistance to Iki island to help establish appropriate aquaculture and mariculture programmes as alternative occupations, thus ensuring jobs and food supply on a continuing basis; government assistance in the construction of artificial reefs and *buri* hatcheries to rebuild the devastated *buri* population around the island; government-enforced reduction of the number of fishing boats allowed in the area to an ecologically sustainable number. The Japanese government was already spending huge amounts in dolphin bounties, machinery and foreign public relations in order to perpetuate the slaughter; these suggested programmes would provide a way to spend this money that would solve the problem of the dolphins *and* the fishermen.

On my final visit to Iki, in February 1980, I planned to follow through with this proposal: to get the endorsement of the Iki fishermen, if possible, and to press for government action.

I didn't get the chance. The day my family and I arrived on Iki, we learned they were already herding the dolphins in towards Tatsunoshima. The next morning we arranged to journey to the Island of the Dragon.

The scene that met us was straight out of Dante. Between about 800 and 1,000 dolphins were in the cove, many beached and dying a lingering, agonizing death. Others were caught in the nets, struggling to get their blowholes above the water's surface to gasp for one more breath. On the beach hundreds more lay dead and dying, blood gushing from spear wounds in their sides. About sixty fishermen were busy with the massacre. While some, dressed in full wetsuits, waded in the chest-deep, blood-red water catching the dolphins and tying ropes to their tails, another twenty or so pulled in unison on a stout rope. A writhing dolphin, pulled by the tail flukes, slipped and slid over the bodies of her friends and relatives and lay gasping and whistling on the beach, while two or three men with spears jabbed until blood came gushing forth. At any moment a dozen or more dolphins were heaving in their last struggle, their life flowing red into the sand. My wife, Suzie, and cameraman Howard Hall constantly changed angles, recording on film this ghastly side of the Dragon Island.

We learned that the fishermen would receive a bounty of $80 per dolphin, half of this paid by the Japanese Government. Dolphin meat, not normally a part of the Iki diet, was being promoted in a full-colour pamphlet produced by a government agency. A huge $147,000 grinding machine, purchased with government assistance, was being employed to grind the dolphins into a mush that would be used as pig feed and fertilizer.

What had begun two years ago as a desperate move by the

fishermen had now become a profitable business. Watching the giant grinding machine do its grisly work, I knew all my efforts to find alternatives had come to nothing.

The following day most of the fishermen occupied themselves by grinding up the dolphins slaughtered the day before. I spent the day buying necessary equipment and that night, in the teeth of a building storm, paddled a small inflatable kayak a mile across the channel to Tatsunoshima, where some 500 dolphins were still awaiting execution.

Untying three ropes, severing one, I opened the jaws of the Dragon. As the winds reached gale force, I realized I would be unable to paddle back to the main island. It was just as well. There were dozens of dolphins left stranded on the beach as the tide fell. I spend the rest of the night helping them to deeper water and the chance of freedom.

Not all the dolphins escaped. Some were injured, and some, I feel, simply made the choice not to abandon loved ones. By the time the fishermen arrived the next morning approximately 250 dolphins had found their way out of the nets to freedom.

I was turned over to the police by the fishermen and subsequently charged with forceful obstruction of the fishermen's business. I spent the next three months in solitary confinement at Sasebo prison. During this time my trial proceeded.

At my trial Milton Kaufman, of the Fund for Animals and Monitor International, testified to the ecological short-sightedness of such dolphin slaughters and the worldwide reaction to Japan's policy of dolphin eradication. Peter Singer came from Australia to testify to the philosophical and moral implications of the dolphin slaughters. Buddhist teachings of reverance for sentient life were discussed, as well as the fact that the small island where the slaughters took place is a national park where such killing is strictly forbidden.

My lawyer, Manabu Arioka, who volunteered his services, tried to apprise me of the differences between Japanese law and US law. I was still caught off-guard. Japanese law allows a judge to refuse bail to anyone who does not have a permanent address in Japan. The trial judge would not accept my Tokyo address as permanent because, as I was a foreigner, my permanent address must, by definition, be abroad. He refused bail. My lawyer objected that such reasoning would deny bail to any visitor to Japan, which would contravene Japan's constitution guaranteeing equal treatment under the law, regardless of nationality. The Judge's response: 'But

Mr Cate is not just any visitor to Japan. He has committed a crime.'
Aside from the rather circular reasoning, this incident taught me
that in Japan, once you are charged, the assumption is that you are
guilty, although theoretically you are innocent until proven guilty.
There is no jury, and the judge has complete autocratic power. He is
not bound by precedent, as are US judges. He has the authority to
credit or discredit any testimony or line of reasoning, without
explanation.

This system has some obvious disadvantages, but it also has some
advantages. Because the judge has control of the outcome of the trial,
he may feel less constrained about what he may allow as testimony.
It is unlikely that in a similar trial in the United States the judge
would allow a philosopher to testify concerning animal rights. In
fact, Peter Singer's testimony on the dolphins' behalf is, as far as I
am aware, the first time such testimony has been allowed in a
criminal court anywhere.

The Japanese system also allows a defendant personally to cross-
examine any witness. This was especially useful, as I had very little
time to confer with my lawyer before entering the courtroom. He had
slight knowledge either of dolphins or of my activities concerning
dolphins in Iki or anywhere else. He had volunteered his services out
of a conviction that what the fishermen were doing was wrong and
that my actions were morally and legally justified. The trial took on a
two-level aspect: I dealt with the moral and philosophical implications, while Mr Arioka dealt with strictly legal matters. For the
most part it was an effective division of labour. The greatest
problems were in the area of communication. They were quite
frustrating.

The court interpreter had a fair command of English, which in
most situations, I'm sure, would have sufficed. However, in this
situation there were many concepts quite foreign to the Japanese
way of thinking. It was very difficult to communicate our view of the
dolphins to the judge. In several instances I intercepted rather
serious misinterpretations, even with my meagre knowledge of
Japanese. The interpreter had a very difficult time with the concept
of ecology, and when he translated testimony concerning the
intelligence of dolphins the courtroom, filled with Japanese reporters
and onlookers, burst into laughter. Obviously something was lost in
the translation. The judge asked Peter Singer, 'If these dolphins are
so intelligent, do they go to school?' It became evident that the
philosophical gap between the Japanese and the Westerners was

even greater than I had realized. Most of my discussions with Japanese had been with the small minority who shared my views concerning ecology and with a few who even shared my concern for the cetaceans. Even these balked, with very few exceptions, when I talked of dolphins as the 'people of the sea'. The thought that any other creature, besides humans, might have language, might have thoughts as sophisticated as ours, might have similar feelings, was totally unacceptable. When I mentioned the size and complexity of the cetacean brain, the judge responded with, 'If dolphins are so intelligent, why do they lead American tuna boats to schools of tuna, only to meet with death themselves?' I didn't know whether to try to correct his misapprehension of the tuna–dolphin situation or to try to deal with the intelligence issue further – or to give it up as a lost cause. The only thing that kept me going was the knowledge that the courtroom was filled with reporters, some of whom just might understand what I was saying.

Perhaps the best communications bridge was Uncle Harry Mitchell, a Hawaiian taro farmer and fisherman, who came over to Japan at my request. He talked with both the judge and Mr Kashii, head of the Iki fishermen's union. I believe his down-to-earth Hawaiian wisdom did more to communicate our concern for the dolphins and the overriding concern for a healthy marine environment than could all of our talk of ecology and animal rights.

In the end the whole trial came to have the farcical appearance of a *shibai*, a Japanese play. After three months in detention and six days in court (the Japanese judicial system allows only two days in court per month, hence the three month detention), the judge issued his verdict and passed sentence. All defence arguments went by the way as the judge limited his considerations to 'forceful obstruction'. I was found guilty, given a six-month suspended sentence and turned over to Immigration. During my stay in Sasebo prison my visa had expired, so I was now labelled an illegal alien to be held in detention for the duration of any appeal I might undertake; if I signed a waiver of my right to appeal, on the other hand, I would be deported immediately. After learning that the appeal process can take three years or more, I signed the waiver. I also learned that I had a choice over deportation: if I paid for my own ticket, I could leave immediately; if I insisted that the Japanese Government pay, there would be a delay of six months, during which time, of course, I would have to remain in detention. I paid.

After the trial I asked my lawyer if he thought the outcome of the trial had been predetermined by higher-ups in government. 'Oh yes,' he responded. I asked what percentage of the cases that go to trial in Japan end up in convictions. 'More than 99 per cent,' was his answer.

Since my return to Hawaii I have frequently been asked, 'Was it worth it?' Certainly the three months in prison did me no harm and probably did me some good. The dolphin slaughters in Iki continued, although the numbers killed the following years were 90 per cent fewer than in 1980. The fishermen reported that the dolphins were much more difficult to herd into the nets.

Other dolphin slaughters have continued in Japan and elsewhere in the world. I fear they are on the rise. Just as terrestrial mammals have been forced off their land and exterminated, so too are marine mammals increasingly becoming the victims of unchecked human expansion. It is a global problem. So to whatever extent my action served to publicize the problem, it was worth it.

However, as I recall my feelings and thoughts of 29 February 1980 I realize that these things were not my major concern. I had witnessed my brothers and sisters of the sea suffering and had had the opportunity to help them. I had really had no choice. Was it worth it? Ask the dolphins.

Tatsunoshima symbolizes to me the plight of our planet. The friendly face of the Dragon shows us the possibility of living peaceful lives in tune with the beauty of our environment, of coexisting with all creatures, including other people of all shapes and colours. The destructive face of the Dragon consumes all in its path, cherishing no life other than its own. Its self-centred rampage can have but one end: extinction. The fire-breathing Dragon springs from the depths of our reptilian past. Can we transcend the demon that lies within us, or are we doomed to destroy our planet, this lovely island in space? Maybe the dolphins have the answer.

A Matter of Change

DONALD J. BARNES

'Don,' an acquaintance of mine said recently, 'I don't mean to question your commitment to the principles of antivivisection, but you were a vivisector for sixteen years. What caused such a quick and radical change in your beliefs?' I have been asked the same question many times, and by one person more than any other . . . myself. The answer has changed as my values have changed, but consistently and in the same direction. Let's take a chronological look at the evolution of my values in order to try to understand.

In early 1941, just a few months before my fifth birthday, my parents somehow managed to buy a 20-acre farm in Southern California. They had migrated with their two young sons from the rural south, where they themselves had quit school early to help support their families by labouring in the fields for as little as 20 cents per day. They neither liked nor understood city life, and our move to our own land promised security with independence.

The land fed us and clothed us. We grew our own fruit and vegetables and a surplus which we sold from door to door for maximum profit, as the large packers and buyers paid poorly for the products of small independent growers.

Animals were integral to our existence. We raised pigs, cattle and chickens for our meat, eggs and dairy products, churned our own butter and drank our milk as it came from the cow, without pasteurization or homogenization. We treated our animals with love and respect, but always in the knowledge that they were on earth not for themselves but to serve us. Butchering was accomplished as expediently as possible with a hatchet and a chopping block for the fowl and a well-placed bullet for the larger animals. Their deaths raised enigmatic questions in my mind but were soon accepted as necessary, for that was the ethos of the farm.

When I was about seven years old (and my brother nine), our father bought us a burro. We had wanted a horse for some time but had been convinced that a horse was economically unjustifiable, as it would contribute nothing but pleasure to the family farm. We had a tractor with huge metal wheels, almost an antique, so we couldn't even use a horse for ploughing. We soon learned that our burro was not to be simply a plaything for us. As my father pruned the branches of the fruit trees or cut down the corn stalks from the field, my brother and I loaded them on the cart and hauled them away from the field or orchard. There is much hauling to be done on a farm, and before we knew it we were performing this essential function daily. Even so, the burro and I became close friends and we spent many blissful hours exploring the surrounding countryside together.

While the burro and the other farm animals were pressed into our service, there were many other animals on our farm which were undomesticated and posed a threat to our way of life. Gophers and ground squirrels burrowed in the soft soil of the orchards, eating our vegetables and the roots of our trees. We irrigated our fields at night to minimize loss of water through evaporation. The water came from a single source and had to be channelled into irrigation ditches dug by hand or with a plough. These ditches followed a rather circuitous path in order to accommodate gravity and the many plants that required frequent irrigation. If a gopher should happen to burrow near an irrigation ditch, we had to fill the burrow with rocks and soil, for it's amazing how much water can disappear into a gopher hole. Skunks, while posing no immediate physical threat, were a constant nuisance; other creatures of the wild, such as rattlesnakes, weasels or coyotes, were seen as encroachers and potential enemies to our chickens and our egg supply. I received 25 cents for each ground squirrel I trapped or shot, and 10 cents for each gopher. I therefore learned early to kill without guilt, for wasn't I doing something to help the family?

After several years our family moved to Colorado and the life on the farm was over for ever. But now I was taken hunting and fishing, and I became proficient in both. We considered ourselves, 'good sportsmen', and I suppose we were in the sense that we always ate what we killed, never exceeded our limit, were conscious of camping etiquette, were careful with firearms when there were other people around and so on. To us, it was a perfectly acceptable way of life, even though we could have done without the meat provided by these activities.

In 1960, while studying for a Ph.D. in clinical psychology and ever mindful of the ethics involved in working with psychiatric patients, I was given a position as graduate teaching assistant at the Ohio State University. My job was to teach principles of learning to second-year college students through the use of operant-conditioning techniques applied to laboratory rats. This was no problem for me, given that my entire background consisted of using other animals for my sake, and I glibly demonstrated the effectiveness of various techniques of training, including the use of electric shock as 'negative reinforcement'.

Six years later, having completed my internship and graduated from the US Air Force Officers Training School, I was assigned to head up the laboratory when the Air Force decided to develop a capability to determine the effects of pulsed ionizing radiation upon the behaviour of non-human primates. (To the Department of Defense, a psychologist is a psychologist: it didn't matter that I was a clinical psychologist.) I was given a relatively large budget ($200,000 to $300,000 per year) and freedom to set up the programme I wanted. I had a crew of enlisted and civilian workers, most of them with college degrees. I was given the opportunity to travel to other laboratories, to speak to funding agencies, to consult with other scientists.

Realizing that the vocabulary of the clinical psychologist was inappropriate for the job, I immediately set about learning something about experimental psychology. I instituted a contractual arrangement with the Department of Psychology, Baylor University, Waco, Texas. Baylor University was to train monkeys at their primate facility in Waco and, further, to provide two or three graduate students to work as 'interns' at the School of Aerospace Medicine under my direction. I learned from these students and from their professors.

The gastro-intestinal system is affected early in the course of radiation injury. Hence we were not at liberty to use food, or 'positive reinforcement' to train the monkeys, for if they stopped 'working' we could not attribute the work stoppage to their inability to work. The animals might simply not feel like eating. We were therefore constrained to use shock avoidance, or 'negative reinforcement', in our experiments. We felt that we must provide the animals with the strongest incentive in order to avoid interpretational difficulties based upon 'motivation'. We therefore bought specially designed shock units from Behavioral Research Systems Electronics. These shock units delivered between 0 and 50 millamperes at 12,000 volts. The output from the shock units was connected to 'shock plates', metal plates under the monkeys' feet and mounted on strong springs to ensure contact with the feet. It was impossible to measure the amount of shock each animal received as skin toughness, perspiration, spring tension, the specific shock unit, etc., were all relatively uncontrolled. The training situation therefore became totally empirical in that the shock unit was turned up until the primate began to respond. In many cases this was a very high shock level, as most of the monkeys were very young and passive and tended to withdraw rather than to strike out when hurt. The more aggressive animals received fewer shocks because they responded more often and were therefore more likely to emit the response desired by the experimenter, at which point the shock would be terminated. But woe to the monkey who withdrew, who began to self-mutilate, who tried to escape: I've seen more than one monkey die from cardiac fibrillation occasioned by repeated shocking.

There are two obvious questions which must be addressed at this point: how could anyone do such things to animals? And why would anyone do those things in the first place? Realizing full well that I will probably never be able to answer these questions to anyone's satisfaction, I'll attempt to reflect my thoughts during the time I was involved in such research.

First, why *wouldn't* I use other animals for my own means? I represented a classic example of what I choose to call 'conditioned ethical blindness'. My entire life had consisted of being rewarded for using animals, treating them as sources of human improvement or amusement. There had not been a single person with the temerity to challenge my behaviour towards other animals. Of course I was kind to animals; of course I loved my pets; of course I would tend to a sick bird, rabbit, dog or cat without question. On the other hand, I would belie my tenderness a moment later by eating a chicken, or a rabbit or a squirrel, or part of a steer. That was different in my mind; that was 'meat'. The word 'meat' is a means of distancing ourselves from the animals we eat, just as 'negative reinforcement' is a means of distancing ourselves from electrically shocking a creature who feels pain as much as, if not more than, we humans do.

I returned to graduate school at the Ohio State University in 1971–72 for a year's study of experimental psychology. At first I spoke openly of the work I had been doing, but I sensed discomfort among my fellow students and some of the professors. They didn't *say* anything – I simply felt their discomfort. I stopped talking about my work. I studied with an ethologist from Britain, with physiological psychologists, learning psychologists, motivational psychologists and social psychologists from the United States and with graduate students from all walks of life. Never was the ethical question broached. The compartmentalization was incredible (now that I look back on it). We'd be discussing on the one hand the effects of early stimulation upon later development, on the other the effects of brain lesions upon visual behaviour. The whole gamut of research was implicitly defined as ethical. There was never any question. Why *shouldn't* I have engaged in such research?

But let's take this conditioning process a step further. During my tenure as a psychologist I considered Harry Harlow a super-person. Dr Harlow, perhaps the best-known of all experimental psychologists, was responsible for conceptualizing the surrogate-mother concept in raising rhesus monkeys. He learned that if one separates an infant monkey from his or her mother, the monkey will probably grow up to be neurotic. Going beyond this simple truth, Dr Harlow did all manner of things to infant monkeys. Not only did he separate them from their mothers, but he also put them in 'pits of despair', where the animals never saw, heard, smelled or in any other way sensed another life. These monkeys became psychotic, as one might suspect if one were to give it a moment's thought . . . which I didn't. Harry Harlow created a 'monster mother' a mechanical device which threatened the infants with all kinds of harm. It is scarcely surprising that the monkeys turned out to be more fearful than their normally raised peers. The bulk of this research was paid for by the American public under the auspices of the National Institutes of Mental Health.

Dr Harry Harlow is not the only person to have carried out this type of research. Others continue to do it. The justification? To develop a model of psychopathology to be applied in work with humans. It is very difficult for me to understand why I did not question the validity of this research twenty years ago. As a practising clinical psychologist, I would never consider going to the literature on non-human animals to try to find a model for a client.

The work simply has no utility. This is another example of 'conditioned ethical blindness', although one does not even have to face the ethical issue to see the fallacies in such research.

We are now ready to examine the second question I raised above: why would anyone do the kinds of experiments I did? I was, of course, given a reason for this research. I was told that the Air Force needed to know the survivability/vulnerability of its weapons systems. In other words, it needed to know where the systems were weakest so that it could bolster up that part of the system. Much research had been accomplished to 'harden' the electronics against the effects of radiation, but the human was also a basic component of most Air Force weapons systems (i.e., airplanes). Hence, it was argued, the vulnerability of the human 'subsystem' demanded definition.

It became my job to determine probability estimates of aircrew functioning following nuclear radiation. If the pilot (co-pilot, bombardier, etc.) became comatose following the receipt of 5,000 rads, why spend an exorbitant amount of time and money 'hardening' the electronic components to withstand 10,000, 15,000 or 20,000 rads? Also, if the human simply underwent a period of 'early transient incapacitation' and could operate the weapons system fifteen or twenty minutes after irradiation, how could we develop an automatic pilot which would get the crew member through this period of incapacitation and still enable him (sexist but accurate) to complete his mission?

These are real questions to the military planner; as an employee of the Department of Defense, they became real problems for me. I'm sure that I don't have to point to the lack of humane consideration inherent in this situation. In contrast to most biomedical research, even the human is seen as expendable to the mission; the goal is to assure that the mission is completed, that the bombs are dropped. No one expects the human operators of these weapons systems to return from their missions. What possible chance of personal consideration does a non-human have in such an environment?

The obvious solution: take the human out of the weapons system. Even though the technology to do exactly that has existed for a decade, it will not be done. Why? Because the future of the US Air Force depends upon having a person in the cockpit. The US Air Force is an entrenched bureaucratic institution. It is self-perpetuating and has erected defence mechanisms to prevent its own annihilation while developing other defensive strategies to defend the United

States against invasion; both systems are sophisticated and 'hardened' against attack. In order to protect the status quo, projects which maintain it are approved; those which threaten its continuation are disapproved. If we can't take the human out of the system, we must find a way to ensure that the system works with the human in it. Hence, billions of dollars are spent on justifying the existing bureaucratic apparatus.

In this role, I accepted the problems as my superiors outlined them for me. How, indeed, does one determine the vulnerability of the human operator to radiation?

First, one must accept an anthropocentric point of view – that is, human welfare is the first priority. Second, one must, at least implicitly (as in my case), assume that the ends justify the means. There is no substitute for humans in biomedical research designed to learn about humans, but one cannot accept this fact if convinced that the problem must be solved. So a surrogate must be found for those experiments which would prove harmful to humans. The non-human primate would appear to be our closest relative; he is the obvious choice.

If there were an extrapolative index, a formula for predicting human behaviour from the behaviour of non-human primates, biomedical science would have a wealth of information. Many of the 'problems' presented to me would have been solved years and years ago, for millions of non-human primates have been sacrificed to this end. There is no such formula. But I didn't realize this simple fact and, being convinced that non-human animals exist for human purposes, blindly accepted the premise that 'close is better than nothing' and set about developing an ambitious programme to irradiate trained monkeys in order to extrapolate the results to hypothetical human situations. Over 1,000 monkeys later, several events occurred which caused me to step back and re-evaluate my position. Although I cannot point to a single causative factor in my conversion from experimenter to animal rights activist, I can recall some of the events.

I must confess that, for some years, I had entertained suspicions about the utility of the data we were gathering. I made a few token attempts to ascertain both the destination and the purpose of the technical reports we published but now acknowledge my eagerness to accept assurances from those in command that we were, in fact, providing a real service to the US Air Force and, hence, to the defence of the free world. I used those assurances as blinkers to avoid the reality of what I saw in the field, and even though I did not always wear them comfortably, they did serve to protect me from the insecurities associated with the potential loss of status and income.

As each day passes it becomes increasingly difficult to comprehend how I was able to close my eyes to the artificiality of the research I was doing. The data we gathered on the behavioural effects of ionizing radiation were used as inputs to 'models' of the operational systems. By this stage the numbers themselves had become 'truths'. The fact that they had been obtained from non-human primates in highly artificial situations was forgotten or ignored. The very fact that they existed to be utilized as inputs to computer-modelled 'war games' justified their validity.

And then, one day, the blinkers slipped off, and I found myself in a very serious confrontation with Dr Roy DeHart, Commander, US Air Force School of Aerospace Medicine. I tried to point out that, given a nuclear confrontation, it is highly unlikely that operational commanders will go to charts and figures based upon data from the rhesus monkey to gain estimates of probable force strength or second-strike capability. Dr DeHart insisted that the data will be invaluable, asserting, 'They don't know the data are based on animal studies.' Needless to say, this confrontation proved devastating to my status as a Principal Investigator at the School of Aerospace Medicine!

In retrospect, I realize that the slow changes in my perception of the research I was doing were accompanied by changes on the empathic, as well as on the intellectual, level. For example, on several occasions during the sixteen years I did research on non-human primates, I took it upon myself to destroy irradiated animals. Although not trained as a physiologist, I found I had the facility to locate a vein while many technicians could not. Rather than cause the monkey further suffering, I began to fill in when the veterinarian was absent. On each occasion a thought occurred to me: 'Do I have the "right" to do this?' I know now that a subliminal voice answered 'No!' but I felt I had no choice. At that particular moment I did not; later it was easy to concentrate on other issues.

In 1979, just over a year before I would leave the laboratory to work for the dignity of non-human animals, my boss approached me with a request: would I talk to a young statistician who had just come into our laboratories to work with us? He had apparently become quite upset upon seeing the monkeys receive electric shock for failing to perform their 'duties' correctly and had commented on the inhumanity of the project. Could I defuse this potentially dangerous situation? Of course! I gave this fellow all the trite arguments. I told him of the 'necessity' for the research; I told him of the reason for using electric shock; I told him why we had to use monkeys. He bought the argument; in the process I began to unconvince myself.

Shortly thereafter I was ordered to radiate four trained rhesus monkeys with 360 rads of gamma radiation and to determine the effect of such radiation upon the monkeys' behaviour over the next ten hours. I objected to doing this experiment for the following reasons. First, I had become an expert on the behavioural effects of ionizing radiation in the rhesus monkey; I knew that 360 rads would not affect the performance of the monkeys during the ten hour post-irradiation observation period. Second, with even the most elegant of experimental designs, a subject population of four is statistically inadequate; even if all four monkeys behaved in exactly the same way following radiation, the results would be scientifically invalid. Third, I had fallen out of favour with my superiors by this time as a result of my questioning of the entire project and had been relegated to the laboratory. I *knew* these monkeys. I was becoming more and more particular about how they were 'utilized'. I didn't want to 'use' these animals in a meaningless project. This is not to say that I would have balked at using them in a project I considered to be important; I had not yet reached that point in my conversion. I took my objections to a staff meeting and presented my position.

The other professionals, including my immediate supervisor, agreed that the experiment would be a negative one; the monkeys would demonstrate no behavioural changes during the 10–hour post-irradiation observation period. They further agreed that the experiment could be done by analysis of existing data, by a thorough literature review. Even so, my immediate superior was frightened to authorize this procedure and would not do so. He did, however, promise to discuss the matter with his supervisor.

The farther one goes up the chain of command, the less competent technical advice is available, states the Peter Principle. This was no exception; I was ordered to accomplish the experiment for political reasons. My reaction was anything but acquiescence; steps were subsequently taken to get rid of me, as I had become a thorn in the side of the bureaucracy. I was fired.

As I reflect upon this situation, I see that values based upon an unpopular ethic are a luxury that many people cannot afford to conceptualize, let alone to embrace. I was being stirred by some disquieting thoughts and feelings, to be sure, but I didn't understand them. As far as I was concerned, I was caught up in a bureaucratic morass, being punished for questioning authority, feeling self-righteous because I knew that it was scientifically improper to waste valuable resources (animals) in the pursuit of poor science. Whatever empathy existed with the laboratory animals was still in its own cage, locked away from my thoughts.

I was hurt, embarrassed and angry. I looked for ammunition, for tools of retribution. I called in the Inspector General, alleging mismanagement and waste of government resources. I filed for reinstatement with the proper authorities. I talked to the press. I wrote to humane organizations and, in the process of composing these letters, began to realize, perhaps for the first time, that my work and the research efforts of my peers had been both inhumane and without redeeming value.

As a biomedical research scientist, I had been shielded almost completely from contact with organizations within the animal advocacy movement. It wasn't so much that I had been ordered not to communicate with individuals or organizations concerned with the rights of laboratory animals, but a bias against any antivivisection philosophy was a 'natural' part of the laboratory environment. During my sixteen years in the laboratory the morality and ethics of using laboratory animals were never broached in either formal or informal meetings prior to my raising the issues during the waning days of my tenure as a vivisector. On at least two occasions support personnel were chastised for unnecessary abuse of their non-human charges, but the question of the cruelty of the research itself remained buried in the all-encompassing and 'beneficent' embrace of medical science.

In my anger and frustration, I had a flash of insight. The research I had been doing, and which was continuing in my absence, was not merely scientifically improper: it was inhumane. I was appalled at my own past insensitivity and determined to put a stop to those projects which I knew to be both invalid and cruel, but I had no idea who to contact. Like so many other people, I had not taken the time or made the effort to become informed about the plight of non-human animals. Two groups came to mind from distant memories: the Society for the Prevention of Cruelty to Animals (SPCA) and the Humane Society of the United States (HSUS). I wrote to the latter organization, and my letter was referred to Dr Andrew Rowan, who replied with interest and recommended that I contact Dr Shirley

McGreal of the International Primate Protection League (IPPL). I did so, and a lively correspondence grew up between myself and Dr McGreal – a correspondence which would eventually lead me into the humane movement.

I won my case for reinstatement and returned to the School of Aerospace Medicine, not to work with animals, for I could no longer do that, but to do research on alternatives to the use of animals. After three months I recommended that the research be terminated. This was not accepted, and I was ordered back to the laboratory. I resigned my position and found employment in the humane movement.

My values are very different today from what they were in 1980. In retrospect, I realize that I held tightly to my conditioned beliefs, releasing them only as they were pried from me by logic and evidence of their inappropriateness. In 1980 I could be pressed to separate research with non-human animals into 'better' or 'poorer' categories. The residual logic of 'necessary medical research' remained to some extent; the anthropocentric view faded slowly away, to be replaced by a broader view of increased respect for other life forms. As a consequence, meat was omitted from my diet, leather from my wardrobe and rodeos and circuses from my options for entertainment. My feelings at the sight of a fur coat changed from grudging admiration to nonchalance, to pity, to disgust and frustration.

Change requires the reconceptualization of many, if not all, of our habits. I didn't change my views quickly, nor did I change them without struggle or resentment. I only hope that in changing my own views I have become able to bring about similar changes in the views of those who unthinkingly continue to experiment today.

Animal Rights in the Political Arena

CLIVE HOLLANDS

The welfare of animals in Great Britain has been a matter for political action since the early days of the last century, when Sir William Pulteney, MP, Lord Erskine of Restormel and Richard Martin (or 'Humanity Dick', as he became known), the Member for Galway, introduced the first Bills into the British Parliament which directly related to the protection of animals – Bills to ban bullbaiting and cockfighting and for the protection of horses, cattle, sheep and dogs. Before then the only legislation on the statute book relating to animals were the Game Acts, designed to protect the landed gentry's game from the ravages of poachers and others rather to give protection to the animals.

Although there may not have been actual laws on the statute book, the agitation and concern for the way in which civilized man thought of and dealt with animals had been growing for a very long time. In order to understand the gradual development of man's thinking, it is necessary to look back over many centuries. The historian Keith Thomas, in his book *Man and the Natural World*, provides a fascinating insight into this period:

> to understand . . . present-day sensibilities we must go back to the early modern period. For it was between 1500 and 1800 that there occurred a whole cluster of changes in the way in which men and women, at all social levels, perceived and classified the natural world around them. In the process some long-established dogmas about man's place in nature were discarded. . . . It was these centuries which generated both an intense interest in the natural world and those doubts and anxieties about man's relationship to it which we have inherited in magnified form.

This anxiety about man's relationship with the natural world and about bringing animals and their welfare into the field of legislative action did not go down well with some sections of the populace in Britain. *The Times* of 25 April 1800, commenting on the introduction of the Bill to ban bullbaiting, was explicit on the matter:

> It should be written in letters of gold that a government cannot interfere too little with the people; that laws, even good ones, cannot be multiplied with impunity, and whatever meddles with the private personal disposition of a man's time or property – is tyranny direct.

Strange as it may seem there are many in Britain, particularly those of the blood sports fraternity who still hold to that view.

The law relating to the welfare and protection of animals in Britain has evolved slowly over the years – for many of those working in the field of animal welfare, far too slowly. In this connection it is interesting to note the views of an eminent Parliamentary Counsellor, Godfrey Carter, whose Stephen Paget Memorial Lecture, delivered on 8 October 1980, touched on the way in which the law develops:

> In a society possessed of free institutions and committed to the preservation of liberty and order, law evolves from a rational assessment of the way in which people think and behave, and of their attitudes towards each other. . . . When public attitudes change, the law changes also. But it is unlikely to change immediately because the change of attitude may be long in coming and slow to be noticed; the forces of conservatism are invariably more powerful in the short term than those of reform. . . . Law cannot exist effectively for longer than it is supported by public opinion. . . . When enough people [defy it], it soon ceases to be of any use.

Nevertheless, however slowly the process of establishing law evolves and irrespective of what other avenues may be explored, at the end of the day if animals are to receive the protection which is their right as sentient creatures, it is political and parliamentary action which is required. As Lord Houghton of Sowerby said at the Trinity College, Cambridge, Animal Rights Symposium at the culmination of Animal Welfare Year in 1977:

> My message is that animal welfare, in the general and in the particular, is largely a matter for the law. . . . There is no complete substitute for the law. Public opinion, though invaluable and indeed essential, is not the law. Public opinion is what makes laws possible and observance widely acceptable.

Lord Houghton's words echo those of Godfrey Carter and make it clear that changing public attitudes as a pre-requisite to legislation is necessary if the animal welfare cause is to succeed.

Before looking more closely at political action, and in particular at the limits imposed by political action, it is necessary to identify more clearly the terms being used; what is meant by animal welfare/ protection/rights, and how great is the task of attempting to change public opinion?

First of all, what is meant by animal welfare? It should not, for example, be confused with conservation or any of the other disciplines falling within the science of ecology. Such issues have considerable importance in their own right, and in some cases have a strong welfare element, the conservation of endangered species such as the whale being a good example. While the value of the work of organizations in the field of conservation cannot be overstated, it can be argued, as far as suffering is concerned, that when the last great whale is killed to feed man's greed for its oil, blubber and meat, never again will one of the most intelligent non-human animals in the world be subjected to such an obscene and lingering death. The death of the last whale will be man's loss, not the whales'.

Neither is animal welfare being an animal lover. Britain is called the 'animal-loving' country of the world, with an estimated 20 million household pets, the majority owned by so-called 'animal lovers' but how many are concerned over the plight of the laboratory rat or the battery hen?

Nor is animal welfare being 'kind to animals', a Victorian concept which comes under the heading of 'charitable good works' and was, indeed, the cornerstone of the Royal Society for the Prevention of Cruelty to Animals and the other early animal welfare societies. The phrase 'kindness to animals' is heard most often on the lips of those who exploit animals. How often on radio and television does one hear factory farmers or scientists saying, 'But we are kind to our animals'?

The best definition of animal welfare or animal rights embraces the concept of dignity: it means *according to animals the natural dignity which is their due as living sentient creatures*.

Another phrase which requires defining is 'public attitudes'. The emphasis here is on the word 'public', which means the great uncommitted public – the silent majority – and not the converted few. Most of those working professionally or in a voluntary capacity in animal welfare live very close, perhaps too close, to the subject, and it is easy to fall into the trap of thinking that the public at large shares similar views.

Taking Britain as an example, the paid-up membership of all the animal welfare organizations in Britain is less than 500,000 out of a population of nearly 60 million, which represents less than 1 per cent of the total, without allowing for the fact that many people belong to as many as half a dozen different organizations.

It is easy to exaggerate support by quoting from public opinion surveys, indicating, for example, that more than 70 per cent of the respondents are opposed to the use of animals for the safety testing of cosmetics and toiletries. It must be remembered that opinion polls, which are commissioned by commercial or charitable organizations, may be conducted by independent opinion survey companies but are designed to produce the response required and depend to a large extent on how the questions are framed. For example, NOP Market Research Ltd, in its survey of April 1983, conducted for the General Election Co-ordinating Committee for Animal Protection, asked the following question: 'Do you think testing of cosmetics on animals should be completely banned by law or is there any need for such law? The result: 75 per cent of all respondents thought such testing should be banned by law. Imagine the response had the question been phrased instead as follows (to use an exaggerated example): 'Would you purchase a hair shampoo which had not been tested for safety on animals and which might therefore permanently damage your hair or your eyes?'

There should be no misunderstanding about the enormous task facing the animal rights movement across the world as it tries first to change in the public's mind the concept of 'kindness to animals' to that of 'animal rights' and then to gain the support of the great silent majority for a cause which provides no apparent material advantages for the human species – indeed, a cause which may disadvantage humans financially as well as in other ways.

Incidentally, but nevertheless on a matter of some importance, there is what a marketing organization would call 'sales resistance' in some areas to the term 'animal rights'. For some reason, many people and politicians who are otherwise sympathetic to the animal welfare cause jibe at 'animal rights'. Perhaps this is because it equates other animals with the human animal. The phrase does mean just that to the activist, hence its popularity in such circles.

However, it should be used with great care and discretion, particularly in political campaigning – to which, having identified and defined the terms to be used, we should now turn.

It has to be said that all the marches, demonstrations and rallies in the world will have no effect whatsoever on political action. Such events may help to focus public attention on animal welfare issues, but they will not change the law. Even the more militant and frequently illegal activities of the Animal Liberation Front and its variants in other countries will not affect government thinking. Successive British Governments have made this quite clear in their response to the violence generated by both sides in Northern Ireland. Other Governments, on an increasing scale, have adopted a similar attitude to terrorist activities, such as the hijacking of passenger airlines for political purposes.

Laws can be made only in Parliament. The animal welfare movement in Britain came to this realization in the 1970s. This is not to say that individual animal welfare organizations had not involved themselves in political activity before then. Such activity, however, had been confined in the main to lobbying on specific issues by individual organizations and was frequently linked to the introduction of Private Members' Bills (such bills, if they are to stand a real chance of becoming law, must not be revolutionary, nor too complicated or opposed to Government policy and they must not involve expenditure). Governments over the years have invariably regarded animals and birds as suitable only for the Private Members' Bill procedure and never for Government action, with the exception of such areas as agriculture, where welfare/protection was not the main objective of the legislation. (This attitude on the part of Governments applies equally to other moral and emotive subjects – for example, abortion and divorce – the fear being that as the issue is not divided along party political lines, the Government could lose control of the legislation on the floor of the House and in Committee through lack of discipline among its own backbenchers.) A first objective therefore had to be to persuade political parties that animal welfare and protection was a responsibility of the Government.

The societies in Britain had discovered during Animal Welfare Year (1976–77), and much to their surprise, that it was possible to work together for a limited objective and that, by so doing, they had more impact on the three Ps (Public, Press and Parliament). This realization led to the setting up, prior to the 1979 Election, of the General Election Co-ordinating Committee for Animal Protection under the chairmanship of Lord Houghton of Sowerby, CH. Mr Jeff Rooker, MP, summed up this minor revolution during a debate in Parliament on 23 March 1979:

> The animal welfare societies as a whole have realized in the last eighteen months or so that they must begin to use the political process as ruthlessly as does any other lobby operating in a democracy. . . . In the last year, particularly following Animal Welfare Year, when many such societies combined effectively for the first time, their efforts have been quite successful.

In fact, the campaign to 'put animals into politics' was more successful than even the most optimistic forecast. It was also, of course, the target for many witty comments; as one *Daily Telegraph* correspondent put it on 4 October 1978:

> There are too many animals in politics already. There are snakes in the grass, leopards who cannot change their spots, elephants who never forget and lots of parliamentarians who think they are the cat's whiskers.

The campaign opened with the political parties' annual conferences in the autumn of 1978 and continued through to the general election in May 1979. The success of the campaign can be measured by the fact that for the first time in the history of the British Parliament, the three major political parties included in their election manifestos commitment to animal welfare and protection.

Politics is the art of the possible, and to achieve success those involved in political action and lobbying must, from the outset, accept the limitations imposed on them by attempting political action. In all elected assemblies there will invariably be found lobbies for and against any measure which comes before the legislature; this may be at a purely party political level, but in the case of reforming measures almost certainly the lobbies will be divided on moral and ethical grounds, with both sides claiming that right is with them. In other areas, particularly animal welfare and conservation, one lobby will, while maintaining a moral stand, be a thinly disguised but extremely powerful lobby representing vested interests.

At this point it is necessary to comment on the difficulties facing those animal welfare societies that enjoy the status of registered charities. This is a problem which is possibly unique to Britain, where charity status, while conferring freedom from all forms of taxation, precludes organizations from becoming involved in direct political action. The RSPCA, in supporting the 1978–79 campaign, had its knuckles rapped by the Charity Commissioners for its press advertising in support of the campaign. As animal welfare issues move more and more into the political arena, it is becoming necessary for organizations in Britian to review the issue of charitable status and of whether the saving in taxes (which in the case of the RSPCA amounts to over £1½ million per annum) makes the forfeiting of their political voice worthwhile.

In the issue of 29 November 1978 the editor of the *Field*, a magazine not particularly noted for its support of the animal welfare cause, discussed the effectiveness of the 1978–79 political campaign:

> Many statements of intent by voluntary campaigning groups sound like the rallying cries of crusaders. Lord Houghton's booklet is couched in careful terms in which the parliamentary or statutory background to welfare campaigns is always stressed. He makes it impossible for his organization to be dismissed as a group of naive enthusiasts with more passion than impact. If his co-ordinating effort is successful, it will mark a very large step forward for what are often described collectively as the 'caring societies'. There is certainly no comparable structure to present counter argument.

This view of the campaign sums up very neatly the important elements of successful lobbying. The slogan-chanting approach used the world over in demonstrations carries little weight when transposed into the legislative forum. What is needed in this arena is material couched in careful terms that provides indisputable facts to back up reasoned argument and urges the adoption of reasonable and responsible measures of reform. This may not sound very exciting to the animal activist, but it is the way to make political progress.

If the animal welfare societies act in a responsible manner, the onus is then placed on the Government to respond positively. Legislation must offer real protection and safeguards for the welfare of animals. The price of implementing such legislation will on occasion take the form of loss of commercial profit or of higher prices. Even so, governments must be bold and fearless in demonstrating that the rights of animals (and not weak and unenforceable regulations) will form the basis for legislation.

The weight which the legislature will give to the material will, to some extent, depend upon the number of organizations supporting it and endorsing the proposals for reform. This fact was accepted long ago by trade unions, employers, students and many others. The 'caring societies' exist in many areas of social reform and are, in the main, voluntary bodies supported by public subscription, which incidentally have to rely more and more upon legacies from the dead for their survival. It has been argued that in a welfare state voluntary organizations are no longer necessary, whereas in practice their work continues to expand. However, when it comes to political action voluntary societies working to alleviate human suffering will endeavour to enlist support from the more formalized professional or government-funded bodies working along similar or associated lines to give added weight to their case.

The situation in animal welfare and protection is somewhat different, since virtually all the organizations concerned are voluntary bodies. In the field of conservation, certain advisory groups do exist, such as the Nature Conservancy Council, the Wildlife Link Committee of the Council for Environmental Conservation and others, which on occasion are able to provide considerable support. However, where welfare is concerned the only body with professional standing which is not linked to the voluntary societies is the British Veterinary Association (BVA). In recent years the Association has taken a much greater interest in ethical issues relating to animal welfare. The formation of an Animal Welfare Committee, which formulates policy statements on such issues as animal experimentation for the Council of the BVA, is one important development; another is the setting up of the BVA Animal Welfare Trust, a registered charity with the prime objective of raising funds to establish a chair in animal welfare at one of the British universities' veterinary schools.

These are extremely valuable moves in gaining greater recognition for animal rights, and their importance has not yet been fully recognized by the voluntary section of the movement. It is true that the BVA's policy statements are often cautious in their approach and, although they go further than might be expected, do not satisfy many in the animal welfare movement. Nevertheless, the more cautious approach, as indicated earlier, is one to which Parliament is likely to respond, particularly when it is the declared view of an august professional body with the standing of the BVA.

At least one of the joint consultative bodies in Britain, the Committee for the Reform of Animal Experimentation (CRAE), acknowledged this fact and, in a series of meetings with the Animal

Experimentation Sub-Committee of the BVA's Animal Welfare Committee and representatives of the Fund for the Replacement of Animals in Medical Experiments (FRAME), produced a modified statement on animal experimentation that was based on the BVA's original policy statement but considerably strengthened, particularly on the issue of pain. This joint statement, 'Animal Experimentation in the UK', approved by the respective councils of the BVA, CRAE and FRAME, was submitted to the British Home Secretary in March 1983.

Unfortunately, the animal welfare societies in Britain did not give their backing to the proposals, since in their view these did not go far enough in recommending the phasing out of certain experiments or imposing a total ban on pain.

In May 1983 the British Government published its intentions for new legislation in a White Paper, *Scientific Procedures on Living Animals*. While accepting some of the BVA/CRAE/FRAME proposals, the Government did not accept the limitations on pain which had formed the basis of the joint proposals. Indeed, the White Paper made it clear that procedures causing severe pain would continue to be permitted for virtually any purpose and that only when animals were found to be suffering *severe and enduring pain* must the procedure be terminated, which is exactly the wording of the pain clause imposed upon licensees under the 1876 Act.

The BVA/CRAE/FRAME view, on the other hand, was that there should be almost a complete restriction on pain for all general procedures, with permitted exemptions in special circumstances:

> If a procedure is likely to cause pain, suffering or distress of more than momentary duration or trivial intensity, which cannot be alleviated, prior authorization by the Secretary of State should be obtained. *Such authorization should only be given when the procedure is judged to be of exceptional importance in meeting the essential needs of man or animals.*

This proposal would not have prevented all painful experiments, but it would have ensured that the applicant for a project licence would have to show the Home Secretary that the proposed work was of exceptional importance in meeting the essential needs of man or animal, and the Home Secretary in turn would have to justify to Parliament, when required to do so, his decision to license a particular project.

Another joint consultative body formed during Animal Welfare Year is the Farm Animal Welfare Co-ordinating Executive (FAWCE).

This represents the majority of the societies concerned with the welfare of farm animals in Britain, as well as a number of independent experts. It is another example of an effective vehicle for continuous lobbying by means of comment on planned revisions in legislation, statutory instruments and orders concerned with the welfare and protection of animals farmed for food through the Government's Farm Animal Welfare Council (FAWC).

The work of CRAE, FAWCE and other similar organizations abroad cannot be overstressed. Campaigns such as 'Putting Animals into Politics' in 1978–79 and again in 1982–83 have an immediate but short-lived impact upon political thinking at a time when politicians are prepared to listen to almost any voice, whereas the work of joint consultative bodies continues throughout the life of a Parliament. The submission of memoranda, meetings with Ministers and, equally important, meetings with senior civil servants ensure that the Government of the day is not allowed to forget the animal lobby.

In mentioning the 1982–83 campaign organized by the General Election Co-ordinating Committee for Animal Protection, which was run on lines somewhat similar to those of the earlier campaign, it is also necessary to mention an offshoot of that committee – the Animal Protection Alliance (APA). The APA was formed by a group of the more radical societies in Britain and attempted to mobilize the animal vote by asking animal welfare-minded voters to put their name on a register of those who would be prepared to change their voting allegiance to the political party offering the best deal for animals in its manifesto. The organizers had hoped for as many as 3 million names on the register, but partly because of the calling of the general election earlier than had been expected and partly, perhaps, because of overoptimism, the number on the register was only just over half a million – a very substantial number nevertheless. It should be noted that whereas the other campaigns had been strictly non-party political (all political parties were urged to include animal welfare and protection issues in their manifestos), the APA campaign was party political in the sense that those on the register were to be advised to vote for the party with the strongest animal commitment.

The animal welfare movement in Britain was the first in the world to involve itself directly in the political arena rather than opting for occasional involvement with a particular piece of legislation relating to animals. The main platform of the 1978–79 campaign was the establishment by the Government of a Standing Council on Animal Welfare and the acceptance by political parties that animal welfare was the proper concern of Government and should not be left, as in the past, to Private Members.

Unfortunately, although some progress has resulted from joint action, there are now signs that certain societies are returning to ploughing their own lonely furrow. The reasons are not far to seek, since where members are concerned it is easier to campaign on an 'all or nothing' ticket than to join forces and follow the more difficult path of gentle persuasion and compromise.

To many the word 'compromise' leaves a nasty taste in the mouth. However, Bernard Rollin, in his book *Animal Rights and Human Morality*, suggests that we all have to face up to this 'harsh landscape of reality' sooner or later:

> To some, our willingness to deviate from the ideal we have set up in the face of what is practically possible may appear as hypocrisy, as 'selling out', as prostitution of one's ideals. But in the final analysis, the question that must always loom before us is this: Are the animals any better off in virtue of our efforts?

Political action will always be concerned with practical possibilities. Animal welfarists must come to terms with this fact. We do animals a disservice when we place our sacred principles regarding rights above achieving some progress in alleviating their suffering. As Lord Houghton has said in discussing the present position, which entails all the problems and dilemmas that have faced other reformers throughout history: 'those who refuse to erect the milestones are not on the march.'

'They Clearly Now See the Link':
Militant Voices

PHILIP WINDEATT

Demonstrations, pickets, sit-downs, break-ins, even letter bombs are constantly in the British media, highlighting animal liberation. In November 1983 2,000 antivivisectionists marched on Biorex Laboratories in north London, resulting in a mass sit-down outside the establishment. Clashes with the police led to the arrest of twenty people; police vans were attacked; and eventually mounted police were brought in to break up the demonstration. Twenty-nine demonstrators were arrested in December 1983 after an anti-factory farming picket of the major meat-trade showpiece, the Royal Smithfield Show, in west London. The demonstrations get bigger, the anger more intense. On differing fronts the Hunt Saboteurs Association intervenes on behalf of the hunted animal on approximately fifty hunts a week, and the Animal Liberation Front (ALF) says not a day goes by without their striking out illegally against those who exploit animals.

The Labour Party certainly felt some obligation to take a position on animal welfare. In its 1983 manifesto it intended to outlaw all forms of hunting with dogs, make snares illegal, transform the Farm Animal Welfare Council into a Standing Royal Commission on Animal Protection, review the outdated 1876 Cruelty to Animals Act and give a 'high priority' to the development of alternatives to animals, phase out 'extreme livestock systems' and ban live food animals. Animals kept in zoos, circuses and safari parks would be included in protective legislation. Although political parties are notorious for not keeping to their manifesto promises, this is certainly something for Labour animal welfarists to consider, and it had massive influence on the animal welfare societies. In 1982 a spate of TV documentaries on animals culminated in *The Animals Film* in the first week of transmission of the new Channel Four. It was watched by 1½ million people, more than the popular rock film *Woodstock* a few weeks later. Animal rights groups continue to spring up in every town, and there have even been allegations that the Special Branch is tapping the telephones of the British Union for the Abolition of Vivisection, surely a sign that a force is emerging for animal liberation.

Nevertheless, it has not always been like that. Just a few years ago there was a sharp divide between the traditional societies and the radical animal liberationists like the ALF and the Hunt Saboteurs Association. The traditionalists still clung to coffee mornings, polite petitioning and letters to Members of Parliament. Since then the water has really muddied. The British Union for the Abolition of Vivisection (BUAV) has been entirely taken over by a young, dynamic force of vegetarian animal libbers. The Northern Animal Liberation League has grown, supporting the idea of mass occupations of laboratories. Its militant style owes nothing to traditional animal welfare. The ALF has grown, and the stand of the Labour Party on animals has made all the societies think twice about their own political positions. Inherently conservative organizations urged their members to vote Labour, and now even radical eyes are once again turning their attention to another crack at 'reforming' the Royal Society for the Prevention of Cruelty to Animals. Animal Aid, built by Jean Pink to a 12,000 membership in a matter of seven years, has certainly been instrumental in reviving the large demonstrations and pickets. The talk among animal libbers is now of strategies, directions, relationships with other human campaigns and the first crack in the wall of animal exploitation. But a Conservative Government has recently been elected for another five years, and it is no friend of the direct activist, whether for animals or for humans. With basic trade union rights under legislative attack, can animal liberationists keep up the momentum? Will they fade away like the radical antivivisectionists of Victorian Britain? Will the anger become absorbed by respectable pressure-group politics? Will the frustration felt by some activists lead to violent attacks against actual perpetrators of animal suffering, like scientists and factory farmers? The anonymous Animal Rights Militia have already sent letter bombs to the Prime Minister. In this chapter I try to unearth the aspirations, inspiration and agitation of activists to whom animal liberation is an all-embracing passion. There are, of course, many more who are equally committed, equally concerned, but the people I have spoken to will influence, or have influenced, the shape and direction of animal liberation in Britain. They all represent different shades of militancy, especially by comparison with their counterparts of twenty years ago. They are all vegetarian or vegan and strongly opinionated about the correct strategy for the future. They are not always in agreement.

*   *   *

I asked Kim Stallwood, 29-year-old campaigns officer of the BUAV, whether his organization, formed in the nineteenth century, was militant:

*

In my definition the BUAV is a militant organization. It's prepared to run risks and prepared to challenge and question. I've had to organize three large national demonstrations now. In April 1982, at the Porton Down Ministry of Defence experimental research station, we had 6,000 people demonstrate and the first example of mass civil disobedience, the biggest ever animal rights demo, with 2,000 going through the fences of the station. In April 1983 8,000 marched to Carshalton in Surrey from south London, some 10 miles, to oppose the BIBRA Laboratories. In November 1983 we had 2,000 people from a much localized appeal who marched on Biorex Laboratory in north London. Obviously BUAV has taken over the role of organizing the big national demonstrations . . . [and is] more confrontational than in the past. We see this as part of our general political campaigning. We see things as they really are: we are up against big business; we are not a sentimental organization wringing our hands, saying how awful animal cruelty is. . . . I want to see the BUAV absolutely polarize the Tory Government, to be specific and personal. I want posters, leaflets, propaganda which has a photograph attacking Government Ministers who are anti-animal like David Mellor, Parliamentary Under-Secretary at the Home Office, responsible for animal experimentation, photographs of experiments saying if you voted for the Tories last June, you voted for this. . . . I would like to see civil disobedience directed towards local Conservative Party offices.

How active is the BUAV?

When I first joined the organization in 1978 it was appallingly archaic and Dickensian. It had a paper membership of 4,000, with hardly any active members. Head office supplied no facilities, not even leaflets! The situation has now been completely reversed. We have about 120 local contacts with a membership of 16,000. We are pioneering the use of computers to supply our activists with print-outs of members, MPs and laboratories in their area. We don't want a passive membership – you can't change society that way. We now have specialists in all areas, politics, our revamped newspaper *Liberator*, defence funds for those arrested and with legal costs, scientific research, all wound together.

Do you support the illegal or almost illegal direct-action animal liberation groups?

Our policy is to support the activists in their direct action tactics morally but not in a physical or financial way. We give them space in our newspaper because we think they have a very important role to play.

How did the last general election result effect you?

We were very disappointed that Labour didn't get in. The move-ment on its own will not achieve animal liberation. We've got to take the issue out into the trade unions, political parties, women's groups, professional organizations and so on. That's how we should use the time until the next election. We will then have a much bigger impact. It's tough because we've got to get over the human prejudice that we are a superior species. But animal liberation gives you an enormous insight into the working of society because when people actually grasp the issues, they start to question their own motivations and values. There's an awful lot at stake in animal lib, a drastic readjustment. People who have just joined the movement on gut reaction will be a bit scared by that description because you are challenging an awful lot of established views, prejudices and ways of life. We are asking people to rebel basically. . . . Our political work is vital, we really have got to slot the issue alongside disarmament, unemployment, and its going to be very difficult and take a long time.

People have really got to start bringing this issue up in the trade unions. If we could get two or three unions to support our campaign against the Government's White Paper on animal experimentation (viewed as pro-scientist, anti-animal), we could see shop workers refusing to handle cosmetics or the lorry drivers refusing to transport materials. The possibilities are endless. . . . It's not only a moral question but has vital social, political and economic aspects to it. The movement only sees it in moral terms, but it's got to understand that the drug companies, for example, are making hundreds of millions of pounds out of abusing animals and making people sick, and it's in their interests we are ill.

But aren't you expecting activists to agitate for perhaps another decade without any reforms?

It depends on what you mean by reforms. We have had concrete reforms like Islington and Newham Borough Councils accepting the Animals' Charter and the outlawing of Club Row animal street market in East London. They are rare, very rare. But we have had real success, in that in the last five years the movement has radically changed. God knows what it will be like in five years' time. That's how you measure things. I'm much more optimistic. . . .

*   *   *

Certainly one of those recent rare success stories has been the campaign for animals initiated by Val Veness as deputy leader of Labour's Islington Council. Way back in 1976 Val Veness, as a councillor, was approached by some local residents who were opposed to the circus that was coming to local council-owned free space. She started reading their literature, agreed with them and ensured that the circus was banned from council-owned land in the borough forthwith. Along with the present local Labour MP, Jeremy Corbyn, she read on the subject:

*

It started off with horror of what was happening to animals, but eventually I started to look at the problem as a socialist. I thought that those who share this planet with us have the right to a life free from pain, distress and exploitation. . . . As a woman, I am oppressed, at the bottom of the pile and just stamping on the next lot down, which in those terms were the animals. . . . If you want real socialism, then other species must be liberated. The whole thing just fell in and linked up. The one things that really clicked with me, and the reason why I attended the Porton Down demonstration to begin with, was the plastic bullets used in Northern Ireland, and the

Porton Down tests on ballistics – animals being used to exploit and keep down another section of humans.

The Animals' Charter is a detailed document intent on eradicating animal abuse in one borough, but how did it come about?

When we returned to council office in May 1982 I began to think out the whole issue. I thought, if you can ban circuses, there must be other things local government can do. I built up a good relationship here with my environmental health officers, and we found a whole lot of legislation that we could use in connection with feral cats, companion animals, pet shops, circuses and even factory farms and hunting. We went to the Co-operative movement because of the junky food in Co-op supermarkets these days. We looked up the Rochdale Pioneers, one of whose demands is to stop the bosses' adulteration of food. So we are trying to shift the whole food policy on factory farming. I want to do something about the dissection of animals in O- and A-level examinations. Did you realize that if you are an ethnic vegetarian, you can't do home economics at O-level because you would be in contact with meat? Now, that's racism. . . . On the practical side we now have a very good feral cat policy: trapping, neutering, vaccination, returning to site and homing the kittens. We have properly trained animal wardens, not dog catchers, and we are looking at establishing our own dog kennels and a clinic where animals can be spayed and neutered cheaply. We have also turned down applications for two further pet shops.

What has been the response from your fellow councillors and from local people?

Our fellow councillors thought it a bit strange at first and used to call us the 'Cat Food Brigade', but I have constantly argued the political link, and Victor Schonfeld's *The Animals Film* has been *the* thing. It actually shows the political links. We have shown the film to the Co-op Party. The councillors have now seen it; we have discussed the issues, and the overwhelming majority here clearly now see the link. Once I go out and argue the point I have no trouble. It's very popular. For example, local people who have been feeding the stray cats are now coming out of the woodwork to talk to us because they know the animals will not be put down. Of course, the press has tried to discredit us, saying that it is birth control on the rates; in fact, it's a saving.

Another Labour Government is needed then?

In terms of political philosophy I can't see a Tory Government making any major reforms in animal welfare. It attacks the very class of people they represent. . . . We fought hard for that commitment to animal rights in the Labour manifesto. I think we can expand it by the next manifesto and then really get some major reforms through.

*   *   *

It can be argued that compared with the plight of animals in experimentation and factory farming, blood sports are a far lesser cruelty. But the anti-blood sports movement attracts many thousands of activists. The Hunt Saboteurs Association was formed way back in 1964 and has always attracted the most militant of animal libbers, offering them a direct, albeit non-violent, approach to stop animals' suffering. With the growth of the movement in the last few years the Hunt Saboteurs have not been left behind. They do not hit the headlines as much as they did in the early to mid-1970s because their activities have become much more accepted in the media's eyes. But they are still out in the field throughout the foxhunting season. They have a membership of 5,000, established local groups and a working relationship with the larger League Against Cruel Sports, which has led the parliamentary campaign to outlaw hunting with hounds. Lin Murray has been an active Hunt Saboteur for the last two and a half years, and she spoke about the state of the art of hunt sabotage:

*

There's been a really big upsurge of people who want to go out lately. It used to be the same old people, but loads of new people are coming in. There are three new groups in London alone, and a couple of new groups in Essex, which is my area. . . . In Essex we are sabotaging up to four hunts a week, with groups going out mid-week.

What tactics are favoured now?

To me the most important thing is the distraction of the hounds. Some people say we are just a load of yobs who go out screaming around the countryside, but it's not the case. Hunt Saboteur tactics are very complicated. We are not interested in the riders; we are interested in what will kill the fox – the hounds and the huntsman – so the sole purpose of hunt sabotage is to sab the hounds. For example, we go on to the 'line' of a fox, and we use our horn-blowing to call hounds over to us rather than the quarry. The fox is a clever animal, and if it can be given just a few minutes, that could mean its life. . . . We pre-beat the area before the meet to scare away animals, lay false trails to confuse the hounds and so on, but we never do anything that could harm animal or human. That would be completely self-defeating and wrong.

Why do people become hunt saboteurs?

Frustration. Going out on a hunt sab, you really think you are doing something. It's your chance to get out there and actually stop it physically. The Hunt Saboteurs Association is also a breeding ground and starting point for animal rights.

Is there a feeling of dispiritedness in the HSA at the failure of the Labour Party in the last election?

No, not at all. You are never going to get a total ban on hunting. Although a Labour Government might put it out, the Tories would stick it back in again. The Hunt Saboteurs are the direct action part of the banning blood sports; the League are more Parliament-orientated, and we leave that up to them. Although we do film shows, talks, leafleting, we are very much involved in the field, saving individual animals.

*

The thing that does not change is the violent response of the hunting fraternity towards the sabs. As the 1983 season opened, Lin talked of current cases of aggression on the part of hunt supporters. As sabs keep strictly to their non-violent tactics and attempt to avoid confrontation, they can be badly battered.

*   *   *

Although movements are not really about individuals, there are two people who have kept anti-blood sports a vibrant movement while others have stagnated: David Wetton, the Hunt Saboteurs Association secretary for over fifteen years, and Dick Course, now executive director of the League Against Cruel Sports. After accidentally coming across a hare-coursing event in the early 1970s, Course vowed to get involved in its abolition and joined the League Against Cruel Sports. His fight since then has had two goals, to radicalize the society he joined, and to ban blood sports. He has also played a leading role in getting the Labour Party to make a manifesto commitment to outlaw blood sports. Under his influence the League has been transformed from a very polite anti-blood sports society, with titled people sitting on its committee, to a much harder, campaigning organization, as he acknowledges:

*

As late as 1978 the vast majority of the animal welfare societies – in fact, all of them – were totally controlled by Conservatives, people who cared deeply about animals, I think, but didn't give a damn about people. They're the kind who lavish a lot of money on a pet poodle while an old tramp might be abused in their own street. I found those people offensive, and the biggest offence, as far as I was concerned, was that although the Labour Party was making sympathetic noises about animals, they didn't give a damn; they were only interested in noises from the Conservative Party. . . .

How different is it now?

Totally different. It's not 'Let's drink tea with the vicar and be "terribly nice" to the mayor' – that's gone. There is now a very high degree of political awareness and, of course, a different type of person. It's very encouraging to see young people involved. All the societies are now radical, even the RSPCA has shifted ground. Many criticize it for being reactionary and Tory, and certainly it is very conservative. But some of the things they are now campaigning for were unthinkable ten years ago.

What was the League's role in the 1983 general election?

Back in 1979 we were out for as many party manifesto commitments as we could get. We did support the Labour Party with a donation of £80,000 from League funds, £30,000 to inform people that anti-blood sports policy was in the manifesto and £50,000 to help Labour win. We demonstrated to the Labour Party that if it was prepared to do what we wanted, we would certainly do everything in our power to get it elected. The same thing needed to apply in the 1983 general election. The 1983 Labour manifesto commitment was the best we could have hoped for in our wildest dreams. It wasn't totally pure, but you've got to bear in mind the difference between philosophy and politics.

*

The League was in fact one of the groups that broke away from the General Election Co-ordinating Committee and formed the more radical Animal Protection Alliance (APA). In October 1982 the APA placed advertisements in the national press asking people to promise their vote to the party that was best for animal welfare. Course claims an 'unbelievable feedback', with up to half a million people pledging their votes for animals before the June 1983 election. The APA was also enthusiastic as a national public opinion poll had declared between 5 and 15 per cent of the population was willing to have the animal issue decide which way it would vote. This would, of course, make all political parties look very closely at this issue if they thought up to 15 per cent of the total votes were in the offing. But the election came a lot earlier than people thought, and other issues decided the outcome of the election. The APA did claim some minor victories, however. Paddy Ashdown, a Liberal and pro-animal, was elected in Yeovil in the West of England. (The APA recommended that Labour voters should switch to Liberal in safe Conservative seats, and they claim that this resulted in a Liberal victory.) Also Robin Corbett, a veteran Labour MP and pro-animal, took a marginal Birmingham seat by a few votes, and he thanked the animal libbers for his very close victory.

If Labour had been elected in 1979, what do you think would have been abolished by now?

Staghunting and hare coursing. They are tiny, minority activities. In 1983 we would then have seen the end of foxhunting and the phasing out of factory farming and of certain experiments on animals.

Considering the recent arrival of Cruise missiles, isn't it mistaken to be so concerned about animals?

I think Cruise missiles help us explain our case. Someone who is willing to press a button that would blow away millions of innocent people is the same sort of person who would hunt down a fox without any consideration for the morality of what he or she is doing. I think these things are inextricably linked; both entail disregard for, and contempt of, life. This is where I think the animal question is at its most important. Because we are desensitizing society, people are prepared to tolerate animal experimentation, factory farming, blood sports, all involving hideous cruelty. . . .

Recently Roy Hattersley, deputy leader of the Labour Party, said that one of the reasons why Labour lost the election was because of its concentration on what he sees as 'peripheral' subjects, and he did name blood sports. How do you feel about that?

A grave danger. If the Labour people aren't looking for the animal vote, then there is no reason to think any of the other parties will. The animal vote will be fragmented. . . . We can't match our opponents pound for pound. The vivisection industry is a multi-million pound one. Our only hope is the ballot box. There is no other issue that attracts the kind of public support we get. But we've got to mobilize that support effectively. . . .

What about demonstrations, pickets, etc?

Expressions like 'animal liberation' and 'animal rights' are counter-productive to electoral possibilities. . . . Demos in the name of animal protection, the reduction of cruelty and unnecessary suffer-ing are very good, attracting media and public support. But it's a very fine balance. The movement is getting stronger and we are losing the cranky image which prevented it from becoming a political issue in the 1940s, 1950s and 1960s, but if people pursue the animal rights issue where it comes into conflict with human welfare (which is happening), we could go right back to where we were. So the stronger we get, the greater the threat from our extremities. . . . Sending letter bombs to the Prime Minister doesn't help us at all. The danger is that we will be viewed as a bunch of nutters; we will become a joke. People are going to sit down and eat meat, and we are going to have to accept that, like it or not. People are going to want to have drugs, cures for cancer, arthritis, etc. We've got to accept that as well. If we can't come up with constructive and more positive alternatives, then all we can do is campaign against some of the more outrageous aspects of animal experimentation, such as cosmetics, alcohol and tobacco testing, psychological tests, weapons, etc.

What sustains you?

I want to win, even it it's only the abolition of hare coursing. I don't want to be a flash in the pan. Headlines in Wednesday's papers wrap fish and chips on Thursday.

* * *

Two groups are in the vanguard of radical animal liberation, the Animal Liberation Front and the Northern Animal Liberation League (NALL). The ALF is illegal, whereas NALL's activities are borderline. The ALF believes in destroying the facilities that cause animals suffering: laboratories, factory and fur farms, slaughter-houses, hunt kennels and all allied equipment, especially that used for transportation. It also believes in rescuing the animals involved and re-homing them. It has a national network of ALF supporters who, though not active themselves, give and raise funds. The NALL is opposed to clandestine, middle-of-the-night operations and believes in mass occupations of laboratories in the light of day. It does not remove animals except for immediate propaganda reasons or unless they are are in 'extreme, external torture' or are stolen pets. It concentrates more on obtaining photographic and documentary evidence of animal suffering. Nevertheless, even such tactics may break a myriad of laws, from disturbing the peace to malicious damage. NALL had about eighty arrests in 1982, of which 50 per cent were bound over to keep the peace.

Ronnie Lee has taken some time off from being an active ALF member and is now an ALF spokesman. Lee's personal history of animal protection has run in tandem with the growth of the Animal Liberation Front. He became involved with Hunt Saboteurs in 1971, attracted by their direct approach to saving animals, but he was dismayed at their failure to sabotage the hunting of foxcubs, which occurs before the foxhunting season proper. Thoughts turned to illegal direct action:

*

In late summer 1972 a few of us formed the Band of Mercy, named after the youth group of the RSPCA in the 1800s. They used to damage guns that were used on bird shoots, and our first actions were against cubhunters. We used to let down the tyres of their vehicles, put tacks in their locks and leave a note to say why we had done it. Then a couple of us heard about a vivisection laboratory being built near Milton Keynes. I looked at it a few times with Cliff Goodman, and we decided to burn it down: £45,000 worth of damage was caused in two attacks. We started to attack laboratory animal-breeding establishments, damaging and burning their vehicles. I and Robin Howard completely destroyed a seal-culling boat in the Wash in June 1974. The seal hunt was called off and has not taken place since, perhaps an early victory for direct action. Cliff and I were eventually caught in August 1974 trying to break into laboratories near Bicester. We were each sentenced to three years' imprisonment but were released on parole after one year. While we were inside Mike Husskisson rescued the 'smoking beagles' (dogs undergoing tobacco-smoking experiments) from ICI, and that cheered us up no end! When we came out we met a lot of people who wanted to get involved in that sort of action, and about thirty of us formed the Animal Liberation Front in 1976. The attack on the Charles River Laboratories was the first ALF activity: vehicles were damaged, and several thousands pound's worth of damage was caused. Then in February 1977 I was caught again after taking mice out of an animal-breeding centre in Carshalton, Surrey. I was imprisoned for twelve months.

What's happened since then?

It's just grown: there is now one ALF action every day. There are ALF groups all over the world – in the USA, Canada, Holland, Germany, New Zealand, Australia, South Africa and France – and we don't always hear of all of them. I reckon we've got between 500 to 1,000 active members who are also involved in more traditional campaigning. ALF groups meet informally, in small cells. Some operate in their locality; others travel 50 to 100 miles for a raid.

What are the aims of the ALF?

To save animals from suffering here and now. To inflict an economic loss on people who exploit animals, resulting in less profit for them to plough back into their animal exploitation business. (For instance, if you damage a lab, they have to increase their security and that's less money spent on animal experiments.) That's the short-term aim. The long-term aim is to increase activities, to escalate events to a point where all of these industries are under threat and can't operate.

What's wrong with traditional campaigning methods?

Well, people have tried them for over a hundred years and they haven't worked. The situation of animals in vivisection labs and factory farms in particular has got worse. All the campaigning hasn't alleviated it. But I don't think direct action is the opposite of parliamentary change; I think it will help it. Parliament will legislate when there is so much pressure in the country, so much trouble, that it will have to legislate. But I can't say when that will be. Direct action has been the main reason why the manifestos of political parties, in particular the Labour Party, are so much better.

Isn't the Animal Rights Militia (ARM) just a logical extension of the ALF? In The Animals Film *you did say that you could foresee a time when a cruel professor could be shot on his doorstep. Is the ARM connected with the ALF?*

No. We don't know who the ARM are. A lot of people suspect that they might not be genuine animal rights people at all. We certainly don't agree with what they did.

Have the ARM letter bombs caused you any lasting damage?

The damage hasn't been as bad as we thought it would be. It was big news at the time, but it seems to have gone very quiet, and I hope it doesn't happen again. I was surprised that the police didn't make more inquiries than they did. Do they know more about who actually did it than they have let on?

How many animals have been saved by the ALF?

Many thousands. This year several thousand rats and mice alone. Through damage, hundreds of thousands.

Have you ever threatened someone who works in a factory farm or lab? Do you see a difference between those who own one and those who work in it?

It really depends on what they do. It would be a bad policy to threaten ordinary workers because they can be a great help to us. We've had quite a lot of inside information from people in labs, for example. We are really after the people who are actually cruel to animals. It's not our policy to threaten people.

Isn't it all hopelessly Utopian?

Why demand tiny little changes when you can demand something so much better? Most animal cruelty is caused by the profit motive. If the profit motive did not exist, the pressure for people to treat animals cruelly would be greatly reduced. But I don't think that's the only reason why animals are mistreated. One of the main reasons is the attitude of people who think that animals are of no consequence.

Aren't you encouraging people to end up in prison?

I think it's the other way round. If I wasn't doing that, I'd be allowing the animals to remain in intolerable conditions. Going to prison for a year, say, is very little by comparison with what a laboratory rat or a battery chicken goes through.

What sustains you?

It's the gut reaction. The philosophical part is very important to explain why it happens, but you've got to have some sort of gut reaction to keep going. A concept that keeps turning over in my mind is that of human imperialism. Although we are only one species among many on earth, we've set up a *Reich* totally dominating the other animals, enslaving them. Thought of in those terms, it produces an even stronger feeling for radical change than people are currently demanding. . . . Animals are so defenceless, unable to fight back, that it makes me very angry.

Fighting to Win

HENRY SPIRA

You start with six albino rabbits. You take each animal and check that the eyes are in good condition. Then, holding the animal firmly, you pull the lower lid away from one eyeball so that it forms a small cup. Into this cup you drop 100 milligrams of whatever it is you want to test. You hold the rabbit's eyes closed for one second and then let it go. A day later you come back and see if the lids are swollen, the iris inflamed, the cornea ulcerated, the rabbit blinded in that eye.

That is the Draize test, named after John H. Draize, a former official of the Food and Drug Administration of the United States. It is the standard test applied to every substance, from cosmetics to oven cleaners, which might get into someone's eye. It is responsible for the suffering and death of hundreds of thousands of rabbits each year.

This test has been the target of the Coalition to Stop Draize Rabbit Blinding Tests, a coalition of more than 400 animal rights and animal welfare groups, which I initiated. The Coalition has been unusually successful for an animal rights campaign, in that it compelled the commercial giants of the cosmetics industry – companies like Revlon and Avon – to respond to our pressure for the development of alternatives to the Draize test. For this reason the story of this campaign is worth telling; there are lessons to be learned about the strategies which work for the animal liberation movement.

THE BACKGROUND

To explain the thinking behind the Draize Test campaign, I need to say something about earlier campaigns in which I was involved, and also about my background before I entered the animal liberation movement. That background is not one normally associated with concern for animals, but it has helped me to bring a fresh approach to problems which have faced animal welfare groups for a century or more.

I was born in Belgium in 1927. At sixteen I left home and became a seaman. I worked on European and American ships, and eventually became an American citizen. At that time the maritime union was corrupt and cared little for the interests of the seamen. I was active in the struggle for union reform but was forced off the ships during the McCarthy period, when loyalty was equated with unquestioning acceptance of the status quo.

In the 1960s I worked on an automobile assembly line. I kept up my political activities by marching for civil rights in the American South and writing for small, leftist publications. Among my writings was a series of twelve articles on J. Edgar Hoover's Federal Bureau of Investigation (FBI), which was then considered sacrosanct. This work gained me the experience of FBI surveillance, which much later gave me some amusement when I obtained my file under the Freedom of Information Act; but it also taught me that careful research can often turn up internal contradictions in what a large organization says and does.

When the McCarthy period was over I returned to the ships. Joseph Curran was boss of the maritime union. While his un-fortunate union members were lucky to earn $5,000 a year, his annual salary was $100,000, and his boast was, 'I've made mine'. To hammer the point home, seamen were forced to use the back door in their own union headquarters, appropriately named the Joseph Curran Building. I became editor of a union paper which challenged Curran. Although our alternative candidate for union president had his skull fractured by lead-pipe-wielding thugs, our small group was instrumental in Curran's eventual resignation and indictment.

At that point I settled for the relatively quiet life of a New York high-school teacher. I still had no inkling of animal welfare as a political issue, although a friend foisted a cat upon me, and I soon began to wonder about the appropriateness of cuddling one animal while sticking a knife and fork into others.

It was then that I came across Peter Singer's essay on animal liberation, published in the *New York Review of Books* in 1973. Singer described a universe of more than 4 billion animals being killed each year in the USA alone. Their suffering is intense, widespread, expanding, systematic and socially sanctioned. And the victims are unable to organize in defence of their own interests. I felt that animal liberation was the logical extension of what my life was all about – identifying with the powerless and the vulnerable, the victims, dominated and oppressed.

New ideas gather strength slowly. In 1974 I heard that Singer was to give a course on animal liberation at New York University's School of Continuing Education. The course was based on the materials that Singer was accumulating for his book, *Animal Liberation*, which would appear the following year. During that semester, between classroom and conversations, it all began to gell.

The confluence of events included my activist background, the personal experience of living with first one, and then two, cats and the influence of Peter Singer. Singer made an enormous impression on me because his concern for other animals was rational and defensible in public debate. It did not depend on sentimentality, on the cuteness of the animals in question or their popularity as pets. To me he was saying simply that it is wrong to harm others, and as a matter of consistency we don't limit who the others are; if they can tell the difference between pain and pleasure, then they have the fundamental right not to be harmed.

In selecting material for his course and his book, Singer based his priorities on the number of the victims and the intensity of their suffering. In one way this was obviously right, but my personal concern was rather: what can we do about it? My background had made me ready to question anything, be it the FBI, trade union bosses, or animal welfare organizations with millions of dollars in their bank accounts. In looking at the immensity of animal suffering and then at the state of the animal movement, I felt that it was going nowhere.

The standard strategy of animal welfare groups seemed to be to send out literature saying: 'Look how the animals are suffering. Send us money!' And then, next month, the group would use the money to send out to the converted more descriptions of atrocities in order to generate more money to mail more horror stories. Moreover, interest was focussed largely on the 1 per cent of animal suffering most conducive to sentimental fund-raising efforts – that of dogs, cats, seals, horses and primates. Thus the 99 per cent of animal pain suffered by animals in factory farms and in the laboratories, by species who did not make it on to the popularity list, was ignored.

Certainly, self-righteous antivivisection societies had been hollering, 'Abolition! All or Nothing!' But that didn't help the laboratory animals, since while the antivivisection groups had been hollering, the numbers of animals used in United States laboratories had zoomed from a few thousand to over 70 million. That was a pitiful track record, and it seemed a good idea to rethink strategies which have a century-long record of failure.

I knew that power concedes nothing without a struggle. The meek don't make it. But audacity must be fused with meticulous attention to programme, strategy and detail.

A few of us met and planned what we could do. We did not want to build a tax-exempt charity to raise money in order to be able to raise more money. We wanted to adapt to the animal movement the traditions of struggle which had proven effective in the civil rights movement, the union movement and the women's movement. We realized that we were surrounded by systems of oppression, all related and reinforcing each other, but in order to influence the course of events, we knew that we must focus sharply on a single significant injustice, on one clearly limited goal. Moreover, that goal must be achievable. The animal movement had been starved of victories. It desperately needed a success which could then be used as a stepping stone toward still larger struggles and more significant victories.

THE CAMPAIGN AT THE AMERICAN MUSEUM OF NATURAL HISTORY

Our first target was on a series of experiments being carried out by the American Museum of Natural History in New York. I started thinking about the Museum during the summer of 1975, when a United Action for Animals leaflet listed the Museum as conducting experiments which involved mutilating cats in order to investigate the effect on their sexual behaviour. The experiments also turned up in a computer search I did of animal experiments being carried out in New York City.

We wanted experiments carried out in the New York City area because we knew it would be easier to mobilize public support and media attention if there were no travel problems. The Museum, conveniently located on Central Park West only a few blocks from where I lived, certainly satisfied that criterion. It also satisfied a still more important criterion: we wanted an issue which we merely had to describe in order to put our opponents on the defensive. Here we had just such an issue: 'Do you want your tax monies spent to deliberately mutilate cats in order to observe the sexual performance of crippled felines?'

We prepared ourselves carefully, without haste. It took us a year to get ready. We launched our campaign in June 1976. The laboratories were dismantled by December 1977. Here is how it happened.

The animal research industry cloaks itself in the guise of noble protector of our health and saver of lives. We wanted to spotlight the lack of real scientific pay-off and the fact that much research exists only to create more tax-supported work for the scientist, at immense cost to animals as well as to the taxpayer. Here was a twenty-year-long sequence of deliberate mutilation of cats, all in order to observe the effects of the particular mutilations on their sexual performance. Our preparations began with my request, under the Freedom of Information Act, for all project proposals, progress reports and other papers. I asked that fees be waived on the grounds that this was in the public interest. As a result, the total cost of this investigation was 62 cents. I had the papers evaluated and summarized by Leonard Rack, MD. This was the beginning of a thinktank composed of first-rate professionals, among them Dr Andrew Rowan, author of *Mice, Models and Men* and a specialist in the field of alternatives to animal testing.

Armed with this documentation, we tried to talk with Museum officials. They refused to talk to us. We then circulated Museum documents which set out how the experimenters planned to deafen cats, blind cats, destroy the sense of smell of cats, and remove parts of the brains of cats. I wrote a detailed exposé for *Our Town*, a Manhattan weekly newspaper. Then we set up pickets outside the Museum. For eighteen months we had pickets or demonstrations outside the Museum every weekend.

The nature of the protest was later described by the Museum director, Thomas Nicholson, in the Museum's 1977 *Annual Report*:

A broad section of the public – by no means limited to antivivi-sectionists – became involved in questioning the research. More than 8,000 letters were received and an uncounted number of telephone calls were taken. . . . [Those] who initiated the campaign in the spring of 1976 kept it alive throughout the year through a well-executed campaign. Advertisements were taken out in the media, attacks were written in humane society publications, letters and telephone calls of harassment (some threatening) were directed at employees and Trustees, demonstrators picketed the Museum on most weekends, inflammatory handbills were distributed, the granting agencies that supported the research were attacked, political intervention was sought and contributors to the Museum (particularly corporations and private foundations) were pressured in various ways.

At first the Museum refused to budge, but the pressure grew. New York Congressman (as he then was) Ed Koch toured the laboratories and didn't like what he saw. After his visit he recorded the following conversation in the *Congressional Record*:

> I asked them to tell me what it is they were actually doing, and they asked me if I would like to go in and see the cats in their cages. I said yes, and I went there, and there were about thirty-five cats. They appeared well-treated, in the sense that they were in clean cages and they did not seem to be in any pain. So I said to the doctor who was explaining what was happening: 'What do you do here? What is the purpose of this experiment?' And she said 'Well, the purpose is to look at the effect of hyper- and hypo-sexuality in cats. We find,' said she, 'that if you take a normal male cat and you place that cat in a room with a female cat that is in heat, the male cat would mount the female cat.'
>
> I said, 'That sounds very reasonable to me.'
>
> Then she said, 'Now if you take a cat, a male cat, and you put lesions in its brain –'
>
> I interrupted and asked, 'What are lesions?'
>
> She said, 'Well you destroy part of the brain cells.'
>
> I asked, 'What happens then?'
>
> She said, 'Well, if you take that male cat that has lesions in its brain and you place it in a room with a female cat and a female rabbit, the cat will mount the rabbit.'
>
> I said to her, 'How does that rabbit feel about all this?'
>
> There was no response.
>
> Then I said to this professor, 'Now, tell me, after you have taken a deranged male cat with brain lesions and you place it in a room and you find that it is going to mount a rabbit instead of a female cat, what have you got?'
>
> There was no response.
>
> . . . I said, 'How much has this cost the government?'
>
> She said, '$435,000.'

After this, 120 members of Congress joined Koch in questioning the National Institutes of Health over its funding of the experiments. A long and surprisingly favourable report on our campaign by

Nicholas Wade appeared in *Science*, 8 October 1976. It seemed that at least some of the scientific community wished to dissociate itself from the experiments that the Museum was conducting.

The Museum was vulnerable. The demonstrations hurt its image, and the cancellations of members' subscriptions that began pouring in were threatening to hurt its budget. Finally the National Institutes of Health stopped funding the experiments, and the Museum dismantled the laboratories where the work had been done.

We had won a rare victory. Perhaps for the first time in American history, the public protests of ordinary citizens had saved animals from suffering in a scientist's laboratory.

Admittedly, it was a small victory. The Museum's experiments had involved about sixty cats. When you consider that about 70 million animals are used in United States laboratories each year, and nearly 4 billion farm animals die annually in the United States, that isn't a great triumph. But it showed that we could win, and we were determined to use this first victory as a stepping stone to larger things.

THE REPEAL OF POUND SEIZURE

Our next target was a New York State law known as the Metcalf-Hatch Act. This law allowed researchers to seize stray dogs and cats from the very pounds ostensibly built to save them from the misery of the streets. For twenty-seven years New York animal welfare groups had been trying in vain to get this insulting law repealed. We felt that it was a betrayal of the public which had worked to create the animal shelters. Both the law itself and the failure of the animal movement to get the law repealed were symbols of the powerlessness and political ineffectiveness of the animal welfare movement. So I organized a coalition and started lobbying the state legislators.

We soon discovered that in all these years no one had tried to talk to the legislator who had been the chief stumbling block in the way of repeal: Senator Lombardi. As chairman of the relevant committee, he had prevented the issue from being even debated. The animal groups had accused him of being in the pay of the pharmaceutical industry and had taken the attitude that there was no point in talking to him. We went the other way. We checked him out and found that he had a good track record; we went to him and indicated that we were not looking to start a fight, but that we wanted to get the issue debated on its merits and voted on. We suggested that whatever his beliefs about the issue, we had the democratic right to have the issue debated. Because we approached him without animosity, we were able to develop a really good relationship with him. He maintained his opinion that pound seizure should not be repealed, but he allowed the issue to be debated, which was crucial. When the debate was over the issue was voted on, and we won. We then put out a press release thanking Senator Lombardi for giving us a fair shake. This was important. It showed that we weren't out to 'get' anybody, but only wanted to get things done for animals.

This was a second victory, and again an important one for our morale; but it was still largely symbolic, involving maybe a few thousand animals. Now it was time to move on to something much more significant.

THE DRAIZE TEST

We had begun by saving sixty animals and had gone on to save a few thousand. Now we decided to take on the Draize test, which involves hundreds of thousands of rabbits every year. We had two reasons for selecting the Draize test as our next target. First, David Smyth, head of the British Research Defence Society, a group which exists to counter attacks on animal experimentation, had admitted in print that the Draize test would be a good candidate for replacement by non-animal-using methods, both because it clearly caused suffering and because the development of an alternative should not present any major scientific problems. So from the start, when we asked for the development of an alternative to the Draize test, we were covered against the criticism that it wasn't possible. Here we had a scientist who was the head of a pro-research group saying that it was possible.

The other reason for choosing the Draize test was that it is very dramatic. For instance, the United States Government Consumer Product Safety Commission had a film which was used to train technicians to do the Draize test. The film shows lye, ammonia, oven cleaner, and then it shows the rabbit, the experimental tool on which these substances are to be tested. The same government department also put out a set of colour slides consisting of close-ups of the eyes of rabbits after they had undergone the Draize test. The slides were supposed to serve as a basis of comparison for technicians seeking to grade the amount of damage caused by various products. They were more appalling than any photographs taken by antivivisectionists, and in view of their origin, they could not be attacked as coming from a biased source.

Adding to the suitability of the Draize test as a target was the fact that the purpose of the whole thing is so trivial. We could pose the issue this way: is another shampoo worth blinding a rabbit? It was so incongruous for the cosmetics industry to be carrying out these tests. The cosmetics industry is trying to sell dreams, but the reality is that they are creating a nightmare for the rabbits. Exposing the reality of what they are doing threatens the whole image of the industry. Blinding rabbits isn't beautiful.

As in the case of our previous campaigns, we used the Freedom of Information Act to document what was happening. We got the official reports submitted by the cosmetics companies to the US Department of Agriculture. These returns showed that companies like Revlon and Avon were performing the Draize test on thousands of rabbits each year. They also showed that the rabbits received no anaesthetics.

Armed with this information, we approached the industry leader, Revlon. We said that we thought they should take the lead in overcoming this problem, and that what was needed was a contribution of a couple of hundred thousand dollars to develop non-animal alternatives to the Draize test. We pointed out that such a sum was no big deal for a company like Revlon, which spends millions on advertising. All we were asking for was one-hundredth of 1 per cent of the company's gross revenues. Leonard Rack even developed position papers showing some good strategies for research that could yield alternatives.

We got as far as the vice-president for public affairs. He had a big office; a butler came and asked us what we would like to drink; he was very polite; but nothing happened. A year passed, during which we had more meetings and there was a lot of correspondence, but still nothing happened. So we organized another coalition, building on our record of success. Now that we had shown what we could do, the normally more cautious, old-established animal organizations were eager to lend their names to our efforts. We ended up with a coalition of 407 organizations, with a combined membership in the millions.

We devised a plan for an advertising campaign which we submitted to Pegeen Fitzgerald, president of the Millennium Guild. She decided on the spot to provide financial support. So one morning in

April 1980 readers of the *New York Times* opened their newspaper to find a full-page advertisement featuring a picture of a white rabbit with sticking plaster over his eyes. Above was a single question: 'How many rabbits does Revlon blind for beauty's sake?' The text beneath gave the answer, described the Draize test and asked readers to write to the president of Revlon stating that they would not use Revlon products until Revlon funded a crash programme to develop non-animal eye irritancy tests.

The *New York Times* advertisement was followed by advertisements in other newspapers. In May 1980, 300 people, some dressed in bunny costumes, demonstrated outside Revlon's New York offices. In September the campaign went international, with demonstrations against Revlon in Britain, Canada and Australia. By December Revlon had had enough. The vice-president for public affairs was replaced along with some of his staff, and his successor began serious discussions with us. Within a few weeks Revlon came up with an offer to make a grant of $250,000 a year, for a minimum of three years, to Rockefeller University, so that it could carry out a search for alternatives.

This was an enormous breakthrough. It transformed the search for alternatives from some kind of flaky antivivisectionist issue to something that received large-scale support from a multi-billion-dollar corporation and was linked with one of the most respected medical research institutions in the country. Once Revlon had done this, it was a simple thing to go to Avon, the second flagship of the industry, and tell them that they couldn't do any less than Revlon. Avon soon put up the money and started a centre for research in alternatives at Johns Hopkins University, again a most prestigious medical school. This set the pattern, and Estée Lauder and a number of other companies soon came into line.

THE LD50

At this point we realized that we had the formula for liberating money from just about every company that experiments on animals and wants to keep its image clean with consumers. But then we decided to re-evaluate what we were doing. This led to two changes. First, we decided to broaden our target. Just as our past successes had given us the strength to tackle larger goals, involving more animals, so now we thought the time was right for doing something about the biggest test of all, the notorious LD50. This test, which has been used since 1927, is so named because it aims to find the lethal dose for 50 per cent of a sample of animals. In other words, the test tells you how much of a chemical, per body weight, kills half of groups of between forty and 200 animals. It is the universal death test: every chemical, every 'new improved' product is automatically tested to find its LD50 value. This merely provides the regulatory agencies with meaningless figures because while you can find a precise LD50 value for a given population of rats, or dogs, or guinea pigs, this can't provide any precise indication at all about how lethal the substance is for humans. Different species vary too much. So who needs to know how many tubes of improved toothpaste will kill half a population of beagles or rodents? But half a century of inertia is difficult to overcome, and the LD50 test causes death and suffering to about 5 million animals each year in the United States alone. So this was a really big target.

The second change caused by our re-evaluation of what we were doing was that we thought that perhaps our strategy was not going to be the best way rapidly to bring down the total amount of pain and death. Our reasoning was that the real expertise for reduction and replacement might reside in the corporations themselves rather than in the universities. The universities, after all, are interested in obtaining more money and doing more research. Perhaps that will prompt them to achieve quick successes so that they can boast of their achievements, but then again perhaps it won't. Anyway, we didn't want to be simply unpaid fundraisers for every medical school in the USA. So from this point we switched our strategy. We went to Procter and Gamble, and we told them we weren't interested in bucks; we wanted an internal plan and programme to reduce and replace the use of animals, and we wanted the plan publicized so that it could be used as a model for other companies to follow. Procter and Gamble went ahead and did just what we asked. They formulated a plan and documented it in a three-page article, 'Taking Animals out of the Labs', which appeared in their house magazine. They set up an 'Animal Science Task Force' to make recommendations on minimizing animal use and suffering in safety assessment, and they agreed to publicize any discoveries in this area so that they could be used by other companies. They also took several practical steps which significantly reduced both the numbers of animals they were using in safety testing and the severity of the pain suffered. For instance, one test which used 300 rats at a time has now been replaced by a battery of tests which does not use live animals at all. Another test involving between 10,000 and 20,000 mice has been replaced by a test using fruit flies.

Procter and Gamble's initiative has now been followed by another major company, Smith, Kline and French, and their plan looks like becoming the industry pattern we wanted. According to industry figures, a number of the major companies have reduced by about 30 per cent the numbers of animals they have used in the past two years. That means an awful lot of animals have been spared suffering and death in laboratories. There is a whole new climate in the area, a climate which encourages the leap from the scientific barbarism of Draize tests and LD50s to the scientific elegance of cell biology.

Increasingly, the scientific press, professional meetings and research centres are focusing on non-animal methods. The Food and Drug Administration responded to our lobbying by reviewing its policy on the LD50, and it has now given a clear signal to industry that it does not require the LD50. This deprives industry of the excuse that the test must be performed because the FDA requires it. So now there is hardly anyone left who will defend the LD50. There is no opposition to overcome except apathy. The LD50 is tilting and needs just one more push to topple it for good.

Similar things are happening worldwide. For instance, West German health authorities have announced that they are reducing by 75 per cent the number of animals they require for LD50 testing. It won't be long before both the Draize test and the LD50 test are things of the past. Then the time will come to face the larger issue, that of using laboratory animals as if they were mere tools for research. The science community must become aware that you don't go around ordering 1,000 rabbits or 10,000 mice in the way you order a case of light bulbs on a Monday morning.

WHY WE WON

Basically, the strategy for all freedom fights or struggles against injustice is similar. The other side has the power, but we have justice on our side, and justice can mobilize people. We need to draw on all available energy and expertise. We need to work out our short-term goals so that we can reach people and eventually bring about fundamental change.

The victories we have achieved show that citizen activism can succeed even against prestigious scientific institutions, multi-national corporations and inert bureaucracies. The lessons to be learned from our successes are implicit in the account I have given, but some of them are worth reiterating.

There are several reasons why we succeeded where other animal groups before us failed. We chose our targets carefully. They were small enough, at first, for us to have a chance of success despite our very limited resources, but at the same time the first small targets could serve as symbolic victories which would lead on to bigger goals. We were meticulous in documenting the abuses against which we were protesting, so that we could not be accused of getting our facts wrong. Credibility is the most precious resource any campaign against injustice can have.

We also tried to accentuate the positive. Many people perceive the movement against animal experiments as negative and anti-science. It would have been a mistake to ignore these perceptions, wrong-headed as they may be. So we offered realistic options to the Draize test and the LD50 test. To support our claim that these options were realistic, we drew on the opinions of scientists and medical people outside the antivivisection movement. We were always saying that there is a better way, that non-animal science is more elegant, less expensive and, in the end, will be more precise and more reliable.

We avoided being personally hostile to our adversaries. Before we took any public stands, we always asked them to talk to us. When they refused, as the officials of the American Museum of Natural History did, that gave us the advantage because we could present ourselves as the reasonable ones and them as the ones who refused to discuss the issue. And when collaborative approaches work, they can provide a very fast track to change.

We did not focus on people's intentions or motives. If humane groups supported us in order to show their members that they were participating in the victories we won, we let them take as much credit as they liked. For us the important thing was to gain their support and to show that our coalition had a broad base. Similarly, if a large corporation reduces the numbers of animals it uses, it isn't important whether it does this because it cares about animals or because it is seeking to avoid unfavourable publicity. The animals who are spared suffering will be better off either way.

It is equally a mistake to claim that research scientists get their jollies from torturing animals. The public won't believe this, and it is no way to get support from anyone in the scientific community. Our aim is not to conquer our opponents. We are not on a macho ego trip. We want to win over our adversaries so that they become our allies. We are not going to achieve this if we start out villifying them. There is no percentage in making anybody lose face. We are interested in getting things done, not in pushing people around. It is good politics to put yourself in the position of those you are trying to change: if we were in their shoes, what would make us want to change?

By tackling the issues one at a time we isolated our opponents rather than ourselves. Few scientists were prepared to support the cat experiments at the American Museum, and much of the research establishment was prepared to agree that cosmetics experiments involving pain to animals should stop. Against a scientific establishment which spoke with one voice, we might not have prevailed.

When we started something, we did not let up until we had finished it. Any organization can shrug off a single protest or demonstration. It is tenacity which pays off and encourages a positive response. Any let-up, unless it is in response to a really major concession, reduces the issue to business as usual, and then nothing happens. And a track record of victories won is a priceless asset when the next struggle is begun.

We avoided bureaucratization by keeping our organization down to an absolute minimum. We have never set up a formal group of our own but concentrated instead on bringing people together to get things done. And we did not see the legislative system as a major target. Legislation is no substitute for direct action against the institutions and corporations that are involved in animal abuse.

If I had to sum up all these points in a single phrase, it would be: keep in touch with reality. Dreaming about how great it would be if animal experimentation were totally abolished does nothing to bring that day closer, and it does nothing to help the animals who will suffer tomorrow and every other day we continue to dream. We need to be realistic about where our society is today and where it may be persuaded to go tomorrow. To liberate some animals today and to have some chance of liberating all the animals eventually, we need to study the realities in a detached way as a guide to action. Who profits by animal abuse? Who holds the levers of power? Who calls the tune?

To fight successfully we need priorities, plans, effective organiz-ation, unity, imagination, tenacity and commitment. We need, too, to remember the words of Frederick Douglass, the black leader of the movement for the abolition of slavery:

> If there is no struggle, there is no progress. Those who profess to favour freedom, and yet deprecate agitation, are people who want rain without thunder and lightning. They want the ocean without the roar of its many waters. Power concedes nothing without a demand. It never did and it never will.

Epilogue

PETER SINGER

The 1980s will be remembered as the decade in which the defence of animals began to make headlines around the world. In Britain, the United States, Canada, France, Australia and West Germany, activists took the law into their own hands. They broke into laboratories and took away the experimental animals they found there. When these masked raiders appeared on television, a wide audience learned for the first time that animal liberation was now a cause attracting the kind of commitment and political outlook more commonly associated with struggles for human rights than with the cosy conservatism of the older and more traditional animal welfare organizations.

Nor was it only in the field of illegal activities that those working for animals were breaking new ground. In the preceding essays we have seen how Clive Hollands helped animal welfare to come of age as a political issue in Britain. Alex Pacheco has described the cool and far-sighted approach which led to the first United States conviction of an experimenter for cruelty to laboratory animals; and although the conviction was later reversed on a technicality, the research community was shaken as it had never been before. Henry Spira proved that even the giant multi-national cosmetics leaders Revlon and Avon could not ignore a campaign against their use of rabbits in eye tests; and that seemingly immovable bureaucracy, the United States Food and Drug Administration, was induced to abandon its support of the notorious LD50 test.

There have, in fact, been important gains not just for laboratory animals, but in all the areas identified in Part II of this book. Some of the biggest breakthroughs have concerned wildlife. The European Parliament voted, in 1983, to prohibit the import of sealskins from the baby seals slaughtered on the Canadian ice-pack; as a result the Canadian seal hunters were left without a market, and the killing of baby seals has virtually stopped. Victory is also in sight in another equally long struggle, against the killing of whales. As Lewis Regenstein has pointed out, the International Whaling Commission has voted in favour of a moratorium on the killing of whales, to come into effect for the 1985–86 season. It remains to be seen, of course, whether the few remaining whaling nations, especially Japan, will comply – but clearly they will be under tremendous pressure to do so.

In farming the problems remain formidable, but at last there are some signs of a reversal of the trend towards more and more confinement for animals. In Britain, consumer resistance to veal from confined calves has led one major veal producer to replace the usual narrow wooden stalls (as described in Jim Mason's essay) by group pens with straw for breeding and for roughage, and room for the calves to move around – admittedly still a long way short of how a calf ought to live, but a sign of progress none the less. More significant still, in the long run, may be the example Switzerland is now setting with its new regulations on factory farming, especially its ten-year phase-out of battery cages for laying hens.

Zoos, too, are showing signs of change. While the abolition for which Dale Jamieson has so convincingly argued will be a long time coming, zoo officials all over the world are starting to show evident embarrassment about the very idea on which their zoos were founded: that it is acceptable to pluck animals from the wild and lock them behind bars so that the public can come and gawk at them.

So the animal liberation movement has made a good beginning, considering its relative youth. Can we expect such progress to be sustained? Is there a real prospect of the movement achieving its far-reaching targets? Will any human society ever acknowledge that animals have rights? Or that non-human animals can be persons, and not just property? Can we really come face-to-face, as Harriet Schleifer asks us to do, with what is involved in the totally unnecessary slaughter of animals for food?

Some say that these targets are Utopian. To take such care for the interests of other species is, they claim, contrary to human nature. Our own species must come first, if there is any question of sacrificing our interests to those of other animals. But why should we accept this claim? Only 200 years ago, it might have seemed just as 'contrary to human nature' for us to take great care for the interests of other races. But we know now that humans can be genuinely concerned for others, whether they are racially similar to us or not. We see this in everyday life, and in the work of voluntary organizations which strive to reduce the sufferings of strangers not only in our own societies, but all over the world. We know, too, that the greatest ethical traditions are built on the idea of caring for others. It was not only Rabbi Hillel and Jesus of Nazareth who summed up the moral law as doing unto others as you would like them to do unto you: Confucius, quite independently, said much the same thing; so does the Mahabharata, one of the ancient Hindu scriptures.

These ethical traditions are among the greatest of human achievements. They have in common the perspective that each of us is only one among others, and that we must see the needs of others as important, just as we see our own needs as important. But who are these 'others'? Nowadays it is unnecessary to defend the idea that the circle of 'others' must include all human beings, irrespective of race, class or nationality; that the circle should be extended to non-human animals is not yet as readily accepted. Nevertheless this proposition is, as we have seen, the logical extension of the process of expansion of the ethical circle. When I see myself as one among others, the relevant point of the comparison is that others also have feelings, others can also suffer or be happy. Any being capable of feeling anything, whether pain or pleasure or any kind of positive or negative state of consciousness, must therefore count.

If we have in our nature the capacity to develop the ethical traditions to which I have referred, and to live in at least partial accordance with their teachings, then why should we not also have the capacity to take this logical next step? The ideas and actions of the contributors to this book give us reason to hope that we do have it within us to take this step. We can bring within our sphere of concern those animals on the other side of the line marking the boundary of our own species. Will we do so? From the preceding essays, one thing at least is clear: the animal liberation movement is here to stay, and there is a growing band of committed activists who will keep up the struggle until real victories have been won.

Further Reading

GENERAL

Clark, Stephen, *The Moral Status of Animals*, Oxford, Clarendon Press, 1977, paperback 1984. Perhaps too academic in style for some, but a forceful argument for change.

Clark, Stephen, *The Nature of the Beast*, Oxford, Oxford University Press, 1983. A philosopher looks at what we know about the nature of animals.

Dawkins, Marian Stamp, *Animal Suffering: The Science of Animal Welfare*, London, Chapman and Hall, 1980. How animal welfare can be scientifically assessed.

Godlovitch, Stanley and Roslind, and Harris, John (eds.), *Animals, Men and Morals*, London, Gollancz, 1972. A path-breaking collection of articles.

Hollands, Clive, *Compassion is the Bugler*, Edinburgh, MacDonald, 1981. An account of the campaign to make animal welfare a political issue, by a central participant.

Magel, Charles, *A Bibliography on Animal Rights and Related Matters*, Washington, DC, University Press of America, 1981. A comprehensive bibliography, with lists of organizations as well.

Midgley, Mary, *Animals and Why They Matter*, Harmondsworth, Penguin, 1984. A penetrating discussion of the difference that species makes.

Miller, Harlan and Williams, William (eds.), *Ethics and Animals*, New Jersey, Humana Press, 1983. A collection of essays by philosophers, scientists and agriculturalists.

Paterson, David and Ryder, Richard (eds.), *Animals' Rights: A Symposium*, Fontwell, Sussex, Centaur Press, 1979. The proceedings of a symposium with activists and philosophers contributing.

Regan, Tom, *All that Dwell Therein*, Berkeley, University of California Press, 1982. A collection of Regan's essays on animal rights.

Regan, Tom, *The Case for Animal Rights*, Berkeley, University of California Press, 1984. The fullest elaboration of the philosophical arguments for attributing rights to animals.

Regan, Tom and Singer, Peter (eds.), *Animal Rights and Human Obligations*, Englewood Cliffs, NJ, Prentice-Hall, 1976. An anthology of writings, from both sides, on the animal issue.

Rollin, Bernard, *Animal Rights and Human Morality*, Buffalo, NY, Prometheus Books, 1981. A philosophical assessment, paying particular attention to the issue of animal experimentation.

Salt, Henry, *Animal Rights*, Fontwell, Sussex, Centaur Press, 1980 (first published 1892). An early classic.

Singer, Peter, *Animal Liberation*, New York, a New York Review Book, 1975; Avon, 1977; Wellingborough, Thorsons, 1983. A new ethic for our treatment of animals.

Thomas, Keith, *Man and the Natural World*, London, Allen Lane, 1983. An historian's account of the development of attitudes to animals in Britain.

Wood-Gush, D. M., Dawkins, M., Ewbank, R. (eds.), *Self-Awareness in Domesticated Animals*, Potters Bar, Universities Federation of Animal Welfare, 1981. This collection is aimed at the more scientific reader.

ANIMALS IN RESEARCH

Rowan, Andrew, *Of Mice, Models and Men: A Critical Evaluation of Animal Research*, Albany, State University of New York Press, 1984. An up-to-date examination by a scientist.

Ryder, Richard, *Victims of Science*, London, Davis-Poynter, 1975; National Antivivisection Society, 1983. Still the best overall account of animal experimentation.

Smyth, D. H., *Alternatives to Animal Experiments*, London, Scolar Press, 1978. Although written by a former president of the Research Defence Society, this book acknowledges the scope for developing alternatives.

Sperlinger, David (ed.), *Animals in Research: New Perspectives in Animal Experimentation*, Chichester and New York, John Wiley, 1981. A useful collection for those with a serious interest in the topic.

FARM ANIMALS AND THE MEAT INDUSTRY

Agriculture Committee, House of Commons, *Animal Welfare in Poultry, Pig and Veal Calf Production*, London, HMSO, 1981. An authoritative government report which comes out firmly against many current practices.

Boas, Max and Chain, Steve, *Big Mac: The Unauthorized Story of McDonald's*,

New York, New American Library, 1976. Every McDonald's customer should read this book.

Brambell, F. W. R. (Chairman), *Report of the Technical Committee to Enquire into the Welfare of Animals kept under Intensive Livestock Husbandry Systems*, London, HMSO, 1965. The report of the first detailed government inquiry into factory farming.

Bryant, John, *Fettered Kingdoms*, Chard, Somerset, J. M. Bryant Ferne House, no date. A slim but powerful discussion of our abuse of animals.

Gold, Mark, *Assault and Battery*, London, Pluto Press, 1983. An examination of factory farming.

Harrison, Ruth, *Animal Machines*, London, Vincent Stuart, 1964. The book that started the campaign against factory farming.

Lappe, Francis Moore, *Diet for a Small Planet*, New York, Ballantine, 1971. This book argues on ecological grounds against meat production.

Mason, Jim and Singer, Peter, *Animal Factories*, New York, Crown, 1980. The health, ecological and animal welfare implications of factory farming, with an outstanding collection of photographs.

Swanson, Wayne and Schultz, George, *Prime Rip*, Englewood Cliffs, NJ, Prentice-Hall, 1982. An exposé of the American meat industry.

VEGETARIANISM

Akers, Keith, *A Vegetarian Sourcebook*, New York, Putnam, 1983. The most comprehensive collection of up-to-date scientific information on the vegetarian diet.

Giehl, Dudley, *Vegetarianism, a Way of Life*, New York, Harper & Row, 1979. A discussion of many aspects of vegetarianism.

Kapleau, Philip, *To Cherish All Life*, Rochester, NY, Zen Center, 1981. A Buddhist view of animal slaughter and meat eating, by an eminent American Buddhist.

Wynne-Tyson, John, *Food for a Future*, London, Sphere, 1976. An argument for vegetarianism on humane and ecological grounds.

WILDLIFE

Batten, Peter, *Living Trophies*, New York, Crowell, 1976. A critical look at zoos and what they do to animals.

Day, David, *The Doomsday Book of Animals*, New York, Viking Press, 1980. How we are driving numerous species to extinction.

Ehrlich, Paul and Anne, *Extinction*, New York, Random House, 1981. Two ecologists look at the problem of extinction.

Myers, Norman, *The Sinking Ark*, New York, Pergamon Press, 1979. Another account of what we are doing to other species.

Regenstein, Lewis, *The Politics of Extinction: The Shocking Story of the World's Endangered Wildlife*, New York, Macmillan, 1975. This book looks at the political difficulties in the way of preserving wildlife.

Useful Organizations

The following is a brief list of some of the more effective organizations working 'in defence of animals'. It is based to some extent on personal experience, and the exclusion of an organization does not indicate that it is ineffective.

AUSTRALIA

Animal Liberation, a radical national organization with state branches as follows:

Canberra, c/o Canberra and Southeast Environmental Centre, PO Box 1875, ACT, 2601.
New South Wales, 257 Broadway, NSW 2007.
Queensland, GPO Box 1787, Brisbane, Qld 4001.
South Australia, PO Box 114, Rundle St, Adelaide, SA 5000.
Tasmania, c/o Environment Centre, 102 Bathurst St, Hobart, Tas. 7000.
Victoria, 5th Flr, 37 Swanston St, Melbourne, Vic. 3000.
Western Australia, PO Box 146, Inglewood, WA 6052.

Outcry, PO Box 15, Elwood, Vic. 3184. The magazine of the Australian animal liberation movement.

CANADA

ARK-II: Canadian Animal Rights Network, 542 Mt Pleasant Rd, #102, Toronto. A network of animal rights activists.

Lifeforce, PO Box 3117, Main Post Office, Vancouver. This Vancouver-based group has done a lot to increase public awareness of animal experimentation.

GERMANY

Mobilisation für Tiere e.V., Postfach 977, 3400 Göttingen.

NETHERLANDS

Nederlandse Bond tot Bestrijding van de Vivisectie, Jan van Nassaustraat 81, 2596 BR 's-Gravenhage.

NEW ZEALAND

Save Animals from Experimentation, PO Box 647, Auckland 1. A forceful opponent of animal experimentation.

SWEDEN

Nordiska Samfundet Mot Plågsamma Djurförsök, Drottninggatan 102, 11160 Stockholm. The largest anti-vivisection and animal rights society in Scandinavia with 36,500 members.

UNITED KINGDOM

Animal Aid, 7 Castle St, Tonbridge, Kent. A large grass-roots organization with branches across the UK.

Animal Liberation Front, PO Box 190, 8 Elm Avenue, Nottingham. A direct action organization.

British Union for the Abolition of Vivisection (BUAV). 16a Crane Grove, Islington, London N7. A venerable organization, recently re-activated by a new and radical committee.

Compassion in World Farming, Lyndum House, High Street, Petersfield, Hampshire. Fights factory farming and promotes more rational ways of feeding the world.

Co-ordinating Animal Welfare, PO Box 61, Camberley, Surrey. Serves to link radicals in different organizations.

Hunt Saboteurs Association, PO Box 19, Tonbridge, Kent. As the name suggests, this group exists to disrupt hunts.

Royal Society for the Prevention of Cruelty to Animals, Causeway, Horsham, Sussex. The oldest society of them all, still wavering uncertainly between the conservatives and the radicals.

Scottish Society for the Prevention of Vivisection, 10 Queensferry St, Edinburgh. This group, under the direction of Clive Hollands, concentrates on parliamentary channels to reform.

Vegan Society, 47 Highlands Rd, Leatherhead, Surrey. Advocates doing without all animals foods.

Vegetarian Society, 53 Marloes Rd, Kensington, London W8. A source of general information on vegetarianism.

Zoocheck, Tempo House, 15 Falcon Rd, London SW11. A newly formed group, Zoocheck seeks the elimination of the traditional zoo.

UNITED STATES

Agenda, PO Box 5234, Westport, Ct 08880. This journal is essential reading for those who want to keep up with news of the animal liberation movement.

American Vegan Society, 501 Old Harding Highway, Malaga, NJ 08328. Promotes a diet without any animal products.

Coalition Against the Draize Test/Coalition Against the LD50 Test, 507 Fifth Avenue, New York, NY 10017. The remarkably successful coalitions put together by Henry Spira.

Farm Animal Reform Movement, PO Box 70123, Washington, DC 20088. Campaigns against factory farming and other abuses of farm animals.

Fund for Animals Inc., 140 West 57th St, New York, NY 10019. This organization often acts forcefully to protect wildlife under threat.

International Society for Animal Rights, 421 South State St, Clarks Summit, Pa 18411. One of the first groups to switch from an animal welfare pespective to an animal rights view. Now concerned primarily with urging the abolition of animal experimentation.

National Anti-Vivisection Society, 100 East Ohio St, Chicago, Ill. 60611. A long-established antivivisection society, now taking a more active role in organizing rallies and demonstrations.

North American Vegetarian Society, PO Box 72, Dolgeville, NY 13329. Promotes vegetarianism on a variety of grounds.

People for the Ethical Treatment of Animals (PETA), PO Box 56272, Washington, DC 20011. An effective and fast-growing new organization, responsible for exposing the Silver Spring Monkeys case.

Trans-Species Unlimited, PO Box 1351, State College, Pennsylvania, Pa 16804. Another relatively new, active group with a strong policy against animal exploitation.

Index

219